Daily Planning for Today's Classroom

A Guide to Writing Lesson and Activity Plans

Second Edition

KAY M. PRICE

Western Washington University

KARNA L. NELSON

Western Washington University

THOMSON

WADSWORTH

Australia • Canada • Mexico • Singapore • Spain
United Kingdom • United States

To our dads

Acquisitions Editor: *Dan Alpert*
Developmental Editor: *Tangelique Williams*
Editorial Assistant: *Lilah Johnson*
Marketing Associate: *Neena Chandra*
Project Manager, Editorial Production: *Belinda Krohmer*
Technology Project Manager: *Jeanette Wiseman*
Print/Media Buyer: *Becky Cross*
Permissions Editor: *Joohee Lee*

Production Service: *Sara Dovre Wudali, Buuji, Inc.*
Text Designer: *Rita Naughton*
Copy Editor: *Heather McElwain*
Illustrator: *Jill Danner, Buuji, Inc.*
Cover Designer: *Norman Baugher*
Cover Printer: *Victor Graphics, Inc.*
Compositor: *Buuji, Inc.*
Printer: *Victor Graphics, Inc.*

For more information about our products, contact us at:
Thomson Learning Academic Resource Center
1-800-423-0563

For permision to use material from this text, contact us by:
Phone: 1-800-730-2214 **Fax:** 1-800-730-2215
Web: http://www.thomsonrights.com

Printed in the United States of America
2 3 4 5 6 7 06 05 04 03

Library of Congress Control Number:
2002102244

ISBN 0-534-53914-9

Wadsworth/Thomson Learning
10 Davis Drive
Belmont, CA 94002-3098
USA

Asia
Thomson Learning
5 Shenton Way #01-01
UIC Building
Singapore 068808

Australia
Nelson Thomson Learning
102 Dodds Street
South Melbourne, Victoria 3205
Australia

Canada
Nelson Thomson Learning
1120 Birchmount Road
Toronto, Ontario M1K 5G4
Canada

Europe/Middle East/Africa
Thomson Learning
High Holborn House
50/51 Bedford Row
London WC1R 4LR
United Kingdom

Latin America
Thomson Learning
Seneca, 53
Colonia Polanco
11560 Mexico D.F.
Mexico

Spain
Paraninfo Thomson Learning
Calle/Magallanes, 25
28015 Madrid, Spain

Contents

Preface

To the Instructor

This book has been written for *general education* and *special education* teachers, and its uses are varied. Those just learning how to plan can use this book to provide or supplement initial instruction on the planning and delivery of lessons and activities. Experienced teachers may also use this book as a tool for reviewing essential planning elements. With this versatility, this text is appropriate for use in either undergraduate or graduate courses, for both *preservice* and *in-service* teachers.

We wrote the first edition of this book because we noticed that many of the hundreds of practicum students and student teachers with whom we worked experienced some common problems. First, just like young students, preservice teachers cannot automatically transfer what they have learned in classes to real-life situations. In the real classroom, the focus is on survival, and beginning teachers seem to forget what they had learned from their training. For example, as they try to figure out how to teach division of fractions to a particular group of fifth graders tomorrow at two o'clock, much of what they had learned about making instructional decisions may be forgotten. Beginning teachers can plan more effective lessons and activities when they have a form that prompts the decisions they need to make.

We also noticed that novice teachers sometimes forget to teach. They like to use exciting and creative approaches and are eager to involve their young students in learning. However, they can have

trouble distinguishing between those occasions when students need the opportunity to practice and develop what they know and when students need to be directly taught new facts, concepts, and strategies. In their eagerness to be innovative, they plan fun activities but are unable to express what they want students to learn. Frequently, when they plan and teach lessons, they advance to providing student practice before they have taught enough to enable students to be successful with the practice. Novice teachers may select teaching methods based on their own interests or emerging styles rather than on the needs of their students. For these reasons, we make a distinction between activities and lessons, based on their purposes, and suggest different types of planning decisions for each. We also focus on clear objectives and evaluation of learning to emphasize the accountability of teaching so that students learn.

Finally, teachers often say they are overwhelmed by the diversity of needs of their students. They routinely find themselves writing plans and then trying to modify and adjust them to meet these diverse needs. Teachers need a more efficient and effective way to design lessons and activities. We stress the inclusion of universal design principles, critical teaching techniques, and diversity strategies during the initial stage of planning. This method of building in strategies can result in a more effective plan in a shorter amount of time.

In this new edition, we have revised and expanded on all of the reasons for writing the first edition. Changes and additions have resulted from extensive feedback we have received from reviewers, practicing teachers, undergraduate students, and principals. The following are some of the highlights provided in our new edition:

■ New lesson and activity plan examples designed for various grade levels, content areas, and group sizes

■ New information about connecting lesson and activity objectives to the state standards for general education and special education teachers

■ More examples of critical teaching skills, such as active participation

■ Ideas for integrating classroom management with effective instruction planning to prevent behavior problems

■ Information about how to plan for the teaching of specialized content such as social skills and study skills

■ Lists of additional resources on various topics

■ An expanded chapter on diversity strategies to include strategies for working with English-language learners

Our book has been used in a variety of ways. We know that principals and teacher in-service providers have used our book as a tool for working with and helping practicing teachers in their buildings or district. University instructors have used it at both the undergraduate and graduate levels. University students have used it at both ends of their teacher preparation programs, during their student teaching, and when planning in their own classrooms. We are confident that our revisions make our second edition even more flexible.

Text Organization

The organization of this book is intended to enable university instructors, school personnel, and teachers to select the level of planning assistance needed. The following examples illustrate how this text may be used:

■ Each chapter can be used if this book is being used as a stand-alone text.

■ If instructors are using the text as a supplement to readings and instruction in courses, they can use sections as summaries or guides to completing practice assignments.

■ If teachers need guidance in critical teaching skills, such as planning lesson openings, the detailed information available in Chapter 6 will be useful.

■ If in-service and preservice teachers need support in writing plans, they can look at the sample plans in Chapters 5, 8, 9, 10, and 11.

■ If teachers are practicing or strengthening certain models or methods of teaching, they can select only those specific chapters or sections.

■ If preservice teachers are attempting to plan lessons and activities and have not yet taken courses that teach certain methods, such as using peers for instruction, they can select those sections of chapters for help.

■ If teachers wish to review the basics of lesson planning, the information in Chapters 4, 8, 9, and 10 will help remind them.

■ In programs that pair general education teachers and special education teachers, lesson or activity plan outlines can provide a format for joint planning.

Acknowledgments

We are grateful for the valuable feedback on our first edition received from students, instructors, public school personnel, and reviewers, from both general and special education.

We would also like to acknowledge our extremely supportive families. Each member has provided us with encouragement during all phases of our project. We give many, many thanks to Walter, Steve, Jerell, and Leah.

We owe a special thanks to Lyn Dyson, our friend and colleague. She again read our manuscript and offered her support and valuable suggestions.

We would also like to thank the following reviewers: Richard B. Walter, Kean University; Nancy Stockall, University of Arkansas; Allan F. Cook, University of Illinois at Springfield; and Barbara Benson, Piedmont College.

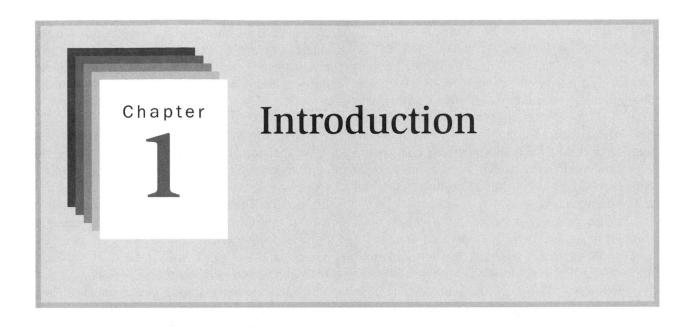

Chapter 1

Introduction

Purpose of Book

Our purpose for writing this book is to help you plan your lessons and activities so that all of your students can learn. You can enhance effective planning and teaching by learning (1) how to select an appropriate plan (that is, an activity or lesson plan); (2) how to write detailed plans that reflect each step of the decision-making process needed for effective teaching (In the same regard, teachers ask students to "show their work" when they are learning to solve math problems.); (3) how to select the planning components needed in various plans; (4) how to include various critical teaching skills in your plans to effectively teach to all students; and (5) which specific diversity strategies can be incorporated into your plans to meet the individual needs of your students. These five topics are emphasized in this book.

To plan effectively, you must first understand for whom you are planning. We begin with a discussion of the diverse student population in schools today.

The Diverse Student Population

The student population in schools today is much more diverse than in years past, and there is no reason to believe that this trend will not continue.

Various groups of students contribute significantly to this diversity.

First, many students are from diverse cultural and linguistic backgrounds. Their presence has created and enriched opportunities to learn about customs, beliefs, and traditions that may be outside the personal experiences of the teachers and other students. Many of those students, however, experience "culture shock" in classrooms where their personal preferences for learning and performing do not match the expectations of their school setting. Making a successful transition to school can be especially challenging for students who do not speak English. (It is not unusual to find several different languages spoken as primary languages by different students within one classroom.)

Students who are "at risk" for school failure comprise another category of students who contribute to classroom diversity. Factors that put students at risk can be found both within our society at large and within our schools. Drug and alcohol use and abuse, poverty, teen pregnancy, physical and emotional abuse, homelessness, and lack of supervision are only some of the societal problems that can cause students to come to school unprepared to learn. Failure to recognize and address student learning problems, irrelevant curriculum, and poor teaching can significantly interfere with student progress in school. While these students have learning and behavioral problems that can interfere

1

with school success, they often do not qualify for special education services.

Finally, students with disabilities have significantly contributed to the diversity of the classroom. Special education law provides most students with disabilities the opportunity to spend their time in both special education and general education settings. It is typical for both the special and general education teachers to provide services to students with Individualized Education Programs (Hallahan & Kauffman, 2000).

There is no question that teaching really is more complex today than it was in years past, for general and special education teachers. Teachers must routinely search for multiple ways to present content. They may need to help their students learn English as well as content. They also teach curriculum that is designed to help students get along with others, learn and study, and acquire important academic content skills. Today's teachers must find ways to honor and accommodate individual student needs and preferences. Meeting the needs of a diverse population of students is our biggest challenge.

Deciding What to Teach

The material in this book will not teach you what to teach, that is, what should be included in your curriculum. We present curriculum information here, however, for two reasons: (1) to help differentiate between curriculum and instruction; and (2) to suggest resources that can be used to locate information and ideas for curriculum development and planning.

Curriculum and instruction, while related, are two different concepts. Curriculum is the "what," the content, to be taught. For example, learning how to divide fractions in math is an example of math curriculum. Instruction refers to the "how" of teaching. Explaining the steps to follow for dividing fractions and showing students how to complete each step is an example of instruction. This book is about instruction—not curriculum—but selecting content to teach is obviously critical to the teaching process.

Teachers must make important decisions about what to teach. If you are a practicing teacher, you know that part of your responsibility is to figure out what your students need to learn—the goals and objectives of the curriculum. If you are a practicum student or student teacher, a classroom teacher who makes these curricular decisions is probably directing you. Important decisions about what to teach are based on the learning and behavioral needs of students.

When teaching students with disabilities, refer to the Individualized Education Program (IEP), the most important source of information to help teachers decide what to teach students with disabilities. Teachers of students with disabilities will need to look at the individualized goals and objectives to provide focus when they plan. Develop daily lessons and activities with individual student's goals and objectives in mind.

Numerous other sources are available to help give direction to teacher planning. The standards that are outlined at the state level are one important source. These standards identify accomplishments in a given content area that are considered important for all students in the state. Generally, all lessons and activities taught will be linked to these standards. (See Chapter 3 for information about state standards.)

Other sources that can aid in developing classroom curriculum are important generalizations or big ideas that are inherent in the content area to be taught. The problem-solution-effect structure used in the study of social studies is an example of a big idea (Kame'enui, Carnine, Dixon, Simmons, & Coyne, 2002) that can be embedded into social studies instruction. Professional organizations in various content areas (for example, the National Council of Teachers of Mathematics (NCTM)), are important sources of subject-specific big ideas. These ideas help to provide a big picture of the subject matter to be taught and can be included in lessons and activities whenever possible.

School district curriculum guides can also aid teachers as they plan what to teach. A group of teachers within the district often develops these guides. The guides can include long- and short-term objectives and related ideas, and activities that teachers who helped write the guide have tried. These guides can help teachers plan lessons and activities that are related to the state standards.

There are also published programs available for purchase in many content areas, (math, social studies, social skills, study strategies, and so on). These programs usually include long- and short-term objectives and all needed materials. Teachers must be sure that program objectives as written meet the needs of their students. If not, they will want to make appropriate adjustments. School district or university curriculum libraries, as well as the Internet, can be good places to start your search for published programs.

Deciding How to Teach

Once teachers decide what to teach, they determine how to best teach it. Fortunately, teachers today have access to many ideas and strategies that have been proven effective through research. This means that even beginning and preservice teachers can add many effective strategies to their repertoire. Educational journals are just one good source of effective techniques considered to be best practice (see Chapter 6 for additional ideas).

Many sources of specific instructional ideas for use in lessons and activities are available, including catalogs, teachers' guides that accompany student texts, Internet sites designed for teachers, books, and workshops. A teacher's creativity can flourish in designing specific activities to be included in instruction.

Effective instructional planning includes providing students with options for learning and expressing information. Teachers write these options into the initial plan. With effective instructional planning, teachers consider the needs of individual students, as well as the needs of the whole group. Address specific strategies designed for the success of these students in a proactive manner. In thinking about planning for the needs of diverse learners, consider concepts of universal design, differentiated instruction, accommodations, and modifications. These concepts are discussed in more detail in Chapter 7. Information about critical teaching strategies that are effective with a diverse group of students will be presented in Chapter 6.

Teaching a Diverse Population

Your ability to be successful in working with a diverse student population begins with a belief that you have a responsibility to do so. If you believe that your job is to teach *all* students, then you will start off much better equipped to meet the challenge. If you believe that your job is to teach only those students who are easy to teach, then your ability to be effective is questionable. You will definitely spend a great deal of your time feeling frustrated.

Equally important, you must believe that you can make a difference in teaching a diverse student population. Beliefs about making a difference may have a significant impact on a teacher's success or lack thereof. We encourage you to examine your beliefs in this area.

There is no question that the diverse classroom of today requires a special kind of teacher. Regardless of age and experience level, effective teachers view teaching as an important and exciting profession. They feel a responsibility to teach all students and see student diversity as a fascinating challenge. Effective teachers plan with the needs of all students in mind. These teachers have a strong desire to learn, and stay current in the field by reading professional journals and taking courses and workshops. These teachers develop an ever-growing repertoire of teaching strategies and methods to use with challenging students. These teachers also believe they can be effective and, therefore, are very effective in diverse classrooms. We hope you are or will become one of these teachers.

The Content and Organization of This Book

This text provides information about the various components of the planning process, and it is organized to provide various levels of planning assistance. This makes it a versatile resource that can be utilized in methods courses, practica, and student teaching. It is also a good resource for practicing teachers.

Many aspects of planning are addressed in the pages that follow. Chapter 2 will help you decide which type of plan to write. Chapters 4, 5, and 8–11 will provide specific information about how to write activity and lesson plans. The sample activity plans and lesson plans located at the ends of Chapters 5 and 8–11 may help you better understand one or more of the planning components. Chapter 3 will aid in writing objectives. Chapter 6 includes information about critical teaching behaviors that should routinely be included in all lessons and activities. Chapter 7 includes many ideas for making your plans appropriate for the diverse student population that you will encounter in the schools. Chapter 11 identifies key planning considerations appropriate for teaching strategies, concepts, and social skills. Finally, Chapter 12 will help you plan for effectively using the assistance of peers in your lessons and activities.

The organizational structure of this text is intended to enable you to select the specific content and the level of detail in planning assistance that you need. The following may guide you in searching for specific material within this text:

1. To understand the differences between lessons and activities, and how to decide when to write which, see Chapter 2.

2. To review the basics of lesson planning, read the information in Chapter 4 and Chapters 8–10.

3. To focus on identifying or implementing critical teaching skills (planning lesson openings, for example), you may benefit from the detailed information available in Chapter 6.

4. To learn or review diversity strategies to help all students succeed, see Chapter 7.

5. To learn or review the key ideas that make up various lesson models, see Chapters 8–10.

6. For learning how to teach specific content (for example, social skills, strategies, and concepts), see Chapter 11.

7. For practicum students practicing certain models or methods of teaching, you can select the appropriate chapters or sections.

References

Brantlinger, E. (1996). Influence of preservice teachers' beliefs about pupil achievement on attitudes toward inclusion. *Teacher Education and Special Education, 19*, 17–33.

Brice, A., & Roseberry-McKibbin, C. (2001). Choice of languages in instruction: One language or two? *Teaching Exceptional Children, 33*(4), 10–16.

Craig, S., Hull, K., Haggart, A. G., & Perez-Selles, M. (2000). Promoting cultural competence through teacher assistance teams. *Teaching Exceptional Children, 32*(3), 6–12.

Cruickshank, D. R., Bainer, D. L., & Metcalf, K. K. (1999). *The Act of Teaching* (2nd ed.). Boston: McGraw-Hill College. (See Chapter 2 in particular.)

Hallahan, D., & Kauffman, J. (2000). *Exceptional Children* (8th ed.). Boston: Allyn & Bacon.

Jordan, A., Lindsay, L., & Stanovich, P. J. (1997). Classroom teachers' instructional interactions with students who are exceptional, at risk, and typically achieving. *Remedial and Special Education, 18*(2), 82–93.

Kame'enui, E. J., Carnine, D. W., Dixon, R. C., Simmons, D. C., & Coyne, M. D. (2002). *Effective Teaching Strategies that Accommodate Diverse Learners* (2nd ed.). Columbus, OH: Merrill Prentice Hall.

Levine, D. U., & Rayna, F. (1996). *Society and Education* (9th ed.). Boston: Allyn & Bacon.

Montgomery, W. (2001). Creating culturally responsive, inclusive classrooms. *Teaching Exceptional Children, 33*(4), 4–8.

Welch, M. (1996). Teacher education and the neglected diversity: Preparing educators to teach students with disabilities. *Journal of Teacher Education, 47*, 355–366.

Chapter 2

Lessons Versus Activities

Introduction

It is important to distinguish between lessons and activities because they have different purposes. Although teachers use both lessons and activities to help their students learn, lessons are used to initially teach knowledge and skills. Activities help students to further process, practice, and generalize knowledge and skills. It is crucial to think carefully about your goals for instruction and to decide when to use lessons and when to use activities.

Lessons and activities each require different planning decisions and tasks. When writing a lesson plan, decide the structure of the teaching so that it lines up with the lesson objective that serves as its foundation. Activity plans need to be congruent also; however, these plans often address the logistics of managing materials and student participation and interactions rather than actual teaching.

Recognizing whether you are going to teach an activity or lesson will help you select an appropriate planning format. When teachers have no clear distinction between activities and lessons, we have noticed a common problem—forgetting to teach! Think of the lesson or activity plan format as a form of scaffolding. It provides support in remembering what to include. For example, the format for a direct instruction lesson plan includes a place to write how the teacher will present or teach the new information, followed by a place to write how students will practice. This ensures that new information is taught thoroughly before students are asked to use the information. In other words, the lesson plan format ensures that you will not forget to teach!

It can be difficult to clearly distinguish between lessons and activities because lessons typically include various activities. Additionally, because lessons vary in length—a lesson might last 30 minutes or 3 days—it can be difficult to determine when a lesson begins and when it ends; therefore, it is hard to know where an activity fits. However, our objective is *not* that teachers will be 100 percent accurate in deciphering lessons from activities. Our belief is that being aware of the differences between the two will help teachers make good teaching decisions.

Primary Differences between Lessons and Activities

Lessons are different from activities in several ways. As stated earlier, one way to distinguish between the two is to look at their *purposes.* The purpose of a lesson is to provide initial instruction on important skills or knowledge. Activities, on the other hand, may have a variety of purposes—learner motivation, additional experience, elaboration of information, additional opportunities for processing and practice, or integration and generalization of skills and knowledge.

Another way to distinguish between lessons and activities is to look at their *objectives*. A lesson has a specific, measurable, short-term objective, and the teacher's intention is that each student will meet that objective by the end of the lesson. Typically, teachers use activities with lessons to help students progress toward long-term objectives or goals.

Because of the differences in objectives, the type of *evaluation* needed for lessons and activities differs. Lessons are followed by a formal evaluation of whether each student can independently meet the objective. The evaluations used with activities are often less formal and less individual.

The following sections provide further information and examples to help clarify the key differences between, and elements of, lessons and activities.

Lessons

As previously stated, the purpose of a lesson is to provide initial instruction on important skills or knowledge, and the objective is for each student to meet a specific, measurable, short-term objective by the end of the lesson.

Lesson Example

In this lesson, an instructor wants to teach students to spell the plural form of nouns ending in *y.* The objective is that students will write the plural form of 10 listed nouns ending in *y* preceded by a consonant, for example, *berry* to *berries.* The teacher instructs the students by explaining the spelling rule, showing examples, providing practice, and giving feedback. The teacher may also begin by showing examples and then leading the students to discover the spelling rule or pattern. Following the lesson, the instructor evaluates by giving a test as described in the objective.

This is a lesson because the teacher is providing *initial instruction* on an *important basic skill;* the instructor is spending time *teaching;* and intends to *evaluate* the students to see if they have met the short-term objective following the lesson.

Definition of Terms

The italicized terms in the previous paragraph are defined as follows:

- **Initial instruction** "Initial" *does not* mean that students have never heard the topic of the lesson before. They will typically have had some previous introduction, and the teacher will use strategies in the lesson to connect the new learning to prior knowledge and experience. If the students do not have the necessary background, then the teacher has selected the wrong objective or lesson to teach at this time. "Initial" *does* mean that the students need formal instruction before they can use the new knowledge or skill. They need more than review and practice.

- **Important basic skill** Important basic skills include academic skills, thinking skills, study skills, social skills, vocational skills, and so on. They are considered basic because they are either important for real-life functioning or they are necessary prerequisites for other important skills. (One could make a case that the skill in the previous spelling lesson example is not important in an age of computers with spell-check capabilities.)

- **Teaching** Teaching can take many forms. It can be highly teacher-directed; it can incorporate peers; it can emphasize discovery. However, teaching means that the teacher does more than provide activities, hoping that students learn something. If no teaching is necessary, you do not have a lesson. Instead, you have either an activity or a time-filler.

- **Evaluate** When writing a lesson objective, a standard is established against which a student's learning is evaluated. The method of evaluating learning is also decided at that time. There are many ways to evaluate—not only written tests. If it is unnecessary to evaluate each student's learning, then you are not providing initial instruction on an important basic skill (in other words, you are not teaching a lesson). If your intention is to provide an "experience," you may have an activity, not a lesson. If your intention is to ask students to demonstrate their knowledge or skill with the help of peers or a teacher, you have an ongoing practice activity, not a completed lesson.

- **Short-term objective** Lessons are intended to help students reach a measurable, short-term objective. A series of lessons, often combined with activities, leads to the attainment of long-term objectives or goals. Long and short are not exact terms. We cannot give exact definitions or numbers, but consider the following example. Mrs. Lopez wants her students to learn to add and subtract fractions with uncommon denominators. She breaks up the long-term objective into several short-term lesson objectives, such as finding least common multiples, converting improper fractions, and so on. She will plan a lesson for each of those short-term objectives. Mrs. Lopez may decide to teach the lesson on least common multiples in 20-minute periods over 3 days. She considers this one lesson because she is not going to formally evaluate until after the third day. She will, however, want to evaluate each student's success before going on to the next lesson. The students will not have received all of the necessary instruction to reach the short-term objective until Day 3.

- **Following** The evaluation of the objective following the lesson may occur immediately after the lesson or may occur one day or several days after the lesson. You may need to provide extended practice before evaluating, or you may have found, through monitoring, that you need to reteach before evaluating. However, if you do not intend to evaluate for weeks or months, you may plan to evaluate whether students meet a long-term objective or goal, not a short-term lesson objective.

Summary

You begin planning a lesson by selecting a specific, measurable, short-term objective. Then you provide opportunities to learn. You follow the lesson with an evaluation to determine whether each student can independently meet the objective.

Activities

Activities are not intended to provide initial instruction and do not include the same evaluation as lessons. Activities may lead up to lessons, be part of lessons, follow up lessons, or extend lessons. Activities have a variety of *purposes*.

Activity Purposes

Activities are designed to provide:

- Motivation for students before beginning a series of lessons.

- Background information, experience, or an opportunity to recall prior knowledge before a series of lessons. (A lesson typically includes an opening with strategies to motivate students or to help them connect this lesson with prior knowledge. We are differentiating this from longer, more elaborate activities used before a series of lessons.)

- Ongoing practice toward long-term objectives or goals.

- Opportunities for students to apply a previously learned skill.

- Opportunities for students to generalize previously learned information.

- Opportunities for students to integrate a variety of knowledge and skills learned from lessons in different subject areas.

Although activities are not associated with a specific short-term objective, they are planned with a definite intention. Teachers develop activities as part of their long-term planning and have a clear purpose for activities that help students reach important goals and objectives. Teachers also use activities to help evaluate student needs and progress. Even though activities are not always paired with formal evaluations of individuals, teachers carefully observe their students during activities and examine the products that students create to decide whether additional activities and lessons are needed.

Activity Examples

The following examples illustrate the wide variety of activity purposes:

■ Before beginning a series of lessons on magnets, Mrs. Troxel plans an activity for which she gives students different types of magnets and materials and has them experiment, make predictions, generate questions, and so on. Her purpose with this activity is to create interest and to motivate the students to learn more about magnets, to make sure each student has experience with magnets before beginning the lessons, and to provide practice on thinking skills. Mrs. Troxel also uses this activity to assess prior knowledge before deciding where to begin lessons.

■ Every day Mrs. Chenier writes a sentence on the blackboard that is full of errors. Students are to copy the sentence and fix the errors. This is an activity that provides ongoing practice on proofreading for errors in capitalization, punctuation, spelling, and so on—not to give initial instruction on written mechanics.

■ Students have had earlier lessons on how to write letters. You now plan an activity in which students write letters to the agricultural extension agent asking for information on rabbit care. (There is a pet rabbit in the classroom.) You may choose to review earlier lessons at the beginning of the activity, but you are not providing initial instruction on letter writing.

■ Students are making a garden in the school yard. They use measuring skills learned in math, information about plant needs for light and water learned in science, and group decision-making skills learned in social skills lessons to select the vegetables to be planted. This is an activity intended to help students integrate and apply skills learned in a variety of subject areas.

■ Following math lessons on the multiplication concept and operation, students can figure out the answers to single-digit multiplication problems, but they are not always 100 percent accurate and they are very slow. An instructor plans a series of practice activities—partner flash card practice and multiplication bingo—to help the students reach the long-term objective, which is that students will write answers to multiplication fact problems (0–10) at a rate of 80 digits per minute with no errors. In this case, the instructor follows each activity with a timed math fact test to chart individual student progress toward the objective.

■ The week before January 15th, Mr. Vandermay shows a video and leads a discussion about Dr. Martin Luther King, Jr. as the first in a series of activities leading up to Dr. King's birthday. His goal is to provide general information about a famous American and to make sure his students understand the upcoming holiday. He has not written a short-term objective and plans no evaluation.

■ Mr. Palm plans an activity for his second graders about polar bears. He reads a story and then helps the students put together a book that includes drawings and sentences about polar bears. Mr. Palm is providing initial instruction, in a sense, because his students do not know many of the polar bear facts discussed in the book. However, he does not really care whether each student memorizes these facts and does not intend to give a test on polar bears. Polar bears are a vehicle for providing ongoing practice on listening skills, fine motor skills, writing complete sentences, and so on. As he looks at the students' books, he will monitor progress ("I see that Ralph is still forgetting to put a period at the end of his sentences."), but there is no short-term objective with a formal evaluation. Mr. Palm may have other goals as well—to pique curiosity about animals and nature or to give the students experience in being authors.

■ Mrs. Eerkes plans an activity to follow a series of lessons on the Civil War. It will be a simulated debate in Congress on the issue of preserving the union versus states' rights. The students will be divided into two groups and given time to research the issues and to plan their speeches. She has several purposes for this activity: (1) to provide practice in public speaking and cooperative planning and research; (2) to encourage a deeper understanding of the issues involved; and (3) to allow the students to demonstrate their knowledge in an alternative way. She knows that this activity will not allow her to be aware of each student's independent understanding, so she has planned other evaluation methods as well.

■ Mr. Floyd plans an art activity in which he will teach his students to tie-dye. He will include many of the elements of lesson planning—step-by-step instruction, demonstrations, and supervised practice. This is considered an activity because tie-dyeing is not an important basic skill (anymore), and because students will each produce a tie-dyed item, but with Mr. Floyd's help. He will not test them later, either by asking them to list the steps in tie-dyeing or by asking them to make a tie-dyed item alone.

Summary

Lessons have been defined very narrowly and activities have been defined very broadly. Lessons have a consistent structure and involve explaining, demonstrating, and supervising student practice. Activities lack one or more of the attributes of a lesson and have many purposes and structures. Both need to be carefully planned.

■ Selecting the Appropriate Plan

When teaching students, whether it is in your own classroom or that of a cooperating teacher during a practicum or student teaching, the two basic types of plans that you will need to write are activity plans and lesson plans. Both require careful thought and become easier and less time consuming to write with practice. As your understanding of important planning components increases, you will be able to make decisions more automatically and fewer details will need to be put in writing.

When you decide on a topic to teach (or are given a teaching assignment by a cooperating teacher), you need to carefully analyze whether you need to write an activity plan or a lesson plan. Ask yourself the questions in Figure 2.1.

Figure 2.1 provides a summary of the decisions that will help you determine when to write a lesson plan and when to write an activity plan.

| **Figure 2.1** | **Lesson Plan or Activity Plan?** |

Ask yourself the following questions:

■ Do I need to provide initial instruction?

■ Is this an important basic skill?

■ Can I write a specific, measurable, short-term objective for this topic?

■ Will I need to spend time teaching (rather than only reviewing or giving directions)?

■ Will I want to evaluate whether each student can independently meet the objective following the lesson?

continued on next page

Figure 2.1   Lesson Plan or Activity Plan? (continued)

If your answer to any of these questions is "no," write an *activity plan* (see "Activity Plans" in Chapter 5).

Write *preplanning* tasks:

- Activity objective
- Activity description
- Activity rationale
- Prerequisite skills and knowledge; key terms and vocabulary

and

- Activity beginning
- Activity middle
- Activity closing

If your answer to all of these questions is "yes," then write a *lesson plan* (see "Lesson Plans" in Chapter 4).

Write *preplanning* tasks:

- Connection analysis
- Content analysis
- Lesson objective
- Objective rationale

and

- Lesson set-up
- Lesson opening
- Lesson body
- Extended practice
- Lesson closing
- Lesson evaluation

Chapter 3

Writing Objectives

Introduction

An effective activity or lesson plan begins with an appropriate, clearly written objective. However, as stated earlier, planning the curriculum is beyond the scope of this book. We are not going to teach you to select or develop appropriate goals and objectives for your students. We are assuming that you know what your students need to learn next.

We are going to teach you a format for writing objectives in a specific, measurable form. Writing those objectives will make it more likely that your activity or lesson and the intended learning outcome will match, and that you will be able to tell if your teaching was effective, whether your students learned. It is essential, however, to remember that objectives can be well written in terms of form and yet not be appropriate or important for your students.

Definition and Purpose

An objective is a description of a learning outcome. Objectives describe where we want students to go—not how to get them there. They pinpoint the destination—not the journey. Well written objectives help teachers clarify precisely what they want their students to learn, help provide lesson focus and direction, and help guide the selection of appropriate practice. Using objectives, teachers can

evaluate whether or not their students have learned and whether their own teaching has been effective. Objectives also help focus and motivate students, and are communication tools to use with other teachers and parents.

State Standards: A Source of Objectives

Most states have adopted a set of standards that provide a description of what students across the state will learn as they progress through the K–12 public school system. The standards are meant to guide the general curriculum and were developed in an attempt to raise the achievement levels of and to standardize the learning expectations for all students in the state. The standards appear as sets of goals in content areas such as reading, mathematics, and the arts, and describe what students will accomplish in each area. State tests, given at various grade levels, measure student progress in relation to the standards.

The 1997 amendments to the Individuals with Disabilities Education Act (IDEA 97) are intended to ensure that special education is also connected with state standards, and that students with disabilities have access to the higher standards of the general curriculum. Therefore, program planning for these students is done with the state standards in mind.

State standards and goals provide focus in schools in several ways. First, they serve as tools around which communication about learning can take place among students, teachers, principals, and parents. Also, they help describe the general curriculum and provide a guide for planning the content of teaching (King-Sears, 2001). This ensures that students, including those with disabilities, have opportunities to prepare for the state tests and learn the content considered important enough to appear in a state standard.

Example of a State Standard

State Standard Mathematics #1

The student understands and applies the concepts and procedures of mathematics.

Component 1.1: Understand and apply concepts and procedures from number sense.

- Benchmark 1 (Grade 4)   Identify, compare, and order whole numbers and simple fractions.

- Benchmark 2 (Grade 7)   Compare and order whole numbers, fractions, and decimals.

- Benchmark 3 (Grade 10)   Explain the magnitude of numbers by comparing and ordering real numbers.

Note that all examples of state standards in this chapter come from Washington state.

■ From General to Specific: State Standards to Objectives

While state standards provide general content ideas, teachers must write their own objectives for lessons, activities, and units. In special education, teachers help develop IEPs that include measurable annual goals and objectives intended to enable students to progress in the general curriculum based on the state standards. A teacher's task is to translate the standards into useful objectives that are used to guide instruction. In this way, the learning outcomes included in the objectives will link to the state standards.

Writing objectives from standards and goals begins with an understanding of how standards, goals, and objectives differ. The following are some of the main differences:

- *Specificity* Specific learning outcomes are described in objectives whereas standards include more general outcome statements. Goals may be general (understand the concept of fractions) or specific (write fractions to describe relationships).

- *Long-Term or Short-Term* Objectives are considered short-term because they describe the learning outcome expected in days, weeks, or months. Goals and standards describe learning outcomes expected to occur at the end of a longer period of time—weeks, months, or years, thus they are long-term outcome statements. In general, objectives are more short term than goals or standards.

- *Uses* Objectives are used in lesson and activity plans and in IEPs. Measurable annual goals are included in IEPs. Goals are also found in units of instruction. Standards are used in state or district curricula or set by professional organizations.

The following examples show goals and objectives that are congruent with state standards.

Examples of Goals and Objectives Related to State Standards

Social Studies (History) Standard 2, Component 2.3, Benchmark 3, Grade 10: Argue both for and against a position (state standard or goal).

- In a role-play situation, students will present an argument that includes three reasons supported with facts, for one side of a controversial issue (for example, capital punishment). (This is a long-term objective or unit goal.)

- Given a list of arguments, students will correctly identify positions supported with facts and positions based on unsubstantiated opinions or beliefs (short-term lesson objective).

Writing Standard 1, Component 1.3,
Benchmark 3, Grade 4:
Write complete sentences
(state standard or goal).

- When writing a paragraph, Leah will include a complete subject and predicate in each sentence by June 6, 2007 (long-term objective or IEP goal).

- Given 10 sentences, students will identify those that are incomplete (short-term lesson objective).

Note that it is our intention to concentrate on specific short- and long-term objectives throughout this book. This means that when we talk about writing objectives for activity plans, for example, we mean writing specific long-term objectives. When we talk about writing lesson objectives, we mean specific, short-term objectives.

Components of Objectives

Well written, measurable objectives include four components: content, behavior, condition, and criterion (Howell & Nolet, 2000). Including these four components will help ensure that your objectives are clear and specific. Each of the four components is briefly described below and examples and nonexamples are provided. Common errors may be noted and suggestions for writing each objective component may be included.

Example Objective

Students will write answers to 20 subtraction problems (two-digit numbers from three-digit numbers with regrouping) on a worksheet, with no errors.

The Four Components of an Objective

- *Content* The content is the subject matter. It tells what the student will learn. In the previous example objective, the content is "subtraction problems, two-digit numbers from three-digit numbers with regrouping." Note that the content is described specifically so

that anyone reading the objective understands what the student will learn.

- *Behavior* The behavior tells what the student will do to show that she has learned. It is a verb that describes an observable action. In the example objective, the behavior is "write." The student will demonstrate knowledge of subtraction by writing the answers to problems.

- *Condition* It is important to describe the conditions—circumstances, situation, or setting—under which the student will perform the behavior. It is the condition that will apply while the student is being evaluated, rather than the learning condition, which must be described. In the objective above, the condition is "on a worksheet," not in a real-world context.

- *Criterion* The criterion is the level of acceptable performance, the standard of mastery, or the proficiency level expected. This component describes how well the students should perform in order to say that they have met the objective. In the objective above, the criterion is "with no errors."

Content

This component describes the specific subject matter to be learned.

Suggestions When Writing the Content

1. Be *specific* enough that anyone reading the objective will understand the subject matter.

2. Be sure the description of content can stand alone, that is, be *"materials-free."* The reader should be able to understand the content of the objective without tracking down specific materials.

3. Be *generic* enough that the emphasis is on knowledge and skills that are important and applicable in a variety of contexts.

Examples of Content

- Add *unlike fractions with common factors between denominators.*

- Write *two-syllable spelling words with -ing endings (for example, hoping, hopping).*

- Compare and contrast *fables and fairy tales.*

Nonexamples of Content

- Add *fractions* (not specific); answer *fraction problems 1–7 on p. 42* (not "materials-free").

- Write *spelling words* (not specific); complete *Unit 4 in spelling book* (not "materials-free").

- Compare and contrast *"The Lazy Princess" and "Lost in the Woods"* (not generic).

Common Error When Writing the Content

A common error is to include content appropriate for an activity or assignment rather than a learning outcome. The following are examples of errors in writing content:

1. Write *adjectives for 10 animals and plants from the rainforest unit.* Are you looking for knowledge of the rainforest or knowledge of adjectives? This may be a good integrated practice activity, but it is not a clear objective.

2. Present *five facts about a bird of their choice.* The content is unclear. We do not know what facts are to be learned. Is the real content using reference books to find facts, making presentations, or summarizing from the unit on birds? Do not confuse an instructional theme with content.

Behavior

This component states what students will do to demonstrate their learning. Write the behavior or performance as an observable verb so outcomes can be measured.

Examples of Behavior

say	write	list
draw	diagram	paraphrase
operate	throw	volunteer

circle	complete	copy
label	predict	calculate
add	design	select
name	hit	laugh
choose	initiate	put in order
define	compare/contrast	

Notice that some of these verbs can be made more specific, for example, one could "define" in writing or orally. You must judge how much specificity is needed, but when in doubt be more specific rather than less. For example, the commonly used verbs "identify" and "recognize" often need further specifics, such as "identify by underlining."

Nonexamples of Behavior

know	realize	comprehend
understand	experience	discover
memorize	believe	appreciate
learn	value	be familiar with

Notice that these verbs may be appropriate when writing general goals, aims, outcomes, or standards. They are not appropriate for measurable objectives because you cannot know that a student "knows" or "comprehends" or has "learned" something unless she does something overt. For example, you may have a goal that your students appreciate poetry. You cannot tell if that objective has been reached unless your students do something (voluntarily check out poetry books from the library or write poetry without being assigned to do so, for example).

Suggestions When Writing the Behavior

1. Decide whether you want students to "identify" or "produce" as you write the behavior component in objectives (Howell & Nolet, 2000). A lesson for teaching students to produce or write metaphors will be quite different from a lesson for teaching students to identify or recognize metaphors written by someone else.

2. Include only one or two required behaviors in an objective. Objectives that include many behaviors (for example, students will research, write, draw, and present) make evaluation confusing and often end up being descriptions of

activities or assignments rather than learning outcomes.

3. Consider including alternate behaviors (write, type, or say, for example) to provide the flexibility to allow all students, including those with disabilities, to be successful.

4. Leave out nonessential or redundant behaviors.

   - "Students will copy the sentences and circle all nouns." Omit "copy the sentences." It has nothing to do with the skill of identifying nouns.

   - Omit "locate" in an example such as, "Students will locate and point to. . . . " If the student is pointing to something, then you can assume he has located it.

5. Omit the phrase "be able to" as in the example "The student will be able to make a speech. . . ." The phrase adds words but no meaning. Remember that the performance is important, not an assumed ability or inability.

6. Do not use the phrase "Student will pass a test on. . . ." It does not communicate specific information about what the student will do or learn.

7. Write objectives for what the students will do, not what the teacher will do. Objectives may be written for one student or a group of students.

Conditions

Describing the evaluation conditions provides additional specificity about what the student will learn. Notice that the *italicized* conditions in the following objectives result in three different learning outcomes.

- Students will write the capitals of each of the 17 western states *given a list of the states and a list of the capitals*. (They will be asked to recognize state capitals. This is really a matching task.)

- Students will write the capitals of each of the 17 western states *given a list of the states*. (They will be asked to recall the state capitals rather than simply recognize them.)

- Students will write the capitals of each of the 17 western states *on a blank outline map*. (They

must recall the names and locations of the states and the names of the capitals in order to write the capitals in the correct places.)

Notice that the different conditions affect the level of difficulty of the objective and will affect the lesson and practice activities that you plan for your students.

Types of Conditions

Various types of conditions may be included in objectives. A very important condition is whether we are asking students to perform a skill in isolation or in context, or in artificial or real-world circumstances. This is important to think about when sequencing objectives and when planning for generalization or transfer of the skill. The information or materials provided—often called the "givens"—may be important to specify. Visualize the evaluation or testing situation and what the students will have available. A third type of condition—a description of the setting or situation—may help clarify the objective as well, especially social skill and learning strategy objectives. Obviously, all conditions need not be mentioned (for example, the lights will be on in the room). However, be sure to include those that communicate important information about the learning outcome.

Examples of Conditions

In isolation or in context

- Computing measurement equivalents *on a worksheet* or *while following a recipe*

- Responding to teasing *in a role play* or *on the playground*

- Correcting punctuation errors *in given sentences* or *while proofreading an essay*

- Pronouncing words *when shown flashcards* or *in a story*

You may want to specify whether the student is going to solve mixed math problems or correct mixed grammar errors. Otherwise, you may only be evaluating whether students can figure out the pattern (for example, all problems require regrouping or all sentences are missing a question mark).

Information or materials provided

- On a diagram
- Given a list of ten nouns
- Given a description of symptoms
- Given an incomplete proof
- Given population figures for each country
- With a calculator, ruler, scale
- Using notes, dictionary, word processor
- From memory, with nothing provided

Setting or situation

- In front of class
- During seatwork; on homework
- In familiar situations; with strangers
- When given directions
- When corrected
- During class discussions
- During teacher presentations
- When working with a small group of peers
- During free time
- When given a choice
- On an in-class test
- In a textbook
- When teased; when angry; when refused

A combination of conditions are often specified

- Given ten problems and a calculator

In some cases— for example, when writing objectives for students with severe disabilities or for very young students—it may be important to specify whether students will be performing the behavior independently or with assistance.

- With or without reminders
- With or without physical assistance
- With or without verbal cues

Note that typically the "default" condition is without assistance.

Nonexamples of Conditions

- *Describing the learning condition rather than the evaluation condition.* It doesn't matter where or when the students learned the knowledge or skill. Remember that objectives focus on outcomes. Avoid using the following conditions: "As a result of my instruction . . . ," "After a lesson on . . . ," "After com-

pleting the weather unit . . . ," "After studying . . . ," and so on.

- *Adding unimportant information.* Avoid using conditions such as, "When asked by the teacher . . ." or "Given a blank piece of paper. . . ." Some conditions are obvious and do not need to be written.

Criterion

The criterion specifies the standard of acceptable performance. It states how well students must perform to say that they have met the objective.

Examples of Criterion

As a total number or proportion

- Comparing or contrasting four key issues
- Using two types of figurative language
- At every opportunity
- In three out of three trials
- At least five times daily
- With no errors
- With ten out of ten correct
- With 90 percent accuracy
- At least three of the steps
- Five paragraphs in length

In terms of time

- Within 10 minutes; per minute
- For one hour each day
- The first time
- For 5 consecutive days
- By September 6

As a variation

- Within plus or minus 1 inch
- To the nearest mile
- Within 1 percent
- To the closest hundredth

As a description or result

- Light bulb turns on
- Liquid disappears
- Until consensus is reached
- Story includes a conflict and resolution
- The strategy selected solves the problem in the fewest steps

Often a combination of criteria is used

- 50 per minute with 100 percent accuracy by March 10
- Backing up opinion with data from three relevant research studies
- Paragraphs include topic sentences and at least three supporting details

Nonexamples of Criterion

Does not pass the "stranger test"

- As judged by teacher
- To teacher's satisfaction

These obviously do not pass the "stranger test" (Kaplan, 1995), that is, they are open to interpretation. A stranger may not interpret them the same way as you do. Remember that one of the purposes of writing objectives is to communicate clearly with students, parents, and other teachers and professionals.

Common Errors When Writing the Criterion

1. *The criterion is too low.* Keep high performance standards, especially for basic skills in reading, writing, and arithmetic. Do not confuse setting criteria in objectives with assigning grades. It will take some students longer to reach an objective. You may want to set gradually increasing criteria—50 percent accuracy by October 1; 75 percent accuracy by November 1; 100 percent accuracy by December 1. However, be sure that the final outcome is high enough. If a student is only 80 percent accurate on number recognition, he is doomed to failure in arithmetic.

2. *The criterion is set arbitrarily.*   Do not make the error of automatically writing 85 percent accuracy for every objective. Set realistic standards and time limits. Establish criteria either by doing the task yourself or by having a successful peer do the task. Do *not* write: ". . . will say the multiples of 10 from 10 to 100 in 3 minutes" or ". . . locate a word in the dictionary in 5 minutes." Try it! If it took you 5 minutes to find a word, you would never choose to use the dictionary.

3. *"Percent accuracy" is misused.*

   - When there are many possible divergent or complex responses, percent accuracy as the criterion does not make sense. One cannot write a story with 100 percent accuracy nor manage anger with 80 percent accuracy.
   - There needs to be a number of responses for percent accuracy to be sensible—not simply correct or incorrect. For example, choose "name the state you live in" or "correctly name the state you live in," rather than "name the state you live in with 100 percent (50 percent) accuracy." Write "turn off the computer correctly" or "without damaging anything," rather than "turn off the computer with 100 percent accuracy."
   - Sometimes percent accuracy works, but it would be too much work to compute. To decide if someone reached 85 percent accuracy in punctuating a story, you would first have to count all of the opportunities for punctuation within the story.

4. *There is no end in sight.*   If the objective is that the student will spell words correctly in all written work, when would you be able to say that a student had met this objective?

Suggestions When Writing the Criterion

1. Think about how many times you want the students to demonstrate the skill during evaluation in order to be confident that they have met the objective. For example, do they need to write their addresses five times to prove they can do it? If Jon responds to teasing appropriately during one recess, are you sure he has learned that skill?

2. Be specific enough so that any evaluator would reach the same conclusion as to whether the student meets the objective.

Avoid writing, "Student will write *descriptive* sentences." This criterion is not specific enough to determine if the objective of the lesson has been met. The following two sentences cannot be evaluated using this criterion: "The bike is big," and "Perched on the seat of the bike, I felt like Hillary on the peak of Everest."

3. Make sure the criterion gets at the skill you want. For example, if the skill you are looking for is writing descriptively, do not make your criterion say that all words need to be spelled correctly. In addition, do not write a criterion solely because it is easy to think of (for example, "Student will underline the adjectives in a given sentence without error.").

In attempting to make the objective specific and measurable, however, do not end up making it trivial!

■ Summary

1. Write objectives that describe learning *outcomes*, not activities or assignments (TenBrink, 1999).

   NOT: Wally will write spelling words missed on the pretest five times each.

   NOT: Students in pairs will take turns throwing dice, adding the numbers together, and stating the total.

   NOT: Students will play a quiz show game in which they divide into two teams and answer questions from Chapter 4 in the social studies book. Each team will ask the other team members questions.

   NOT: Ben will write letters to the main character in the story.

2. **Keep objectives clean and simple; save creativity for instruction.**

   NOT: Students will demonstrate their understanding of the reasons that pandas were endangered by graphing the average number of panda babies born and the number of pandas who died per year for the last 10 years.

   NOT: Students will create a poster that demonstrates their knowledge of modern Mexican culture.

3. **Be sure to write objectives that represent *important* learning outcomes!**

   NOT: Michelle will write the names of the counties in each state in the United States from memory without error.

Examples of Measurable Objectives

- Given ten sets of five pictures, four of which are related—belong to the same category, such as vegetables or tools—students will point to the one in each set that does not belong, without error (lesson objective).

- Students will correctly state temperatures, with an accuracy of plus or minus 1 degree, shown on pictures of five thermometers depicting temperatures between –20 degrees F and 95 degrees F (lesson objective).

- Randi will write correct answers to five of five inference questions on a grade level reading passage (IEP objective).

- Students will return the change from $1.00, using the fewest possible coins, for four purchases, with no errors (long-term unit objective).

- When the fire alarm sounds for a fire drill, students will form a line within 30 seconds and leave the building following the correct route, without teacher prompting (lesson objective).

- Kathi and Chuck will correctly compute the amount of wallpaper needed to cover a wall of given dimensions (lesson objective).

- When teased by peers, Jorge will respond by ignoring, walking away, or quietly asking the person to stop in eight out of eight observed opportunities by May 1 (IEP goal).

- Richard Michael will complete all of his independent seatwork assignments during class with at least 90 percent accuracy for 2 consecutive weeks (IEP goal).

A Final Thought

We wish to restate the importance of beginning your lesson or activity planning with a clear idea of what you want your students to learn. Writing a specific objective will cause you to think this through. It has been our observation that, when teachers experience frustration with a particular lesson or activity, it is often the case that they are unable to clearly state what students were to learn. Writing a clear objective is well worth your time.

Practicing Writing Objectives: Study Suggestions

Once you have mastered the skill of writing clear objectives, planning useful activities and lessons will be easier and less time consuming. Following are strategies to help you become accurate and fluent at writing objectives. As with other writing tasks, editing and rewriting will always be important.

1. Study the component names and definitions. Paraphrase them.

2. Review the lists of component examples. Explain why each example fits the definition. Create your own examples.

3. Practice writing your own objectives.

   a. Think of a general instructional goal, such as the following:

      - Know how to use an index
      - Learn baseball skills
      - Understand cell division
      - Distinguish between fact and fiction
      - Resolve conflicts nonviolently
      - Do homework

   b. Specify the content (index becomes subject index in textbook, for example).

   c. Specify the behavior (know how to use becomes locate page numbers for topics).

   d. Add necessary conditions (for example, given a textbook and a list of topics).

   e. Add criteria (no errors, within 30 seconds).

   Notice that there are many possibilities for each component. You may wish to practice writing a variety of objectives on one topic.

   f. Put the components together into a one- or two-sentence objective. For example, given a textbook and a list of topics, the student will locate page numbers for topics in the textbook's subject index with no errors, within 30 seconds.

   g. Examine for clarity and conciseness and rewrite as necessary. For example, given a textbook, the student will write the correct page number from the index for four out of four listed topics within 2 minutes.

4. After you have written an objective, critique it following these self-evaluation steps:

   a. Are all four components present? (Label them.)

   b. Is each component correct?

      - Content specific? Generic? Materials-free?
      - Behavior observable?
      - Evaluation condition described?
      - Criterion specific? Measurable? Realistic?

   c. Does the objective need editing? Is it wordy? Is it awkward?

   d. Does it pass the stranger test?

   e. Does it represent an important learning outcome?

References

Howell, K. W., & Nolet, V. (2000). *Curriculum-Based Evaluation: Teaching and Decision Making* (3rd ed.). Belmont, CA: Wadsworth/Thomson Learning.

Kaplan, J. S. (1995). *Beyond Behavior Modification* (3rd ed.). Austin, TX: Pro-Ed. (4th edition in press).

King-Sears, M. E. (2001). Three steps for gaining access to the general education curriculum for learners with disabilities. *Intervention in School and clinic, 37*(2), 67–76.

Lignugaris/Kraft, B., Marchand-Martella, N., & Martella, R. (2001). Writing better goals and short-term objectives or benchmarks. *Teaching Exceptional Children, 34*(1), 52–58.

Matlock, L., Fielder, K., & Walsh, D. (2001). Building the foundation for standards-based instruction for all students. *Teaching Exceptional Children, 33*(5), 68–73.

TenBrink, T. D. (1999). Instructional objectives. In J. M. Cooper (Ed.), *Classroom Teaching Skills* (6th ed.). Boston: Houghton Mifflin.

Walsh, J. M. (2001). Getting the "big picture" of IEP goals and state standards. *Teaching Exceptional Children, 33*(5), 18–26.

Chapter

4

Lesson Plans

■ Introduction

Putting together a daily lesson is the end result of a complex planning process. This process begins when the teacher determines the overall curriculum to be taught. The curriculum is based on an analysis of student needs, on district or state standards, generalizations or big ideas from the subject area, and on a student's Individualized Education Program (IEP). Once the curriculum for the year or for a particular unit is identified, the teacher divides the content into individual lessons and writes specific lesson objectives, making sure each lesson clearly fits with the goals of the overall curriculum. The teacher finally selects a lesson model—direct instruction, informal presentation, structured discovery—that will work best to meet the objective of a specific lesson.

Teachers use lessons to help students attain a specific short-term objective. Lessons typically have a clear beginning and ending, and they will last a few hours at the most. Lessons are followed by an evaluation of each student's learning in relation to the selected objective(s). Series of lessons that lead to the attainment of long-term objectives or goals are often combined into a unit of instruction. Remember that lessons may be developed for individuals or small groups of students as well as for the whole class.

Lessons can be used to teach specific skills and information directly or to give students the opportunity to discover information on their own or with their peers. The type of content that can be taught through lessons is extremely diverse. Teachers typically use lessons to teach academic content; to develop study skills, social skills, and problem-solving skills; and to promote higher level thinking.

Examples of Lesson Objectives

The following objectives help demonstrate the wide variety of skills and knowledge that can be addressed in lessons.

■ When teased in a role-playing situation, students will talk through each of the five problem-solving steps.

■ On a list of 25 sentences, students will circle the complete subject in all sentences.

■ Given a list of 10 assignments, students will accurately transfer all of them to an assignment calendar.

■ Given 5 2-step multiplication and division problems, students will find the answer and write or draw a description of the problem-solving process they used.

■ Generic Components of a Lesson Plan

A lesson plan is a written description of how students will progress toward a specific objective. It clearly describes the teacher's statements and actions, which hopefully result in student learning.

All lesson plans include the following seven generic components:

1. Preplanning tasks
2. Lesson setup
3. Lesson opening
4. Lesson body
5. Lesson closing
6. Extended practice
7. Evaluation

The specific content of the components will vary with different lesson models because each model enables students to progress toward an objective in a different way.

The following descriptions of each component include two parts: the purpose of the component and a summary of the type of content that might be included. Our intent is to help you generate ideas, not to list everything that must be included in each component in every lesson plan. It is up to you to select or generate the specifics that are appropriate for the lesson model, the subject matter, and the students being taught. As you plan each component, be sure you are planning for the diverse needs of your students (see Chapter 7).

The components are described here in the order in which they would appear in the lesson plan. This is not necessarily the order in which they will be written. When preparing to write a lesson plan, refer to "Sequence for Writing the Components of a Lesson Plan" in this chapter and to Chapters 8–10 for information about the specific model you will be using.

Component 1: Preplanning Tasks

The purpose of this component is to help you thoroughly think through the content to be taught and the best way to teach it. This is a good time to think again about how this content connects with the larger picture, for example, the state standards and the gener-

alizations or big ideas within the subject area. Generally, this component consists of the following:

■ *Connection Analysis*   The lesson planning should begin by identifying the *generalization or big idea, state standard,* or *IEP goal* that you will address in your lesson.

■ *Content Analysis*   The next step is to decide on the specific content to be taught. This is accomplished by completing a thorough content analysis, which helps you think in detail about the content you will be teaching. In turn, this allows you to determine the best way to teach the content.

The term *content analysis* is a general one. The following are various types of content analysis: a *subject matter outline,* a *task analysis* or a *concept analysis,* a *principle statement,* definitions of *key terms or vocabulary,* and a list of *prerequisite skills and knowledge.*

The type of content analysis done depends on *what* is being taught. When you plan to teach a concept, for example, a concept analysis will always be included. When the point of the lesson is to teach a skill or procedure, you would always include a task analysis. When teaching information about a topic, a subject matter outline works best. A clearly written principle statement is included when teaching about a cause and effect or an if-then relationship. All lessons may have a number of key terms and vocabulary that need to be defined in ways the students will understand. A listing of prerequisite skills and knowledge would also be routinely considered as part of a content analysis. This analysis will help determine whether the content is appropriate for the students and will also help you write the objective. A content analysis is a critical preplanning task. Time spent on analyses will save time later, as the rest of the lesson or activity plan will fall into place more easily (see Chapter 6).

■ *Objective*   Select and write a clear, specific, worthwhile lesson objective. The objective must contain a behavior, the content, the condition, and the criterion so that you can specify, in detail, what is to be learned and how well the students are to learn it (see Chapter 3).

■ *Objective Rationale*   Once you have written the objective, you need to actively think about and evaluate its importance and relevance. Reread it and ask yourself the following questions: Why should my students know how to do this? How will my students benefit from this learning? Does this objective connect to a state standard? Does it relate to an important big idea? Does it lead to an IEP goal? When you are satisfied with your answers to these questions, you will have an objective rationale. If your answers to these questions help you determine that the objective is not important, write a new one.

Ask yourself the following question also: Does my objective really represent what I want my students to know? For example, do I really care if they can name three types of penguins, or is the purpose actually to practice following directions? If practicing following directions is the purpose, you would need to write an activity plan, not a lesson plan.

■ *Lesson Model*   Now you are ready to determine the best way to teach the objective. This decision can be based on the objective itself, the students, the time available, or the type of content being taught (very abstract or difficult, for example). Lesson models presented in this text are direct instruction (Chapter 8), informal presentation (Chapter 9), and structured discovery (Chapter 10).

Avoid making the mistake of selecting activities and methods and then trying to make up an objective for them.

Component 2: Lesson Setup

The purpose of the setup is to prepare students for the beginning of the lesson. A lesson should not begin until you have the students' attention (they are physically turned toward you, they are listening to you, and so on). Also, you can prevent problems by explaining behavior expectations to students right up front, rather than waiting for problems to occur.

■ *Signal for Attention*   Signal to the students to gain their attention; have them look at you and listen to you so the lesson can begin. In some cases, students are ready and a simple "Let's get started" or "Good morning" is a sufficient signal for attention. In other cases a stronger signal— such as turning the lights off and on or ringing a bell—is needed to attract their attention. It is important to wait for everyone's attention and to acknowledge it (see Chapter 6).

■ *Statement of Behavior Expectations*   It is important to explain the rules and procedures that apply to the current lesson, that is, how you expect the students to act during the lesson. It is not necessary to review all classroom rules and procedures, just those most pertinent to the current lesson (raising hands, getting help, for example). The statement of behavior expectations should be written in language that is positive, is appropriate to the age of the students, is specific, and is clear. You should consider stating expectations at each transition within the lesson, rather than stating them all at the beginning (see Chapter 6).

Component 3: Lesson Opening

The purpose of the lesson opening is to help prepare students for the learning to come. You will typically want to let students know what they can expect to learn, why it is important and how it builds on what they already know. You will also want to get them excited about learning. Planning the lesson opening consists of selecting one or more strategies from each of the following categories:

■ *Motivate and Focus Students*   To motivate and focus students, tell or show them the lesson objective, use an attention-getting "set," or tell the purpose, rationale, importance, or application of the lesson objective.

An opening generally includes a statement of the objective and the objective purpose. When you state the objective, you tell students in their terms, what they will know or be able to do at the end of the lesson or activity. The objective purpose lets the students know why the knowledge or skill they are learning is important to them, for example, how it will help them in their daily lives or how it will help them in school. Students respond positively when they understand why they are learning what you are teaching.

■ *Connect New Learning* To help students see relationships between known information and the new learning, discuss how the learning connects to personal experience and prior knowledge, review earlier lessons or skills, preview upcoming lessons, present an advance organizer, or show a graphic organizer.

Openings can be elaborate or simple but it is important that all lessons (and activities) have one (see Chapter 6 for more ideas).

Component 4: Lesson Body

When creating the lesson body, remember that the specifics of the body will depend on the lesson model selected (see Chapters 8–10 for more information).

The initial instruction, related directly to the lesson objective, occurs in the lesson body. For this reason, Component 4 is considered the heart of the lesson. The majority of planning time and teaching time is spent on the lesson body. The body is where the content is presented through explanations, examples, demonstrations, or discoveries, and where students begin to process and practice the new skills and knowledge.

While the specifics of the body vary with the lesson model, the lesson body should always include the following:

■ *Diversity Strategies* These strategies help ensure that the needs of all students are being met (see Chapter 7 for ideas).

■ *Active Participation Strategies* Plan frequent, varied opportunities for students to be involved, to rehearse, and process the new learning (see Chapter 6 for ideas).

■ *Checks for Understanding* These are specific active participation strategies designed to help teachers monitor student progress toward the objective. A teacher's goal is to check individual student learning throughout the lesson (see Chapter 6 for ideas).

In this section of the lesson, it is important to present information using multiple methods so that all students can be successful. Present information verbally, by demonstrating and in writing (for example, on a transparency, a white board, a poster, or a handout). Other aids that can add interest and clarity to the presentation of information are sound recordings, pictures, diagrams, objects, models, and video recordings with captions and verbal descriptions.

Component 5: Extended Practice

The purpose of the extended practice component is to plan for the development of high levels of accuracy and fluency and to provide application opportunities so students can generalize the skill or knowledge. (This is not the same as the initial supervised practice that may have been included in the body of the lesson.) Students will usually need extended practice opportunities prior to evaluation. These opportunities are often provided through activities, seatwork, and homework that help students master, transfer, and retain the information or skill. Monitoring this practice will provide students with important performance feedback and help you determine when students are ready to be evaluated. Decisions in this component will have to be made about the following:

■ *Practice Opportunities* Describe the plan for providing practice opportunities during and following the lesson. These are in addition to supervised practice that was provided during the body of the lesson. Remember that distributed practice (many short practices) is more effective than massed practice (one long practice). Remember also that some students may need a great deal of extended practice, while others may need enrichment activities. Be sure that students have an opportunity to practice individually prior to evaluation.

■ *Related Lessons or Activities* It is useful to determine and list the other lessons or activities that will build on this objective and provide opportunities to generalize, integrate, and extend the information.

Component 6: Lesson Closing

The lesson closing helps students tie the material together. It may follow the body of the lesson, or it may follow extended practice. Lesson closings can be elaborate or simple, but there always needs to be one.

A lesson closing may include a review of the key points of the lesson, opportunities for students to draw conclusions, a preview of future learning, a description of where or when students should use their new skills or knowledge, a time for students to show their work, and a reference to the lesson opening (see Chapter 6 for more ideas).

Component 7: Evaluation

The purpose of the evaluation component is to let you and your students know if learning has occurred. It also helps you determine whether it is appropriate to build on the current lesson or whether you need to reteach or change the lesson model, methods, or materials.

The lesson evaluation is actually planned when the lesson objective is written. Look back at the objective to be sure the evaluation matches the objective, and then describe when and where the evaluation will occur. For example, if the objective is to "write a paragraph with a topic sentence," you might plan to have the students write the paragraph tomorrow morning in class. Regardless of when you ask them to write it, they must not be the practice paragraphs they wrote with peer or teacher help. Remember that evaluations need to be of each individual student's independent performance. Do not confuse teaching and testing.

Monitor the students during the body of the lesson and during extended practice to give you an idea of when to formally evaluate. There is no sense in giving students a test that you know they will fail. Students may be evaluated again later (on a unit test, for example). They may also be evaluated on an ongoing basis. For example, you could evaluate paragraph construction in their journal writing. Learning must always be evaluated following the lesson, regardless of other evaluations planned. This evaluation is essential for deciding what to do next (see Chapter 6).

■ Editing Tasks: Evaluating the Written Plan

Editing tasks are undertaken after you have finished the first draft of your lesson. Editing helps you examine and evaluate what you have planned so you can make necessary adjustments. The goal of the adjustments is to help ensure that all students will be challenged and successful, and that the lesson will go smoothly. Completion of the editing tasks leads to the finished plan.

■ *Examine Lesson Congruence*   It is imperative that the various components in the lesson match (the body of the lesson and the evaluation must both match the lesson objective). The following is an example of a lesson in which none of the components match:

- *Objective:* Students will write sentences that include adjectives.

- *Teaching:* The teacher shows and tells how to identify adjectives in a sentence.

- *Practice:* Students are asked to list adjectives that describe a given object.

- *Evaluation:* Students write the definition of adjective.

Making your plan congruent ensures that you are teaching toward the objective you selected and that students are evaluated on what they were taught and what they practiced.

■ *How to Determine Congruence*

1. Reread or paraphrase the objective.

2. Look at the teaching part of the lesson body and ask yourself the following questions:
    - Am I *explaining* the skill or information described in the objective?
    - Am I *demonstrating* the skill or information described in the objective?
    - Am I having students *practice* the skill or information stated in the objective?

3. Look at the evaluation section of the plan and ask yourself this question:
    - Am I *testing* students on the very same thing I explained, demonstrated, and had them practice?

If your answer to all questions is *yes,* then your plan is congruent. If you answered *no* to even one question, revise before completing your final plan.

■ *Examine Critical Teaching Strategies* Be sure that you have included all applicable critical teaching skills (best practices). These are very important in helping all of your students learn (see Chapter 6).

■ *Examine Diversity Strategies* The lesson plan must be designed to meet the needs of diverse learners. Have you built in alternatives that will allow all students access to learning? Have you included accommodations or modifications for individuals? Strategies should be written directly into the plan (see Chapter 7).

■ *Examine Active Participation Strategies* It is of utmost importance that you plan for your students to be actively engaged in the lesson. A reasonable goal would be to give frequent opportunities to participate by using a variety of strategies.

■ *Examine Checks for Understanding* Consider carefully the strategies you select to help you monitor whether students understand the material you are presenting in your lesson. The most effective checks for understanding are those strategies that enable each individual student to respond and be given feedback.

■ *Examine Behavior Management* Sometimes great lessons fall apart because student behavior has not been considered in the lesson plan equation. Management problems can be prevented by planning ahead for how partners should work together, for distributing materials, for transitions between activities within lessons, and so on. This increases chances of lesson success. Therefore, after the lesson plan has been written, go back through it and write in specific management strategies. Ask yourself the following questions:

· *When planning for student needs, ask,* Do I need to do additional management planning because of the needs of the students (incorporate stronger reinforcement, rearrange seats, select partners, use precorrection plans, for example)?

· *When planning for logistics, ask,* Do I need to do additional management planning because of the kinds of things I am doing in

the lesson (for example, lots of equipment and material needed, many transitions within the lesson)?

■ *Materials or Equipment* Another task is to decide what special or unusual materials and equipment are needed for the lesson. It may make sense to list only those materials and equipment not readily available in the classroom. Items such as pencils and paper would not need to appear on the materials list, whereas a hot plate, test tubes, or waxed paper might need to be listed. You can list the materials or equipment in the plan wherever it is most convenient for you.

■ *Housekeeping* Make sure you plan for the distribution of materials, safe use of equipment, cleanup, and so on.

■ *Assistants* Plan what paraprofessionals, volunteers, or peer tutors will do during the lesson if they are available.

Steps in Writing a Lesson Plan

Writing a lesson plan requires a series of decisions. Even before starting to write the actual lesson plan, decisions must be made about what exactly is to be taught and how best to teach it. Experienced teachers are able to do more thinking and less writing when they plan lessons because of their experience. They do, however, often write fairly detailed plans when they prepare to teach new content. This helps them to think through what is the best way to teach the information they will present. In general, the best way to become fluent in writing lesson plans is to practice. As experience grows, teachers will need to write less because certain aspects of the lessons will become second nature.

All of the generic components presented in this chapter should be included in every written lesson plan until you gain the necessary experience to reduce your written planning. The order in which the various components of the plan are written, however, does not necessarily correspond to the order in which they appear in this chapter or to the order in which they would be presented to the students. For example, it makes more sense to write the lesson body before the lesson opening, but when the lesson is presented to the students, you would obviously present the lesson opening before the lesson body. It is also important to note that, although Components 2–7 are the only ones actually presented to the students, the preplanning tasks component is equally as important and should be completed in writing.

The following is a suggested sequence for writing the components of a lesson plan:

Sequence for Writing the Components of a Lesson Plan

1. Component 1 (Preplanning Tasks)
2. Component 4 (Lesson Body)
3. Component 5 (Extended Practice)
4. Component 7 (Evaluation)
5. Component 3 (Lesson Opening)
6. Component 6 (Lesson Closing)
7. Component 2 (Lesson Setup)

Remember to complete editing tasks as well.

 Writing a Useful Plan

When you write a plan for a lesson (or an activity), it is important to consider two factors. First, you must be able to refer to your plan with a quick glance rather than reading it in front of the students. Secondly, if you are writing plans for others to read, remember that your instructor, cooperating teacher, supervisor, principal, or substitute must be able to follow your main ideas.

How to Write a Reader-Friendly Plan

■ Use an outline format whenever possible—major headings, subheadings, bullets, numbers, and indenting.

■ Label the transitions from one part of the lesson or activity to another. State directly what is going to happen (for example, "transition to lab stations" or "explain partner rules").

■ Use a variety of font sizes and appearances—uppercase and lowercase, bold, and underline.

■ Use key words and phrases rather than long narratives.

It is impossible to make a rule that determines how much detail should be included in your plan. It is safe to say, however, that any explanation that may be complex or have the potential to be confusing should be put in writing to help ensure it is complete, accurate, and clear. For example, if you are going to teach your students how to write paragraphs, you would not simply write, "Explain each part of a paragraph." This is too brief because the key information you need to emphasize during the lesson is not planned. You would have to rely solely on your memory to ensure that the key information your students need to know is, in fact, presented to them. It can be very difficult to remember all of the key information when you are up in front of a room full of students. You will not want to write every single word you will say to the students either. Something in between is preferable. The following example outlines key information.

Topic Sentences

■ Usually, but not always, the first sentence
■ Describes the main idea
■ Tells what the paragraph is about

 Summary

Lesson plans are written for topics in all subject areas. Variations in lesson plans result from the specific characteristics of the model of instruction being used in the lesson. Regardless of the lesson model however, important components must be included in all lesson plans. The content within the component will vary somewhat depending on the model used.

Note that memory tasks need special planning. See Chapter 6 for more information.

■ **References**

Arends, R. I. (2000). *Learning to Teach* (5th ed.). New York: McGraw-Hill.

Borich, G. (2000). *Effective Teaching Methods* (4th ed.). Columbus, OH: Merrill, an imprint of Macmillan Publishing.

Callahan, J. F., Clark, L. H., & Kellough, R. D. (2002). *Teaching in the Middle and Secondary Schools* (7th ed., Part 2, Module 4). Columbus, OH: Merrill/Prentice Hall.

Cartwright, P. G., Cartwright, C. A., & Ward, M. E. (1995). *Educating Special Learners* (4th ed.). Boston: Wadsworth.

Lasley II, T. J., Matczynski, T. J., & Rowley, J. B. (2002). *Instructional Models: Strategies for Teaching in a Diverse Society* (2nd ed.). Belmont, CA: Wadsworth/Thomson Learning.

Moore, K. D. (1999). *Secondary Instructional Methods* (2nd ed.). Boston: McGraw Hill.

Orlich, D. C., Harder, R. J., Callahan, R. C., & Gibson, H. W. (2001). *Teaching Strategies: A Guide to Better Instruction* (6th ed.). Boston: Houghton Mifflin.

Chapter 5 — Activity Plans

■ Introduction

Teachers typically use a wide variety of activities during the school day. Some of these activities are necessary routines to organize and manage all of the tasks that need to be done, such as correcting homework or getting ready to go home. Others are meant as fun or relaxing activities to provide a break for students, such as listening to music or singing a song. Certain activities occur daily, such as math timings. Others may happen only occasionally, such as watching a fun video. This chapter is not about how to plan these types of activities, except in those cases where the activity is quite complex, for example, morning opening activities.

This chapter is about how to plan for activities that are directly related to the curriculum—activities that extend, supplement, or enrich lessons. The purpose or rationale for any given activity may not be immediately apparent to an observer, but it is very clear to the teacher.

Purposes of Activities

As discussed in Chapter 2, teachers use activities that relate to the curriculum with various purposes in mind. Activities can often provide the following:

- ■ *Motivation* for students before or during a series of lessons (for example, planning class fund-raising activities during a unit on economics).

- ■ *Background information* or enrichment of the students' knowledge and experience before or during a series of lessons (for example, taking a field trip to a salmon hatchery while studying resource conservation).

- ■ *Ongoing practice* toward long-term objectives, such as playing math games to increase fluency on addition facts or completing art activities that provide practice using fine motor skills or following directions.

- ■ Opportunities for students to *apply or generalize* a previously learned skill (for example, having students plan and maintain a daily meal and snack plan that meets good nutrition requirements).

- ■ Opportunities for students to *integrate* a variety of skills learned from lessons in different subject areas (having students practice their writing skills by writing letters to the editor of the local newspaper about pertinent social issues being discussed in social studies, for example).

- ■ *Differentiation of instruction* by dealing with the same content but at different levels. For example, an activity could involve setting up different poetry tasks at various stations and assigning students to stations based on their skills and interests.

It is important to note that various components of a *lesson plan* may have the same purposes as noted for activities; for example, the opening of a lesson may be intended to motivate students. In addition, lessons always include practice activities (see supervised and extended practice components), and they sometimes incorporate activities to supplement the presentation of information. For example, a teacher may show a videotape about the main parts of the heart and their functions during a lesson on the circulatory system. When activities are part of a daily lesson, they should be included within the lesson plan itself. When activities are part of a series of lessons or unit, or when activities are long and complex, it will be helpful to write a separate activity plan.

Teachers typically decide what activities will be used while planning units of instruction. Teachers may also plan additional activities based on their assessments of student progress. For example, teachers may find that students need more practice in identifying adjectives than originally planned.

Generic Components of an Activity Plan

An activity plan is a written description of exactly what the teacher will do and say to help students prepare for and complete an activity. The plan may consist of a set of questions to ask the students, a set of explanations that help tie the current activity to other learning, or step-by-step procedures and directions.

All activity plans contain the same generic components, even though the content of each component will vary greatly, depending on the type of activity planned. For example, a plan to show and discuss a videotape will look very different from an activity plan for a complex art project. The following explains the purpose of each component and suggests the kinds of decisions that need to be made in each. This is designed to help guide you through the steps for planning your activity. When you are ready to actually write an activity plan, refer to Figure 5.1 "Writing an Activity Plan."

Component 1: Preplanning Tasks

Typically, teachers will develop various activities and lessons to help students progress toward longer term objectives. Keeping this in mind, the preplanning component of the activity plan is to help you think through how the current activity connects with important learning outcomes.

One essential part of this component involves developing a thoughtful connection between the objective of the activity and its purpose. This process begins by identifying the *activity objective.* This is the long-term objective within which the current activity fits. This objective is specific and needs to include all four essential components. In addition, be sure you can identify the *generalization or big idea,* the *IEP goal,* or the *state standard* to which the objective connects.

Remember that an activity objective is different from a lesson objective because students will not necessarily meet the objective by the end of the activity. Students may not be expected to meet the objective for a number of weeks or months. In summary, activity objectives are generally considered long-term objectives, whereas lesson objectives are considered short-term objectives. An example of an activity objective is that students write a paragraph that includes a topic sentence, three supporting detail sentences, and one closing sentence.

Another important part of this component involves selecting an activity that will help students progress toward long-term objectives and then writing an *activity description.* Once you have decided on the objective, brainstorm activities that will bring about this outcome. Be creative. Consider variety, novelty, and student interests. Think about the diversity in your classroom and what kinds of activities would be flexible enough to provide opportunities for all students to be challenged and successful. Select an activity that best fits the objective and the students (or you may choose to plan several alternative activities to meet student needs).

Note that if you are a practicum student or student teacher, your cooperating teacher may already have decided on the topic and the type of activity. For example, she may ask you to plan an art activity that will fit with the unit on Northwest Native Americans or to find a book to read to the students that introduces the theme of friendship.

Once you have selected the activity, write a short description (one or two sentences) that summarizes it. This task will help you distinguish between the desired outcome (objective) and the actual activity. An activity description might appear as the following: Give students packets of color-coded sentence strips. Each packet includes one topic sentence strip and three supporting detail sentence strips. Working in pairs, students will place supporting detail sentences under each topic sentence strip.

Avoid making the mistake of selecting an activity first and then trying to justify it by making up an objective and rationale.

The final task in thinking about the objective is to construct an *activity rationale.* This is a description of how the current activity will help students progress toward the objective. When you plan the rationale, you may wish to refer to the broad purpose for the activity (for example, to motivate, enrich, practice, integrate, apply, or generalize).

The rationale provides the important connection between the long-term objective and the current activity. It requires thinking through carefully why students need to do the activity. Rationales such as "I thought it would be fun . . ." or "I happen to have this videotape . . ." are definitely questionable. Activities ought to be fun and motivating, of course, but they also need to result in important learning. An activity rationale might look like the following: This activity is intended to provide ongoing practice in identifying topic and supporting detail sentences. Physically moving the topic and detail sentence strips may make the connections more concrete to the students. In addition, the opportunity to talk through decision making with a peer partner may increase understanding.

Note that the activity rationale is really a rationale for the current activity rather than for the long-term objective. The rationale for the long-term objective would have been determined when the objective was written.

Examples of Activity Objectives, Descriptions, and Rationales

Example #1

- *Activity objective*   Students will write answers to addition facts (0–20) at the rate of 80 digits per minute with no errors (State Mathematics Standard: "Add, subtract, multiply, and divide whole numbers").

- *Activity description*   Students will play a bingo game in which math fact questions (for example, 5 + 3 = ?) are called out and students cover the correct answer on their bingo card.

- *Activity rationale*   The game format is intended to increase interest and motivation in gaining accuracy and fluency on math facts.

Example #2

- *Activity objective*   Students will identify and describe the contributions of at least three Americans important in ending slavery (State History Standard: "Examine and discuss historical contributions to U.S. society of various individuals and groups from different cultural, racial, and linguistic backgrounds").

- *Activity description*   I will read a story to the students about Harriet Tubman and ask questions that will help them identify the important contributions she made in helping people escape slavery through the Underground Railroad.

- *Activity rationale*   Reading to the students provides an alternative method of gaining background information, and it helps the students with reading problems. This story is only one of the activities that will be used to teach about Harriet Tubman. Students will also watch a videotape and search the Internet for information.

The other main preplanning task is to think through necessary *prerequisite skills or knowledge* as well as *key terms and vocabulary.* It is very important to carefully consider what information or skills your students need to be successful in the current activity. Review, teach, or provide scaffolds or supports as appropriate. It is equally important to identify key terms and vocabulary words that need to be defined and taught. Be sure that you teach terms using language your students will understand.

Component 2: Activity Beginning

The purpose of the activity beginning is to prepare students for participating and learning in the new activity. The activity *setup* includes both a signal for attention and a statement of behavior expectations. An *opening* is also included in the activity beginning.

You will need to decide on a signal for gaining the attention of the students, as well as methods of regaining attention during the activity. If the activity will involve a lot of noise or student movement, you will probably want to use a strong signal for attention, such as ringing a bell or flicking the lights (see Chapter 6).

It is also necessary to think about your expectations for student behavior during the activity and how you will explain them to the students. This applies to the classroom rules as well as procedures that need to be followed during the current activity. For example, may they draw while listening to the story? Are there special rules for using the materials? May they ask for help from peers? Stating your expectations directly is an important strategy for preventing behavior problems. Plan what you will say and when you will say it. Write your *statement of behavior expectations* (see Chapter 6).

It is very important that you think about how you will help students understand the purpose of the activity, and how it connects with long-term objectives, with their prior knowledge, and with their personal experience. You will also want to capture their interest right away and motivate them to participate. Write your plan for the *opening* (see Chapter 6).

Component 3: Activity Middle

The activity middle is a specific description of what the students and the teacher will do during the activity. This will be the most detailed and longest section of the plan and must be thought through carefully.

The planning decisions in this section will be very different depending on the type of activity. However, there are certain planning elements that should always be considered because they will help meet the diverse needs of the students. One key element is to provide information both verbally and visually, which is an example of a *critical teaching skill*. For example, write the rules for a game on a poster as well as saying them to the students, or demonstrate the preparation of a microscope slide as well as providing a list of procedures (see Chapter 6). Another key element is to

incorporate *active participation* by all students during the activity. For example, when asking questions during a story, have students say their response to a neighbor rather than calling on only one or two volunteers. Many active participation strategies serve as *checks for understanding* so that you can monitor student learning. For example, students can hold up fingers to show how many syllables they hear in a word (see Chapter 6). A third element is to plan provisions, that is, *diversity strategies,* which consider individual strengths and weaknesses. These might include allowing options, such as (1) having students work individually, with partners, or in small groups, or (2) allowing students to make a presentation rather than writing a report (see Chapter 7 for many additional ideas).

It is important to remember the following:

- Provide information both verbally and visually.
- Incorporate active participation.
- Plan provisions for individual differences.

Think about your activity—what you will be doing, what the students will be doing, and what you will need to communicate to your students. If the students will be listening to or watching something (readings, films, or demonstrations, for example), you will need to plan a set of questions to ask or a series of explanations to make. If the students will be creating something (writing, drawing, or building, for example), you will need to plan a set of directions to give and perhaps plan to show an example of a finished product. If the students are going to be doing something (such as performing experiments or playing a game), you will need to plan a set of procedures or rules.

You may need to provide the following:

- *A set of questions* Plan questions to ask before, during, and after reading a story, playing a musical selection, or taking students on a nature walk. It can be difficult to ask good questions spontaneously. Planning some of the questions in advance will help you ask clear and thought provoking ones. It will also help you think through the purposes of the questions. For example, when you are reading a story with your students, you may want to ask questions to emphasize vocabulary words, predicting, the meanings of figures of speech, making inferences, summarizing, main ideas, or character, setting, and plot.

◾ *A series of statements or explanations* Prior to a presentation, explain that the videotape they are about to see presents three major factors that contribute to child abuse and that, when the video is over, they need to be prepared to discuss them. Telling students what to watch or listen for will help them focus. Planning these statements in advance will ensure clarity and brevity.

◾ *A list of directions* Provide step-by-step directions for the book covers students will be making for the short stories they have written. Displaying the directions in writing, as well as stating the directions to the students, is very important and will save much repetition. Planning the directions in advance will ensure clarity and completeness.

◾ *A sample of a finished product* Provide an example of a completed book cover. Seeing a completed product can be very helpful in understanding what to do and what is expected. Be sure to clarify whether students' products need to look exactly like the sample or whether you are looking for variety and creativity. If the steps in making the product are complex, consider showing samples of the product at various stages of completion.

◾ *A list of procedures* List procedures for how to experiment with each magnet, how to find partners or form groups, how to share tasks, where to get or how to use materials or equipment, and so on. In addition to stating the procedures, showing the written list or even acting them out is helpful.

◾ *A list of rules* List rules for the quiz show game the students will be playing to review social studies information prior to their test. Again, providing a written summary of the rules as well as stating them and demonstrating them is a good idea. Be sure to plan all needed rules to avoid confusion, arguments, and wasted time.

Be sure to plan how you will check for understanding after explaining directions, procedures, rules, and so on. For example, you may ask specific questions—What do you do first? How do you find your partner? —or call on individuals to summarize the directions. Simply saying, "Does everyone understand?" or "Any questions?" is not effective (see Chapter 6).

Component 4: Activity Closing

The activity closing helps students tie it all together. Decide whether it will be important to review key ideas and to preview future lessons or activities. It may be necessary to provide an opportunity for students to draw conclusions, describe their problem-solving process, or show what they created. You may wish to formally assess progress toward a long-term objective. Activity closings do not necessarily need to be time-consuming and elaborate, but there should be a meaningful ending of some kind for all activities (see Chapter 6).

◼ Editing Tasks

Once you have written the activity plan, you are ready to conduct editing tasks. Reread your plan and evaluate whether you need to make adjustments in any of the following areas:

◾ *Critical Teaching Strategies* Include all applicable critical teaching skills (best practices) that will help all of your students learn (see Chapter 6).

◾ *Congruence* It is very important that various components of the activity plan match; for example, the activity middle must reflect the activity objective (see Chapter 6).

◾ *Diversity Strategies* Your activity plan must be designed to meet the individual needs of diverse learners. Strategies to meet these needs must be written directly into the plan (see Chapter 7).

◾ *Active Participation Strategies* Remember to include a variety of strategies to keep your students involved in the activity (see Chapter 6).

■ *Checks for Understanding* It is especially important to carefully consider the strategies that will be used as checks for understanding. These give you an opportunity to monitor progress (see Chapter 6).

■ *Managing Student Behavior* There are numerous issues to think about regarding the management of student behavior, such as clarification of behavior expectations, rules, and applicable procedures, explanation of positive and negative consequences, presentation of what students should do if they finish early, and so on (see Chapter 6).

■ *Materials and Equipment* Be sure you know where to locate any materials or equipment not readily available in the classroom. You can write the list of materials or equipment wherever it is most convenient for you.

■ *Housekeeping* Make sure you have planned for the distribution of materials, safe use of equipment, cleanup, and so on.

■ *Assistants* Determine what paraprofessionals and others will be doing to assist. Decide whether or not you will need extra help to implement the activity, such as parent volunteers, and arrange for it.

Write any needed adjustments into the appropriate section of your plan. (See "Editing Tasks: Evaluating the Written Plan" in Chapter 4 for more information.)

Writing a Useful Plan

Remember that when you write your activity plan, it is important that your final draft serve as a useful resource for you and those who observe you. (See "How to Write a Reader-Friendly Plan" section of Chapter 4 for guidance.)

Summary

There are many types of activities you can plan for your students, but they should all have a clear purpose. Be sure you can state the important objective that the activity will help your students meet.

Figure 5.1 summarizes each component in an activity plan. Notice that Component 1 is not presented to the students. Instead, you are asked to think through the objective of your activity and think about its purpose. When you write your activity plan, first write Component 1, then Component 3, then Component 2, and finally, Component 4.

Figure 5.1 Writing an Activity Plan

The content of the components in Figure 5.1 tells what typically would be included in each component of an activity plan.

COMPONENT 1: PREPLANNING TASKS

Prepare the following:

■ *Activity objective* State the long-term objective for the activity as well as the generalization or big idea, the IEP goal, or the state standard that is being addressed.

■ *Activity description* A brief summary or description of the activity itself.

continued on next page

Figure 5.1   Writing an Activity Plan (continued)

- *Activity rationale*   Describe how the current activity helps students progress toward the long-term objective.
- *Prerequisite skills or knowledge* and *key terms or vocabulary*   Describe those needed for success in the activity.

COMPONENT 2: ACTIVITY BEGINNING

Prepare the following:

- *Setup*   This includes a *signal for attention* to make sure students are listening and a *statement of behavior expectations,* which informs students how to act during the activity.
- *Opening*   An opening shows students how this activity connects to yesterday's lesson, to personal experiences, or to prior knowledge. It also helps to motivate or focus the students (stating the activity rationale, for example).

COMPONENT 3: ACTIVITY MIDDLE

Prepare the following:

- A description of what you need to communicate to the students. Depending on the type of activity, you may need one or a combination of the following: a set of questions, a list of statements or explanations, a list of rules, a list of procedures, a sample of a finished product, and a list of directions.
- A description of how you will effectively communicate this information to the students (use of critical teaching behaviors, visual supports, demonstrations, checks for understanding, diversity strategies, active participation, and so on).

COMPONENT 4: ACTIVITY CLOSING

Prepare the following:

- A description of how you will end the activity. Your closing may involve a class review, students drawing conclusions, teacher previews of future learning, students showing work, or an evaluation procedure (if appropriate).

Remember to use editing tasks to evaluate your plan!

Tic-Tac-Toe Spelling

This is a large group activity plan.

I. PREPLANNING TASKS

A. Prerequisite skills or knowledge: How to play Tic-Tac-Toe

B. Key terms or vocabulary: NA

C. Long-term objective: Given a list of 15 words that contain one to three syllables and end in "–ing," students will write (or spell orally) all words correctly. Students are given lists that match their skill level (one, two, or three syllables, for example). State writing standard: spell age-level words correctly.

D. Activity description: A Tic-Tac-Toe game where partners quiz each other on their spelling words. Correct responses result in placing an X or O on the tic-tac-toe board.

E. Activity rationale: This game is intended to provide students a fun way to practice and memorize their spelling words. This format also provides practice in giving and taking constructive feedback.

F. Materials: Worksheets with 25 tic-tac-toe grids on each, transparency of grids and rules.

II. ACTIVITY BEGINNING

A. Signal for attention: "Attention, please."

B. Behavior expectations: "Keep eyes on me and raise hands to ask questions when you have them."

C. Opening

    1. Review: "You are studying words that end with '–ing'. Give me some examples."

    2. Objective and purpose: "Tic-Tac-Toe Spelling will help you memorize correct spelling of words, so you can use these words in your writing; you won't need to look up words in a dictionary."

> *Active Participation (AP) = Call out answers.*

III. ACTIVITY MIDDLE

A. Show a transparency of five Tic-Tac-Toe grids, game directions, and sample word lists.

B. Explain and model directions for the game with a teaching assistant as partner.

    1. "Exchange spelling lists with your reading partner."

    2. Partner roles.

        a. Partner 1 (*X*) asks Partner 2 (*O*) a word from her list.

        b. Partner 2 spells. If correct, Partner 2 places an *O* on a Tic-Tac-Toe square; if wrong, no *O* is placed.

        c. Partner 1 places a check if correct or a minus if incorrect by the word spelled (to keep track of accuracy and to ensure that all words are asked).

      d. If partner spells word correctly, say "You're right" or "Good spelling."

      e. If incorrect, say "The word _____ is spelled _____. How do you spell _____?"

3. Reverse the roles.

      a. Partner 2 (*O*) asks Partner 1 (*X*) a word from her list.

      b. Partner 1 spells. If correct, Partner 1 places an *X* on a tic-tac-toe square; if wrong, no *X* is placed; a check or minus is placed by the word.

C. State expectations for partner work. Remind students of classroom rule: respect others; talk about the skill, not the person when giving feedback.

D. Check for understanding (CFU): Have *two students come to the front of the room and model* the game procedure as I ask other students specific questions about the game rules and expectations: "What does the speller do if the word is spelled correctly?" "What does the asker do?" and so on.

> *AP = Tell partners, and then call on nonvolunteers.*

E. Pass out materials: Tic-Tac-Toe grids. "Get out your spelling lists."

F. Play the game: Play for 20 minutes. Complete as many games as possible.

IV. ACTIVITY CLOSING

A. Preview the next related activity: "Tomorrow, we'll do another practice activity to help you memorize words."

B. Practice one final time: Partners take turns quizzing each other on misspelled words (if no words are misspelled, use "challenge words").

Treasure Hunt

This is a large group reading practice activity.

I. PREPLANNING TASKS

A. Long-term objective: Given a set of instructions (and materials) necessary to complete a product or a process (a complex drawing, a first aid technique), students will follow the directions so that the product or process works as intended. State Reading Standard: Read and understand information to perform a specific task.

B. Activity description: Students will work in pairs (a more skilled reader will be paired with a less skilled reader.) Each pair will be given a set of directions to read and follow. They will be sent from one location around the school to the next. Each time the pair arrives at a new location, they will find a new set of directions to read and follow. The last clue will bring them back to the room and to their seats where they will find a riddle that must be solved together to figure out what the "treasure" is.

C. Activity rationale: This activity is designed to provide a motivating introduction to our next reading unit, which is called "The Purposes of Reading." Our focus in this unit will be on reading information to perform tasks (for example, recipes, first aid manuals, maps).

D. Prerequisite skills and knowledge: Read with comprehension

E. Key terms or vocabulary: NA

F. Materials: (a) 10 sets of directions that will send partner groups to six locations throughout the school and grounds; (b) 10 cards on which a riddle about the treasure is stated; and (c) two transparencies: one with the game rules and partner roles, and one for partner assignments.

G. Let the principal and other staff know that the students will be moving around the school.

II. ACTIVITY BEGINNING

A. Signal for attention: "Eyes up here."

B. Behavior expectations: Look, listen, and participate

C. Opening

    1. Motivate. Say, "Today you are going on a hunt inside and outside of school to find a treasure."

    2. State the objective and rationale. Say, "In our next unit, we will be learning about times when careful reading is important, such as when following directions. Suppose that your friend gave you directions so you could go to her soccer game and you didn't read the directions carefully. What would happen? (You wouldn't find the game.) Your hunt for treasure today is another example. You must read carefully to find the treasure."

III. ACTIVITY MIDDLE

A. Show the transparency of directions for the treasure hunt and partner roles.

B. Explain and demonstrate the directions. Role-play the directions with a student using different clues that will send us around the classroom.

    1. Work with a partner. Partner 1 reads Clues 1, 3, and 5, while Partner 2 checks, and *both* follow the directions. Then reverse the roles for Clues 2, 4, and 6.

    2. Read the clues *carefully.*

    3. Follow the directions.

    4. Read all six sets of clues.

    5. Find the treasure (within 20 minutes).

C. CFU: Ask questions about the treasure hunt directions; for example, "Who reads the first direction? How long will you have?"

> *AP = Call on nonvolunteer, then unison response*

D. State behavior expectations for the hunt.

    1. Walk from place to place.

    2. Keep voices quiet so other students and teachers do not readily notice you.

    3. Stay with your partner.

E. CFU: Ask questions about behavior expectations such as, "Show me how you will move from place to place. Show me the kind of voice you use so as not to disrupt others."

> *AP = Unison response*

F. Assign partners. Show a list of partners on the transparency. Remind the students of class rule: Use language and actions that are polite, kind, and including, and to apply this to assigned partners.

G. Begin the game on a signal. After 20 minutes, students should end up back at their seats.

IV. ACTIVITY CLOSING

A. Review.

    1. Say, "Today, we saw an example of a type of task that requires very careful reading."

    2. Ask, "Why was it important to read carefully?"

> *AP = Turn to partner, call on nonvolunteers.*

B. Preview tomorrow's lesson.

    1. Say, "In our next reading unit, we're going to be learning about other kinds of tasks that require careful reading in order to complete."

    2. Ask, "Can you think of examples?"

> *AP = Brainstorm*

    3. Say, "Tomorrow we'll begin our unit and see if some of your ideas are included."

C. Say: "Now it's time to enjoy your treasures."

Chapter 6

Critical Teaching Skills

Introduction

It is essential to incorporate various important skills and strategies into all of the plans you write. They should be included regardless of whether you are planning a lesson or an activity, and regardless of the subject matter and makeup of the class you will teach. These skills reflect best practice and should become part of your teaching skill repertoire.

The skills we have chosen to include in this chapter represent various instructional purposes. Some of these strategies help with thoughtful preparation and planning of the subject matter to be taught. Other techniques help focus students during instruction. Some of the strategies address methods for monitoring student learning progress. A final group of skills are important to the management of student behavior.

Planning the Content to Be Taught

A thorough analysis of the content of the lesson will help you to teach it effectively. The analysis typi-

cally involves examining the essential ideas contained in the content and how they are connected.

Content Analysis

A content analysis is prepared in the beginning stages of planning a lesson. The content analysis could contain one or more of the following: a *subject matter outline*, a *task analysis* or a *concept analysis*, a *principle statement*, definitions of *key terms and vocabulary*, and a list of *prerequisite skills and knowledge*. The content analysis allows you to consider thoroughly what you will be teaching.

Subject Matter Outline for Organizing Declarative Information

A subject matter outline is a standard outline of the specific content to be covered in the lesson. They are most always written for lessons designed to teach specific declarative information (for example, an informal presentation lesson on the causes of the Civil War). The body of the informal presentation lesson consists of a subject matter outline and is used to guide the teacher's delivery of information.

The following outline format promotes clear organization of information.

Malignant Melanoma

1. Three Types of Skin Cancer
    a. Basal Cell Carcinoma
    b. Squamous Cell Carcinoma
    c. Malignant Melanoma—can be fatal
2. Risk Factors of Malignant Melanomas
    a. Sun exposure
       - Repeated sunburns
       - As a child, 80 percent of damage is done
    b. Fair complexion
       - Caucasian
       - Redheads and blondes
    c. Family history: increased risk if parents or siblings have melanoma
3. Detection: Know the A, B, C, and D of Melanoma
    a. Asymmetrical
       - A line through the middle would not create equal sides.
       - Most moles and freckles are symmetrical.
    b. Borders
       - Uneven: scalloped or notched edges
       - Normal mole: smooth, even border
    c. Color
       - Begins with varied shades of brown, tan, or black
       - Progresses to red, white, or blue
       - Normal moles are an even shade of brown
    d. Diameter
       - Larger than normal moles: 6 millimeters or 1/4 inch in diameter
       - Normal mole is smaller

Task Analysis for Teaching Procedures or Strategies

A task analysis is generally used when you plan to teach a how-to lesson; that is, you want your students to do something at the end of the lesson that they cannot presently do. Procedures or strategies are generally what you want your students to do and they are best organized using a task analysis.

A procedure is a series of steps that leads to the completion of a task (Smith & Ragan, 1999). Procedures can be academic (how to convert degrees Celsius to degrees Fahrenheit), social (how to join in a group), or describe a classroom routine (what to do with a late assignment).

Strategies are a subcategory of procedures. Howell and Nolet (2000) define strategies as procedures that students follow to combine subtasks into larger tasks. Strategies are techniques that help students learn (how to take notes from a lecture), study (how to memorize lists of items), or get organized (how to maintain an assignment calendar).

A task analysis can be written in two ways, depending on the specific content to be taught. It can be written as a list of sequential steps that must be followed in order (how to do long division, for example). It can also be written as a list of various subskills that must be completed but not necessarily in a certain order (how to write out a check, for example). The following examples illustrate how to write task analyses.

How to Alphabetize to the First Letter

1. Underline the first letter of each word in the list.
2. If all letters are different:
    a. Say the letters of the alphabet in order.
    b. As you say each letter, scan the underlined letters.
    c. Stop each time you say the name of an underlined letter.
    d Write the word that contains the letter you said.
    e. Continue until all words are used.

How to Proofread Sentences

1. Skim the work and check that:
    a. all sentences begin with a capital letter.

b. all sentences have an appropriate end mark (period, exclamation point, or question mark).

2. Fix any errors.

The most efficient way to conduct a task analysis is to perform the task yourself while writing the steps, including the thinking process you follow. However, there are cases where the process you follow may be different from the process followed by a child or beginner. The task analysis will help you plan the presentation of information and demonstration.

Concept Analysis for Teaching Concepts

It is important to do a concept analysis prior to concept teaching. This type of content analysis helps the teacher think through and write down exactly how the essential elements of the concept will be explained. A concept analysis includes: (1) a definition of the concept, (2) a list of the critical attributes that are distinguishing features or characteristics found in all examples, (3) a list of noncritical attributes that are nonessential characteristics not found in all examples, (4) a list of examples, (5) a list of nonexamples, and (6) a list of related concepts, if helpful or needed. Here is an example of a concept analysis.

Concept Name: Proper Nouns

- *Definition*   A proper noun is a noun that names a particular person, place, or thing.

- *Critical attributes*   A proper noun, which names a particular person, a particular place, or a particular thing, is capitalized.

- *Noncritical attributes*   The position in the sentence and the number of words are noncritical.

- *Examples*   Seattle Mariners, Golden Gate Bridge, Harriet Tubman, Amsterdam, Curtis Kerce, Orcas Island, Washington State, UW Huskies

- *Nonexamples*   baseball team, bridge, woman, city, man, island, state, football team

- *Related concepts*   Common noun

Principle Statement for Teaching Principles

Principles are relational rules that prescribe the relationship between two or more concepts. They are often described in the form of if–then, cause–effect, or "rule of thumb" relationships. Principles can be complex or simple, and there are examples of principles in all content areas (Smith & Ragan, 1999).

Examples of Principles

- When water reaches 32 degrees Fahrenheit, it freezes.

- If your payment arrives late, then you will need to pay a late fee.

- When a wasp's food supply dwindles toward the end of the summer, it is more likely to sting without provocation.

- If there is little or no prenatal care for a pregnant mother, then the risk of a premature birth increases.

- When effective memorization strategies are used for studying, then retention of information is usually greater.

- Regarding rounding numbers, when a number is 5 or more, round up.

Be sure that you plan in advance how the principle will be explained to your students. It can be difficult to correctly or accurately explain the principle spontaneously during the lesson or activity. Begin by writing out the complete principle statement; include the condition and the result or the action that needs to be taken. Next, consider carefully which words are best used as part of your explanation. Finally, be sure that you plan many, varied examples to illustrate the principle. It is important that your students can *apply* the principle to unknown examples, not just state it (Smith & Ragan, 1999).

Key Terms and Vocabulary

Another type of content analysis is to identify and write out the definitions of key terms or specialized vocabulary words that will be used in the lesson. The definitions need to be written in words that the students will understand. It is important to do this in advance so incorrect or incomplete definitions are avoided. Terms are not as easy to define on the spot as they would seem.

Student dictionaries and textbook glossaries can be good places to start when trying to write a clear definition for a particular term. Generally, though, this is only the first step. Suppose you are preparing a list of vocabulary words as part of a reading lesson: One of the words is "myth." You locate a dictionary definition that says a myth is "a story rooted in the most ancient religious beliefs and institutions of a people, usually dealing with gods, goddesses, or natural phenomena." Suppose that you write this definition into your lesson plan. The next day, when you introduce the word "myth" to your second graders, you suddenly realize that, not only do they not understand the entire definition, they do not even understand some of the words that make up the definition. Therefore, all definitions need to be reviewed and restated in words the students will understand.

A variety of strategies can help you to increase the chances that your students will understand the definitions provided. The following are suggestions of such strategies.

CLARIFYING KEY TERMS AND VOCABULARY

The following strategies will help your students understand the definitions you provide:

- Provide students with both verbal and written definitions.

- Provide pictures, models, and other visual aids to help illustrate important terms.

- Have students write terms and definitions in their notes or locate them in their text.

- Provide students with a list of terms to learn that can be used as a reference throughout a series of related lessons or a unit.

- Post word banks and semantic webs in the classroom.

- If memorization of terms is necessary, provide memorization strategies and time to practice. Flashcards, computer games, and mnemonic devices can all be used for practice.

Be consistent in the terms you use with students. For example, if you decide to use the term "subtract," do not randomly alternate with "minus" or "take away." This can be confusing when learning new information.

Prerequisite Skills and Knowledge

One part of a content analysis is determining prerequisite skills and knowledge that students must have to be ready for a particular lesson. Sometimes these would be broad skills; being able to read is a prerequisite skill for using encyclopedias as a resource when writing reports. Sometimes the prerequisite skills are more specific; for example, long division requires skills in estimating, multiplying, and subtracting; using adjectives is dependent on knowing about nouns; and being able to prepare food from recipes is contingent on being able to measure ingredients. It is certainly not necessary, nor desirable, to list all prerequisites. However, it is important to consider these factors.

Choosing the Analysis

The following guidelines will help you choose the type of analysis to prepare:

- Write a *concept analysis* when you plan to teach a concept.

- Include a *task analysis* when the point of the lesson is to teach a procedure or strategy, that is, a "how to" lesson.

- When teaching about a topic (that is, declarative knowledge), a *subject matter outline* will be most beneficial.

- Write a complete *principle statement* (the condition and the result or action to be taken) when the objective of the lesson is to teach a principle.

- *Key terms and vocabulary* words are important to consider in every lesson or activity. Be sure that words are defined in terms that the students will understand.

- It is always important to consider *prerequisite skills and knowledge* as part of a content analysis. This will help you write the objective and determine whether the content is appropriate for the students you are teaching.

Content Analysis and Lesson Model

There is a relationship between the type of content analysis and the type of lesson model used. A task analysis, which includes steps in a procedure or strategy, generally fits with a direct instruction lesson model. A subject matter outline, which organizes declarative knowledge, is usually used in an informal presentation lesson. A concept analysis, which describes a concept in detail, may be used in structured discovery or direct instruction lessons. A principle statement, which describes a relationship between concepts, may fit in direct instruction, structured discovery, or informal presentation lessons. Most lessons will have key terms that need to be considered, as well as prerequisite skills or knowledge that may need to be taught or reviewed.

The content analysis helps you organize the content you will teach into an organized framework that benefits both you and your students. Preparing this framework also helps strengthen your understanding of the material. As you communicate the analysis to your students, you provide them with a structured way to consider the content. This can have a very positive impact on student learning and retention.

A Special Note about Memorization Tasks

Declarative knowledge is factual information and it can be broken down into categories. Smith and Ragan (1999) describe several types of declarative information: facts and lists (the movie begins at 8:00, steps to follow in the reading comprehension strategy), and labels and names (the parts of a volcano, words and their definitions, the names of states and capitols). These types of declarative knowledge are the focus of this section.

When facts, lists, labels, and names are presented in lessons, the intent is generally that students memorize the information for future use. Students may need to remember the factual information so they can build on it in future lessons and activities.

Memory tasks need special planning. Generally you would not write a single lesson plan when planning for students to memorize significant amounts of information (a long list of steps to follow for a reading strategy or to solve math story problems, a list of states and capitals, chemical symbols, math facts, and so on). This type of information is often initially introduced in a lesson, but needs to be followed by a variety of activities designed to aid memorization. Follow lots of practice (frequent and distributed) with the evaluation.

When you are planning your lesson or activity, determine what new information (steps, vocabulary words, content facts, for example) students will need to know or do to meet the lesson objective. Ask yourself this question: Do my students need to memorize the information? If you answer *yes,* then you may need or want to revise your objective, and plan memory devices (mnemonics, for example) as appropriate, with an adequate number of practice opportunities within the lesson. If your answer is *no,* then plan which visual supports are needed to give students access to the information (posters, transparencies, and so on).

Focusing Attention

One of the biggest challenges teachers encounter is keeping students involved, interested, and learning. Many effective teaching practices can be incorporated into your plans that can help you meet this challenge. One practice is to use active participation strategies that help keep students engaged during instruction. Teachers can also use effective questioning skills and provide strong openings and closings for lessons and activities. Be sure to consider these ideas when planning.

Active Participation

Active participation means getting all students to respond by talking, writing, or doing something—usually overt—that is directly related to the lesson or activity. Any technique that brings about student involvement is an active participation strategy. Most lessons and activities eventually involve all students in active practice or processing of some sort. However, it is very important that students are asked to actively respond right from the start, during the opening of a lesson or activity, for example.

Importance of Active Participation

Active participation strategies are valuable for several reasons. First, by using these strategies, students are kept engaged, and it is more likely that they will learn, retain, and process the information presented. Next, various active participation strategies allow the teacher to check for understanding early and often during instruction. When students are involved in lessons or activities made interactive through the use of active participation strategies, they are also more likely to be attentive and less likely to be off task. These lessons and activities are likely to be more fun and interesting for students and teachers.

Types of Strategies

There are many kinds of active participation strategies that can be incorporated into lessons or activities. Recognizing the variation of strategies in terms of their response type and purpose can help in selecting appropriate strategies to use at various points throughout lessons and activities.

One way to think about active participation strategies is by the type of response they require. First, *written responses* involve writing answers on a chalkboard or think pad, for example. Calling out answers or discussing main ideas with a partner are examples of *oral responses*. Finally, *signal responses* include strategies such as pointing or holding up fingers.

Another way to think about active participation strategies is by their purpose. Most strategies can be loosely organized into four main categories. First, *involvement strategies* (choral reading, for example) are designed mainly to keep students alert and attentive. *Rehearsal strategies* (unison responses) are used to provide students with opportunities to practice or rehearse the information being presented. *Processing strategies* (Think-Pair-Share, for example) help increase comprehension by providing opportunities to think about, mull over, or discuss content to develop a deeper understanding of the material. Finally, *check-for-understanding strategies* (for example, response cards) give the teacher feedback about each student's understanding.

Many strategies serve several purposes. As you read through the specific strategies below, notice how various strategies easily fit into more than one category. For example, unison response can be both an involvement strategy and a rehearsal strategy; response cards can be both a check-for-understanding and an involvement strategy. The organization of strategies by response type and purpose is simply a general guideline to consider when you select strategies. It is far more important to select an appropriate variety of strategies to use in your plans than it is to spend time trying to figure out in which category a strategy fits.

Note that numerous strategies are designed to be used in response to teacher questions. Considering that teachers ask a large number of questions each day, it is very important to carefully consider how students will participate during question-asking situations. Be sure to select response strategies that will involve as many students as possible during these sessions. An important point must be made here: The act of asking a question is not an active participation strategy, whereas the strategy used for getting a response from students is.

INVOLVEMENT STRATEGIES

A major goal of involvement strategies is to keep students alert and attentive during instruction. The following are some examples of how to achieve this goal:

1. Ask for *unison responses* from the whole class or from rows or groups. Say, "The name of this river is . . . Everyone?" Make sure that everyone is, in fact, responding.

2. Ask students to *respond through hand signals*. Say, "As I point to each number, put thumbs up if you would round upward."

Strategies 1 and 2 work well as response strategies when questions require brief answers.

3. Have students *stand to share answers* (Kagan, 1992). Students stand up when they have an answer. The teacher calls on one student to share the answer. Everyone with the same or similar answer sits down. Students continue to answer until everyone is sitting down.

4. Have students do *choral reading* of content text as an alternative to "round robin" reading. Students can read whole sentences or

paragraphs as a group. Teachers can stop at various places and have students fill in words or phrases when they are reading.

5. Have students *take notes* during teacher presentations. Skilled note-takers can write their own notes; provide students challenged by note-taking with partially completed notes.

6. Use covert strategies such as a *think about* or *visual imagery*. Saying to the students, "Imagine for a minute what it would feel like to be teased about the color of your skin," or "Think about a time when you helped a friend." Use visual imagery by asking students to "picture" something in their minds (for example, "Try to imagine how the ferocious lion looked.").

7. Use a *think to write preview* to get students thinking about today's topic. Give students 3 minutes to write down everything they know about the topic.

8. *Brainstorming,* followed by the teacher calling on individuals randomly, gives all students an opportunity to participate.

REHEARSAL STRATEGIES

9. Ask a question, and then ask students to *say the answer to their neighbor.*

10. Ask partners to *take turns* summarizing, defining terms, or giving examples.

Strategies 9 and 10 work well when you are asking questions that require somewhat longer answers. They are also effective when many students are eager to speak but there is not enough time to call on each student individually. Students who are uncomfortable speaking to the entire class may readily speak to a neighbor or small group.

11. Use the *pausing technique* (Guerin & Male, 1988; Salend, 1998). Stop for 2 minutes after every 5–7 minutes of lecturing. Have students discuss and review their notes and the content presented (they can rehearse important points or discuss how the information relates to their own experiences, for example).

12. *Drill partners* work on facts they need to know until they are certain both partners know and remember them all (Johnson, Johnson, & Holubec, 1991).

13. *Board workers* work together to answer questions. Each student has a role: one student is the Answer Suggester; one acts as Checker to see if everyone agrees; and one is the Writer (Johnson, Johnson, & Holubec, 1991).

CHECK-FOR-UNDERSTANDING STRATEGIES

14. Ask everyone to *write down an answer* on paper, on a small blackboard, on a dry-erase board, or on a magic slate. Then have them hold it up so you can see it. For example, tell everyone to write an adjective that describes your chair.

15. Ask students to respond using student *response cards* or other objects. Say, "Hold up the green card if the word is a noun," or "Hold up the isosceles triangle" (Heward et al., 1996).

16. Ask for *finger signals* from everyone. "Students hold up numbers of fingers to respond to mastery questions (e.g., 'How many sides on a triangle?'). Other gestures can also be used. For instance, 'I will watch while you draw a triangle in the air'" (Guillaume, 2000, p. 51).

Strategies 14–16 work well when questions require brief answers. They allow you to check the understanding of all students and provide opportunities for the students to respond or rehearse in a variety of ways.

PROCESSING STRATEGIES

17. Ask students to think about the answer to a question. Have them then discuss the answer with their neighbor. Call on pairs to share their answers, such as in *Think-Pair-Share* (Lyman, 1992).

18. Ask a question, and then ask students to share and discuss their answers in small groups, such as in *Buzz Groups* (Arends, 2000).

19. Ask a question, and then call on individual team members to answer, such as in

Numbered Heads Together. After you ask a question, the students in each team (who have numbered off) put their heads together and make sure everyone knows the answer. Then, call out a number and students with that number provide answers to the whole group (Kagan, 1992).

Strategies 17–19 are especially effective when the content you are teaching is complicated or difficult. They also work well when you want long and varied responses. Keep groups accountable for involving all members by asking the students to record all answers, to defend their method of reaching consensus, or you may pick one student at random to speak for the group.

20. *"Bookends* is a cooperative learning strategy whereby students meet in small groups before listening to an oral presentation to share their existing knowledge about the topic to be presented. The groups also generate questions related to the topic, and these questions are discussed during or after the oral presentations" (Salend, 1998, p. 231). This technique could also be used with a group discussion or a videotape presentation.

21. Have students complete a *think to write review* in which they write what they learned. Give students 3–5 minutes to write down everything they learned in the lesson or activity just taught.

Individual Student Responses

The strategies mentioned previously are designed to get all or most students in the class to respond at once, to have *everyone* actively participating. Occasionally, teachers may use a repetitive question and response pattern: the teacher asks the question and a student is called on to answer, the teacher asks another question and another student is called on to answer, and so on. In this case, only one student is participating at a time.

If you use the call-on-individuals strategy, we encourage you to consider two techniques that will make your selection random: (1) randomly draw cards or Popsicle sticks with student names on them or (2) use a seating chart and mark names of students who have already answered. It is never appropriate to call on nonattending students with the intent of embarrassing them. If you call on a nonattending student as a management technique, then prompt the student by repeating the question. The purpose of calling on students at random is to keep everyone involved and on their toes.

Number of Strategies to Include

A desired goal when planning lessons and activities is the frequent use of active participation strategies. Cegalka (1995) suggests that teachers plan for students to respond in some way, several times during each minute of a lesson. The three-statement rule—the teacher will make no more than three statements without having students make a response—typifies the importance of student participation during lecture presentations (Christenson, Ysseldyke, & Thurlow, 1989).

It may be impossible or impractical or unnecessary to try to specify an exact number of responding opportunities that should be included in any lesson or activity. Instead, consider (1) using strategies during all parts of the lesson or activity (the opening, closing, and all parts in between); (2) using numerous strategies that focus on the key ideas you are trying to emphasize (have students say the main points to a partner); and (3) adjusting the number of strategies based on student learning and behavior (if you notice that many students are confused, increase their opportunities to rehearse or process information). In summary, remember that having students actively rehearse information will help ensure the transfer of that information into long-term memory.

Active Participation and Hands-On Activities

We want to make a distinction between active participation strategies and hands-on activities. Both provide students an opportunity to be involved during lessons and activities, but they do so at different times. By nature, hands-on activities promote active participation, but active participation strategies do not usually include a hands-on activity.

Having students paint a picture of a story's main character or create a color wheel to be used in subsequent lessons are examples of hands-on activities. Having students choral respond, say answers to a partner, or discuss main ideas with a small group are examples of active participation strategies. Students are involved in all of the activities and strategies mentioned; however, notice the difference between the hands-on activities and active participation strategies themselves. The hands-on activity is the end in itself, whereas active participation strategies are part of the means to the end.

Summary

Many active participation strategies can be used during lessons and activities. The kind of strategy you select for any given part of your plan depends on the needs of the students. For example, if your students need opportunities to process information presented, then use a strategy such as Numbered Heads Together. Select a strategy such as written responses so that you can monitor individual student understanding. In all cases, your goal should be to select a meaningful variety of strategies to use.

Opening a Lesson or Activity

Another critical teaching skill is to help students focus attention and make connections through the use of openings. The opening is the component where the actual lesson or activity begins. Its function is to help prepare the students for learning. It can include strategies designed to motivate and focus the students, and strategies that help students see the relationship between the new knowledge or skill and other learning. Generally, an opening includes both kinds of strategies.

Openings may be simple or highly elaborate. When deciding what to include or exclude in the opening, consider variables such as student background, experience, and prior knowledge of the content; prerequisite skills or knowledge; the abstractness or concreteness of the content; whether this is the first lesson or activity in a series; probable student interest and motivation; and the amount of time available for teaching.

Strategies for Openings

You can select ideas for openings from the following two main categories. However, stating the objective and purpose should almost always be a part of the opening.

1. *Strategies to motivate or focus the students:*

   a. Tell or show the objective (write the lesson objective on the board); describe the evaluation (tell students that at the end of the lesson, they will write two complete sentences in which adverbs are included and used correctly).

   b. Tell the purpose, rationale, importance, and application of the lesson or activity objective (tell students the current math lesson will help them double check the change they receive after a purchase).

   c. Use an attention-getting "set" that relates directly to the lesson to capture student interest (jokes, stories, riddles, songs, poems, demonstrations, video clips, and so on).

   d. Preview the sequence of activities in the lesson (tell students they will read and take notes from their texts and then work in cooperative groups to construct a study guide for their upcoming test).

   e. Provide a key idea or generalization as an advance organizer (explain that all foods fit into five basic food groups and that each group is a primary source of specific nutrients prior to providing information about specific foods or food groups).

   f. Preview lesson content through a graphic organizer (show students a concept map of the parts of a paragraph).

   g. Provide initial examples that are humorous or personalized (include the names and interests of students in the classroom in initial story problem examples).

2. *Strategies to help students see relationships between the new knowledge or skill and other learning:*

   a. Connect the learning to personal experience and prior knowledge (have students brainstorm examples of rhyming words as a way of beginning a lesson on poetry).

   b. Review earlier lessons or activities (conduct a quick review of regrouping in the *ones* column prior to teaching regrouping in the *tens* column).

c. Preview upcoming lessons or activities (explain that the vocabulary words being learned in the current lesson will help students understand the story to be read tomorrow).

d. Show students an outline of the whole unit (show students the table of contents that will be used for the packet of information they will assemble during the respiratory system unit).

e. State the relationship of the objective to a more long-term goal (explain how learning conversational skills will help students gain and maintain friendships).

f. Connect to other subject areas (explain that the letter to be written to a local city council member, as part of the social studies lesson, will be written in exactly the same format learned in language arts).

g. Present a graphic organizer (show a concept map for the unit on test-taking skills with the topic of this lesson on multiple choice tests highlighted).

STATE THE OBJECTIVE AND OBJECTIVE PURPOSE

One of the most effective strategies to use in the opening of a lesson or activity is to tell students directly what they will learn and why. Generally, students respond more positively when they understand what is expected of them and why the learning is valuable.

When students are told directly what they will be expected to know or to do by the end of the lesson, the teacher is *stating the objective*. For example, "You are going to learn the difference between reptiles and amphibians," or "At the end of the lesson, I will ask you to circle the amphibians from a list of animals." The statement of objective is made using words that are appropriate to the age and grade level of the students. It may also be appropriate to show the students the objective in writing and have them write it in their notes.

The *objective purpose* is what the students are told about the value or rationale of the lesson. It also is stated in student terms and lets the students know why the knowledge or skill they are learning is important to them, how it will help them in their daily lives or in school, for example.

Asking Questions

The hundreds of questions the typical American teacher asks on a typical day (Gall, 1984), and the various reasons for asking them speaks to their value. They play an important role in all lessons and activities.

Sometimes questions play a major role in lessons. They are the key instructional component. Orlich et al. (2001) suggest that "next to lecturing and small-group work, the single most common teaching method employed in American schools (and, for that matter, around the world) may well be the asking of questions" (p. 240). Inquiry lessons, for example, depend heavily on asking questions to facilitate learning, as do discussion lessons.

Sometimes questions play a supporting role. None of the models we present in this book, for example, use questions as the major teaching strategy. Instead, questions support instruction in two ways. First, they are used to provide review, rehearsal, and enrichment of the information being presented (for example, "What might have been another way to solve this problem?"). Secondly, they are used to monitor students' understanding of the information being presented (for example, "What is the second step of the editing process?"). The questions used in the sample lesson and activity plans that are included in this book are all questions that play a supporting role.

Types of Questions

We can think of questions according to their purposes and also according to the types of response they require. The four types of questions presented below each elicit a specific type of response from students. Knowing when and why to use each of the question types will help you construct questions that fit your purpose.

A *convergent* question is used when you are looking for one correct answer ("What are the three parts of a friendly letter?"). Convergent questions, for the most part, elicit short responses from students and focus on the lower levels of thinking—that is, the knowledge or comprehension levels (Orlich et al., 2001).

Examples of Convergent Questions

■ What is the name of the NFL team headquartered in Seattle?

■ Where is the Amazon River located?

■ Who is the hero in this story?

■ When was the Declaration of Independence signed?

■ Which two major league baseball teams hold the record for the most wins ever in the regular season?

Convergent questions often begin with the following types of stems: who, what, when, where, list as many as you can think of, and how many. Convergent questions can be especially effective during recitations commonly used in teacher-led lessons. They promote active participation by providing students with an opportunity to rehearse and review information, and provide teachers a way to check for student understanding.

A *divergent question* is used when you wish to evoke a wide range of student responses. This type of question also typically elicits longer student responses (Mastropieri & Scruggs, 2000). Divergent questions can help promote higher-level thinking and problem-solving skills. They can be especially useful when you want students to consider issues in depth, such as during an extended practice discussion activity used to enrich informal presentations. The fact that this question type will have numerous correct answers can make its use appealing.

Examples of Divergent Questions

■ How would . . . be different if . . .

■ What would be another logical ending for this story?

■ You have been given the power to stop racism. What would you do first? Why?

Question stems that will likely encourage divergent responses are *"What could happen if . . . ?"*, *"How many ways . . . ?"*, or *"How else might this have happened?"*.

Note that the divergent question has no single right answer but it can have wrong answers. Borich

(2000) states that "this is perhaps the most misunderstood aspect of a divergent question. Not just any answer will be correct, even in the case of divergent questions raised for the purpose of allowing students to express their feelings. If Johnny is asked what he liked about *Of Mice and Men* and says 'Nothing,' or 'The happy ending,' then either Johnny has not read the book or he needs help in better understanding the events that took place. A passive or accepting response on the teacher's part to answers like these is inappropriate, regardless of the intent to allow an open response" (p. 240).

A *low-level question* is one that is usually convergent in form and involves repetition or restatement of previously covered information. It is often used in basic skills instruction, or in early stages of learning (Mastropieri & Scruggs, 2000). These questions are important building blocks leading to higher level or divergent questions. It is unlikely that a student can analyze or evaluate information without an understanding of basic facts and information.

Examples of Low-Level Questions

■ According to the graph . . .

■ Define the term . . .

■ What is a synonym for . . .

■ Which picture represents . . .

Examples of question stems that could be used for this type of question are *name, list, define, identify, who,* or *where.*

High-level questions ask students to make inferences, to analyze, or to evaluate, and are often divergent in form. They require more in-depth thinking to answer than do low-level questions. The cognitive complexity of these questions (Arends, 2000) helps students go beyond the basic facts, and to think about them in a more complex, perhaps new way. These questions can help to enrich a student's learning.

Examples of High-Level Questions

■ How were the hero and villain alike?

■ Given what you know about stock . . . , how would you rate . . . ?

- Explain why this circuit works.
- Create a rubric which takes the quality and quantity of . . . into consideration.

Some question stems that could inspire high-level thinking are *evaluate, compare,* or *create.*

You have undoubtedly noticed the overlap among question types; for example, a convergent question is often also a low-level question. The important thing to remember is that questions should be planned to fit the purpose for which they are designed. For example, if your objective is to give students an opportunity to rehearse and review basic facts being presented, then convergent, low-level questions will probably be best to help you reach that objective.

Guidelines for Planning and Delivering Questions

It is always best to plan questions in advance. This is especially true for beginners or for experienced teachers who are planning to teach new or difficult content. Think about the following guidelines as you plan your questions (Borich, 2000):

- Plan in advance. It can be difficult to come up with questions that meet your goals when you are in front of a group of students.

- Be clear and concise. For example, "How do the cones of volcanoes vary?" is a clear question, as opposed to "We've studied three kind of volcanoes. They all have different kinds of cones and their cones vary in a number of ways; for example, some are larger than others—what would be the things we would study in the cone of a volcano that would tell us about the volcano type and why?"

- Use vocabulary that is appropriate for the age and ability of the students (ask first graders "What do you think Harry Potter meant when he said . . . ?," rather than, "What is your interpretation of the verbalizations of Harry Potter when he said . . . ?".

- Be short enough for students to remember (do not ask, "What are some of the ways we can preserve energy, water, and timber resources; why do we need to preserve these resources; and what techniques can we use to communicate the need for resource preservation to others in the community?").

- Follow questions with time for students to think (see wait-time 1 and 2). Provide adequate wait-time for more meaningful, thoughtful student responses.

- Follow questions with redirections, prompting and probing as necessary. These cues can help students recall information and formulate more complete, complex answers.

- Follow questions with honest feedback. Correct responses can be acknowledged or praised. Incorrect responses need to be corrected so students do not learn or practice incorrect information (see the section on *feedback* in this chapter).

- Avoid ridiculous questions ("How many of you have ever seen a cloud?").

INVOLVE ALL STUDENTS

When you ask questions of your students, your goal should be to involve as many of them as possible. See ideas for specific response strategies under active participation.

WAIT-TIME

No discussion about questions would be complete without also talking about the importance of wait-time. Wait-time 1 and wait-time 2 are both variations of the idea that students need time to formulate answers to questions.

Wait-time 1 refers to the time between when a question is asked and when a student answers (Rowe, 1986; Orlich, 2001). When students are provided 3–5 seconds after a question is asked, more students usually respond, more responses are correct, and the responses are generally more complex (Rosenberg, O'Shea, & O'Shea, 1998).

Wait-time 2 is the time between when a student apparently finishes a response and when the teacher redirects, prompts, or moves on. Adequate think time at this point in the questioning sequence generally results in more elaborate answers because students are given a chance to add to or modify their initial responses (Rosenberg et al., 1998).

Consider some special points when planning wait-time. First, low-level, convergent questions usually do not require much wait-time. Generally, the purpose of these questions is factual recall so the student generally either knows or does not know the answer. Second, higher-level or divergent questions need more time. Also, some individuals seem to need additional thinking time to respond to higher-level questions (Mastropieri & Scruggs, 2000). Finally, during fluency-building drills and practice activities, for example, when speed and accuracy are being developed, wait-time is not desirable (Rosenberg, O'Shea, & O'Shea, 1998).

Summary

Questions can encourage students to think about and act on the material the teacher has presented (Borich, 2000). They can be used to enrich content learning and help students review and rehearse information. Questions can also be crafted to help teachers monitor the learning of their students. Arends (1997) states that "beginning teachers should keep in mind one important truth, that is, that different questions require different types of thinking and that a good lesson should include both lower and higher-level questions" (p. 214). Questions can play varied and valuable roles in all lessons and activities. (See the resources listed at the end of this chapter for more information about questions.)

Closing the Lesson or Activity

The closing is an ending to a lesson or activity. All lessons and activities should include a closing that gives students one more opportunity to review the learned material. The closing can help create a smooth transition from one lesson or activity to the next.

Strategies for Closings

The closing can help tie everything together for students. It may include one or more of the following:

1. A *review of the key points* of the lesson or activity (for example, after reading a biographical sketch to her students, Mrs. Meurer reviews

major accomplishments of the life of Langston Hughes).

2. *Opportunities for students to draw conclusions* (Mrs. Vossbeck helps students examine the relationship between lack of supervision and juvenile crime).

3. A *preview of future learning* (for example, following an activity designed to create interest in an upcoming unit on the solar system, Mr. Maberry gives a brief explanation of unit lessons and activities that will occur in the next few days).

4. A *description of where or when students should use their new skills or knowledge* (Mrs. Weidkamp reminds students to try out their new social skill of "joining in" at recess).

5. A *time for students to show their work* (Mr. Isom has students share the three-dimensional shapes they constructed during the math lesson).

6. A *reference to the lesson opening* (Mrs. Begay restates the lesson objective as she prepares to begin the evaluation portion of her lesson).

Visual Supports

Using visual supports effectively is a critical teaching skill. Visual supports can increase the effectiveness of instruction by making information, explanations, and directions more comprehensible to learners. They are very helpful in teaching vocabulary, giving directions, building background knowledge, clarifying difficult concepts and strategies, and in providing scaffolds for new learning.

The following four categories provide some idea of the broad range of visual supports from which to choose.

1. *Real objects, animals, or people, working models, models, multimedia presentations, video or audio recordings, computer graphics, photographs, drawings, or maps.* Incorporating these as props in your instruction will help make new information more real and clear to students, especially when they can see, hear, and touch what they are learning about.

2. *Gestures, demonstrations, or role plays.* These are especially helpful in teaching actions and procedures.

3. *Writings.* Providing information in writing so students can read it as well as hear it spoken by the teacher is very helpful to many learners. The teacher can use posters, a whiteboard, overhead transparencies, handouts, labels, books, magazines, newspapers, and computer text.

4. *Graphic organizers.* These are used to depict connections and relationships among ideas. Show graphics during instruction, or students can be asked to fill them in as part of brainstorming, during presentations, while reading, with peer partners or in groups, and as practice or evaluation activities. Examples of graphic organizers are outlines, concept maps, diagrams, webs, T-charts, story maps, word banks, Venn diagrams, compare and contrast charts, problem–solution–effect charts, note taking guides, and so on.

Various visual supports can be combined during instruction. For example, when teaching students how to put together a completed circuit, the teacher can demonstrate using real objects and provide written directions with diagrams, as well as giving directions verbally.

Visual supports can be ordered from catalogs or borrowed from libraries, museums, and universities. Teachers can make files of photographs and drawings, and collect objects from garage sales. They can bookmark Internet sites and put photos, drawings, and diagrams on transparencies and slides. Computer software and the Internet have greatly expanded what is available to teachers.

■ Monitoring Student Progress

Monitoring allows both you and your students to know how they are progressing. It is imperative that you set up opportunities during lessons and activities to help you determine whether or not the students are grasping the desired learning. After all, that is the purpose of your planning. You need to know the kind of progress they are making toward the objective you planned, as well as when they meet the objective. It is equally important that you let your students know how they are progressing by giving them useful feedback. Several techniques will help you monitor progress.

Check for Understanding

A check for understanding (CFU) is a monitoring opportunity. Using active participation strategies helps make a check for understanding more reliable because students respond overtly in some way. Answering questions verbally, showing thumbs up or thumbs down in response to questions, writing information on a piece of scratch paper, and holding up a response card are examples of overt responses that could help monitor for student understanding and progress during a lesson or activity. Checks for understanding should be done early in both lessons and activities and continued at appropriate times throughout (when content needs to be rehearsed or when directions are given, for example). These strategies should be noted directly in the written plan.

The most effective CFUs are those that monitor the understanding of every individual student at once (having each student write an answer on a white board, for example). When you call on an individual student to answer a question, you can only evaluate the understanding of that one student. (See active participation for more ideas.)

Monitoring Seatwork

Supervised practice often takes the form of seatwork. It is very important to monitor student work at this point so that students are not practicing errors. The following are suggestions to help you monitor student work:

■ Move around quickly at the beginning to make sure each student gets started quickly.

■ Check on students you think might have difficulty, but do not spend too much time with any one student.

■ Do not just wander; look carefully at each student's work.

- Monitor all students, not just those who raise their hands.

- It may be best to have students complete just a few examples before correcting.

- Use peers to help monitor ("Compare your answers to questions 1 and 2 with your partner and let me know if they are different.").

- If there are many errors or questions, stop and reteach.

Feedback

Teachers assist students as they learn new information and skills by giving feedback on their performance. Feedback refers to statements that are made to students about the accuracy or inaccuracy of their responses. Feedback is sometimes used in combination with praise ("That's correct! Great!") for correct responses. Negative feedback for incorrect responses is most effective when it is combined with a statement, an example, or a demonstration of the correct response. That is why it is often called corrective feedback. Corrective feedback is academic and should be delivered respectfully. It focuses on the lesson content rather than the personality of the student. All feedback should be specific rather than general ("Your definition of photosynthesis includes all key points!" rather than "Nice job!").

Note that sometimes practicum students and student teachers feel reluctant to give corrective feedback because they are afraid it will hurt a student's feelings if she is told the answer is wrong. Consider this example: Ms. Rogers is teaching a lesson on nouns. After some initial instruction, she has students brainstorm new examples of nouns. Cindy calls out "sit." Ms. Rogers says, "Well . . . yes . . . , that could be a noun" and then calls on Jerome. Ms. Rogers did not want Cindy to feel badly because her answer was wrong, so she gave Cindy and the rest of the students inaccurate information about what she was teaching. Ms. Rogers could have said, "Cindy, that's a great example of a verb. Remember that a noun names a person, place, or thing. Can you think of an example of a thing that someone would sit on?" This response would have

given Cindy, and the other students, an additional reminder of the definition of a noun.

Evaluation

The evaluation section of a lesson plan is where the teacher writes a clear description of the method that will accurately determine whether or not the students have mastered the lesson objective. The importance of this section seems obvious, yet it is frequently overlooked or addressed as an afterthought. The information gathered through evaluation helps to make sensible planning decisions for the future. It allows teachers to determine whether they should build on the current lesson or whether some or all of the information needs to be taught again.

When the lesson objective is written, the evaluation is also planned. A well written objective contains a clear description of what students will do that will provide evidence that learning has occurred. Consider the following objective: "When shown a blank diagram of a volcano, students will label all five parts correctly." It is easy to "picture" what will be happening during the evaluation of this objective. At the end of the lesson, an unlabeled diagram of a volcano will be passed out, and students will label the various parts. They will be doing the labeling without help from anyone (no "hints" from the teacher, no help from a partner). Remember that evaluation is used to determine an individual student's independent performance in relation to an objective.

Evaluation is often more complex than that described in the volcano example. The evaluation may occur in steps or at various times or locations. This additional information should be explained in the evaluation section of the plan. For example, imagine that you want to teach students to use a reading comprehension strategy. The lesson objective is "Students will use all steps in the XYZ strategy when reading for information in content area texts." You decide to teach the lesson over 2 days. The steps of the strategy will be taught on the first day and the application of the steps on Day 2. The following is an example of how you might consider the evaluation:

"I will not be able to test the objective at the end of the first day because all of the necessary content will not have been taught. I will, however, test to see that my students have learned the strategy steps because, if there is confusion, I will need to reteach rather than go on to the application step. The evaluation completed after instruction on Day 1 will be the strategy steps written from memory."

"I can evaluate the objective following Day 2 because students should have the information and practice needed to successfully meet the objective. The evaluation will consist of my observing individual students performing the overt strategy actions during short content area reading assignments throughout the day."

At times it may also be desirable to include a description of a long-term objective and evaluation that relates to the short-term objective for the day. The long-term objective for the reading comprehension strategy might be, "Students will use all steps in the XYZ strategy whenever reading for information in content area texts." Obviously, students could not be evaluated on their use of this strategy when the teacher no longer has contact with them on a regular basis. However, plans should be included to provide ample generalization and review opportunities for the remainder of the school year. This will increase the likelihood that the strategy will be used following this year. Plans are needed to monitor use of the strategy during these times. The teacher may wish to make a note of this plan in the evaluation section of the lesson plan.

Students need to be monitored carefully during the lesson—especially during individual supervised and extended practice—so it can be determined when they are ready to be formally evaluated. Evaluation should occur only when students are ready, which may or may not be when the teacher had planned for evaluation to occur. This definitely speaks to the importance of having a backup plan for when students progress more quickly or less quickly than expected.

As objectives are planned, it should be remembered that evaluation is not necessarily a paper and pencil test. It can take many forms. Learning may be evaluated by asking students to complete worksheets, make oral presentations, answer questions verbally, make products, perform, or participate. Strive for relevance in evaluation methods and look to routinely using a combination of techniques.

As a note of caution, try not to have the evaluation be affected by unrelated skills. For example, an evaluation technique, such as asking students to create a bulletin board to show their understanding of the life cycle of the salmon, may actually be an evaluation of their artistic or organizational skills.

Managing Behavior

You may have a great lesson or activity planned, but if your students are misbehaving, they will not be able to take advantage of what you have to teach. Some basic techniques—some of which can be incorporated directly into your plan—will increase the likelihood that your students will attend and behave when you teach. One strategy helps you gain attention, while another involves telling students exactly what you expect from them. Preparing students to behave appropriately before problematic situations is a third strategy to explore carefully when you prepare to teach. Finally, an effective management technique is to give attention to the appropriate behaviors your students may display.

Signal for Attention

It is important to have your students' attention before starting your lesson or activity. A great deal of instructional time can be wasted when the teacher has to repeat instructions or directions because he did not have the students' attention. In addition, students may learn that they do not need to listen. To gain the students' attention, position yourself so you can see the faces of all your students and ensure that all of the students are looking at you (Colvin & Lazar, 1997).

An effective signal for attention can be used to gain the attention of the students. The signal is used as part of the "activity beginning" and "lesson setup" components. Signals can be verbal— "Attention, please," "Eyes up here," "Give me five!" They can be visual—flicking lights off and on, making mime movements. Or they can be auditory— clapping hands, ringing a bell, turning on music. The following are suggestions for using signals effectively:

■ Teach the students the signal that means they are to pay attention.

■ Explain and demonstrate what attention means: "Stop where you are," "Look at me," and "Listen with your mouth closed."

■ Practice until the group is able to respond to the signal in a specified amount of time (for example, five seconds). Make it fun. Time the students and then challenge them to reduce the amount of time it takes to get everyone's attention (play "Beat the Clock"). Periodically repeat the timing and the practice.

■ Following the signal, the teacher should remain silent. Make the students responsible, giving no reminders, warnings, or nagging.

■ Remember to acknowledge students for learning and performing this skill.

■ Encourage the students to help each other respond to the signal quickly through nudges, whispered reminders, and so on.

■ If the students enjoy competition, divide the class into teams that compete against each other to see who is the quickest to respond to the signal.

■ Be sure you are ready to begin as soon as you have their attention.

■ Make sure you are not starting until you have everyone's attention.

■ If, after your best efforts, students remain slow to give their attention, implement natural consequences. For example, "We need to spend 45 minutes on math today. Any time wasted will have to be made up during free time."

Statement of Behavior Expectations

One of the best ways to prevent behavior problems is to tell students clearly, in specific terms, the rules and procedures that need to be followed during the lesson or activity. It is important to have rules and consequences clear in your own mind before attempting to communicate them to the students. It is also important to carefully consider the class-room procedures that will help the current lesson or activity run smoothly. Consider the following suggestions when determining your behavior expectations:

■ Consider your goals for student behavior. Remember that the purpose of rules and procedures in the classroom is to facilitate student learning, not to establish obedience and conformity for its own sake.

■ Consider the activity or lesson and what will be happening during it. Does it include teacher presentation, small group work, or the use of breakable equipment? What behaviors will help the lesson or activity go smoothly, efficiently, safely, and allow everyone to learn?

■ Determine what previously taught procedures students will need to use. Should you review them at the beginning of the lesson or activity?

■ Recognize that you will need to be especially clear about those rules that vary by situation (talking during tests versus talking during partner work).

■ State your expectations for talking, being out of their seats, asking for help, and what to do when finished.

■ Consider how you can best communicate the expectations to the students. The following suggestions may help you:
  - Write the statement of behavior expectations in advance, making sure the language is appropriate for the students. Behavior expectations should be stated firmly and directly, but politely.
  - Be specific. Say, "Ask permission before using someone else's materials," rather than, "Respect others."
  - State *dos* rather than *don'ts* ("Raise hands," rather than "No talkouts").
  - State expectations for different parts of the lesson or activity. Rather than stating them all at the beginning, state them at the transitions (before you read the story, before doing seatwork, and so on).

■ Be sure to follow through with your expectations. The following guidelines will help you to do this:

- Do not state them and then ignore them.
- Be consistent. For example, if you stated that students must raise hands, then do not respond to callouts.
- Acknowledge students for following the rules and procedures. Be specific ("You remembered to put your paper in the assignment box").
- Plan the consequences for not following the rules.

Your students are more likely to behave appropriately if they know what you expect from them. Be sure to state expectations clearly and directly. It will be well worth your time to plan out how and when you will communicate this information to your students.

Note that if you are a practicum student or student teacher, you must clearly establish expectations for student behavior. Do not assume that, because the students understand and follow the cooperating teacher's rules, they will automatically behave the same way with you.

Precorrection

If, based on past problems, you predict that students will have difficulty behaving appropriately during a particular lesson or activity, use a technique called precorrection. The idea is to correct the problem *before* it happens. For example, in previous lessons when you have had your students work in small groups, they have not completed much work. You want to use small group work in class tomorrow and you want to build strategies into your lesson that will prevent or precorrect the problem behaviors.

The following steps for planning precorrection are adapted from Walker, Colvin, and Ramsey (1995):

1. Think about the *context* of the problem behavior (during small group work) and what the *problem behaviors* are (arguing about sharing materials and taking turns, talking about unrelated topics, not finishing tasks).

2. Pinpoint the *appropriate behaviors* with which you want to replace the problem behaviors (share materials, take turns fairly and efficiently, talk about relevant topics, and finish tasks on time).

3. In the lesson or activity plan, note the *changes to the context* you will make, the supports and structure you will provide (form smaller groups, change group composition, assign roles). This is a very important part of precorrection.

4. Expand the "stating behavior expectations" part of your plan by not only *stating the appropriate behaviors* (from Step 2 above), but also *teaching* the behaviors by demonstrating them and providing a brief practice. For example, show the students one way to decide who goes first and let them try it.

5. Plan how you will strongly *reinforce the appropriate behavior* after the lesson or activity (extra time for computer games).

6. Plan the *prompts* (reminders, encouragement, corrective feedback, and praise) you will use during the context of the behavior, (small group work).

You will find it is more efficient and positive to prevent misbehaviors than to wait and react to them after they occur.

Acknowledging Appropriate Behaviors

Once you have stated your expectations for appropriate behavior to your students, it is very important to acknowledge that behavior when you see it. And, it is essential to pay more attention to appropriate behavior than to inappropriate behavior. Sprick, Garrison, and Howard (1998) recommend a ratio of 3 to 1, that is, paying attention to desirable behavior at least three times as often as paying attention to undesirable behavior. (Mathur, Quinn, and Rutherford (1996) recommend a ratio of 5 to 1 for students with emotional or behavioral disorders.) This will help prevent behavior problems during your lessons and activities. Unfortunately, many of us find it more natural to notice and respond to inappropriate behavior. We expect and take for granted appropriate behavior.

Sometimes teachers do acknowledge appropriate behavior, but do so in a repetitive and general way, such as constant "good job" comments (Sprick, Garrison, & Howard, 1998). Sometimes teachers offer attention to students that does not fit their age, cultural background, or personal preference, such as public praise. Another problem is only to pay attention to a few compliant behaviors (being quiet, sitting still), while ignoring important learning and social behaviors (discussing, persevering, and helping).

There are so many things to think about when teaching. These suggestions may help you remember to pay attention to appropriate behaviors:

1. List in your plan some of the behaviors you hope to see during your lesson or activity (for example, rereading directions before asking for help, disagreeing without personal attack, sticking with a task even with many distractions, and raising a hand to speak). Some of these will be part of your statement of behavior expectations. Thinking about these behaviors ahead of time will help you notice them.

2. Plan several memory strategies—string on finger, reminder note in plan, marbles in pocket—to help you remember to acknowledge appropriate behavior throughout your lesson or activity.

3. Plan various ways to acknowledge appropriate behavior, such as smiles, nods, verbal feedback ("When you finished your work early you found a book to read"), specific praise ("Excellent! You shared your materials with your group members without being reminded. Well done!"), and specific encouragement ("You must be proud of yourself for turning your homework in on time").

4. Self-monitor your ratio of attention to appropriate and inappropriate behavior and write an objective for yourself.

Summary

The critical teaching skills that have been included in this chapter help increase the chances that all of your students will learn. They add focus and clarity to lessons and activities, help prevent behavior problems, and provide suggestions for monitoring student learning. It is important to include these strategies in your initial planning of all lessons and activities.

References and Suggested Readings

Arends, R. I. (1997). *Classroom Instruction and Management.* New York: McGraw-Hill.

Arends, R. I. (2000). *Learning to Teach* (5th ed.). San Francisco: McGraw-Hill. (See Chapter 12 in particular.)

Borich, G. D. (2000). *Effective Teaching Methods.* Columbus, OH: Merrill. (See Chapter 7 in particular.)

Boudah, D. J., Lenz, B. K., Bulgren, J. A., Schumaker, J. B., & Deshler, D. D. (2000). Don't water down! Enhance content learning through the unit organizer routine. *Teaching Exceptional Children, 32*(3), 48–56.

Boyle, J. R., & Yeager, N. (1997). Blueprints for learning: Using cognitive frameworks for understanding. *Teaching Exceptional Children, 29*, 26–31.

Bromley, K., Irwin-DeVitis, L., & Modio, M. (1995). *Graphic Organizers: Visual Strategies for Active Learning.* New York: Scholastic Professional Books.

Cegalka, P. T., & Berdine, W. H. (1995). *Effective Instruction for Students with Learning Difficulties.* Boston: Allyn and Bacon.

Christenson, S. L., Ysseldyke, J. E., & Thurlow, M. L. (1989). Critical instructional factors for students with mild handicaps: An integrative review. *Remedial and Special Education, 10*(5), 21–29.

Colvin, G., & Lazar, M. (1997). *The Effective Elementary Classroom.* Longmont, CO: Sopris West.

Dye, G. A. (2000). Graphic organizers to the rescue! Help students link—and remember—information. *Teaching Exceptional Children, 32*(2), 72–76.

Forte, I., & Schurr, S. (1996). *Graphic Organizers & Planning Outlines for Authentic Instruction and Assessment.* Nashville, TN: Incentive Publications.

Gall, M. (1984). Synthesis of research on teachers' questioning. *Educational Leadership, 42,* 40–47.

Guerin, G. R., & Male, M. (1988) *Models of Best Teaching Practices.* Paper presented at the meeting of the Council for Exceptional Children, Washington, DC

Guillaume, A. M. (2000). *Classroom Teaching: A Primer for New Professionals.* Columbus, OH: Merrill.

Heward, W. L., Gardner, R., Cavanaugh, R. A., Courson, F. H., Grossi, T. A., & Barbetta, P. M. (1996). Everyone participates in this class. *Teaching Exceptional Children, 28*(2), 4–10.

Howell, K. W., & Nolet, V. (2000). *Curriculum-Based Evaluation: Teaching and Decision Making* (3rd ed.). Belmont, CA: Wadsworth/Thomson Learning.

Jacobsen, D. A., Eggen, P., & Kauchak, D. *Methods for Teaching: Promoting Student Learning* (6th ed.). Columbus, OH: Merrill Prentice Hall. (See Chapter 6 in particular.)

Johnson, D. W., Johnson, R. T., & Holubec, E. J. (1991). *Cooperation in the Classroom.* Edina, MN: Interaction Book.

Kagan, S. (1992). *Cooperative Learning.* San Juan Capistrano, CA: Kagan Cooperative Learning.

Kellough, R. D. (2000). *A Resource Guide for Teaching: K–12* (3rd ed). Columbus, OH: Merrill, an imprint of Prentice Hall. (See Chapter 10 in particular.)

Luckner, J., Bowen, S., & Carter, K. (2001). Visual teaching strategies for students who are deaf or hard of hearing. *Teaching Exceptional Children, 33*(3), 38–44.

Lyman, F. T., Jr. (1992). Think-pair-share, think-trix, thinklinks, and weird facts: An interactive system for cooperative thinking. In N. Davidson and T. Worsham (Eds.), *Enhancing Thinking through Cooperative Learning,* 169–181. New York: Teachers College Press.

Mastropieri, M. S., & Scruggs, T. E. (2000). *The Inclusive Classroom: Strategies for Effective Instruction.* Columbus, OH: Merrill.

Mathur, S., Quinn, M., & Rutherford, R. (1996). *Teacher-Mediated Behavior Management Strategies for Children with Emotional/Behavioral Disorders.* Reston, VA: Council for Exceptional Children.

Orlich, D. C., Harder, R. J., Callahan, R. C., & Gibson, H. W. (2001). *Teaching Strategies: A Guide to Better Instruction* (6th ed.). Boston: Houghton Mifflin Company. (See Chapter 7 in particular.)

Rosenberg, M. S., O'Shea, L., & O'Shea, D. J. (1998) *Student Teacher to Master Teacher: A Practical Guide for Educating Students with Special Needs.* Columbus, OH: Merrill.

Rowe, M. B. (1986, January–February). Wait time: Slowing down may be a way of speeding up. *Journal of Teacher Education, 23,* 43–49.

Salend, S. J. (1998). *Effective Mainstreaming.* Columbus, Ohio: Merrill.

Smith, P. L., & Ragan, T. J. (1999). *Instructional Design* (2nd ed.). Columbus, OH: Merrill.

Sprick, R., Garrison, M., & Howard, L. (1998). *CHAMPs: A Proactive and Positive Approach to Classroom Management.* Longmont, CO: Sopris West.

Vallecorsa, A. L., deBettencourt, L. U., & Zigmond, N. (2000). *Students with Mild Disabilities in General Education Settings: A Guide for Special Educators.* Columbus, OH: Merrill, an imprint of Prentice Hall.

Walker, H., Colvin, G., & Ramsey, E. (1995). *Antisocial Behavior in School: Strategies and Best Practices.* Pacific Grove, CA: Brooks/Cole.

Chapter 7

Diversity Strategies

Introduction

Classrooms are made up of highly diverse individuals. They may include students from a variety of cultural and linguistic backgrounds, students with varied gifts and talents, students with different kinds of disabilities, and students with learning and behavior problems. Every teacher's goal is to teach so that all students are successful. With the diversity present in today's classroom, however, it often seems an unreachable goal. A one-size-fits-all approach to instruction is clearly ineffective. Writing separate lesson plans for each student in a full class is not realistic. So, what can teachers do to move toward that goal of instruction that results in success for all learners? They can plan inclusive lessons that incorporate effective teaching strategies, the principles of universal design and differentiated instruction, and make accommodations and modifications that will help each student learn.

Planning for Diversity

The most efficient way to meet the needs of all students is to consider those needs up front—as you design lessons and activities—rather than solely trying to adjust for individuals after the fact. Incorporating best practice and building in alterna-

tives that will allow all students access to your instruction is the way to start. These are strategies that you will always include in your lessons and activities. Other accommodations and modifications will be included based on the makeup of your class.

Critical Teaching Skills

Before you consider making specialized accommodations for the diverse needs of your students, make sure you have included effective teaching strategies in your lessons and activities. These are research-based best practices that you should always incorporate. The following are examples of such best practices:

- Communicate rationales for what students are to learn.
- Vary types of instruction and grouping.
- Ensure high levels of responding.
- Provide regular reviews.
- Communicate clear expectations.
- Monitor student performance.
- Provide positive and corrective feedback.
- Maintain a brisk pace.

Many of these critical teaching skills are described in the rest of the book, especially in Chapter 6.

Universal Design

It is also important to incorporate the principles of universal design into your lessons and activities. Orkwis and McLane (1998) state that, "In terms of learning, universal design means the design of instructional materials and activities that allows the learning goals to be achievable by individuals with wide differences in their abilities to see, hear, speak, move, read, write, understand English, attend, organize, engage, and remember" (p. 9). Universal design is usually applied to architecture (for example, designing buildings with automatic doors that are essential for people in wheelchairs and handy for people carrying things), instructional technology (voice activated programs), and the design of curricular materials (digital textbooks, for example). These principles can also be applied to lesson and activity development as well. The key idea is to build in alternatives and flexibility, not to add them on later. It is also important that all learners benefit. For example, video captions may benefit everyone in a noisy classroom—not only individuals with hearing impairments or English-language learners.

You can build these universal design alternatives into your lesson and activity plans in several ways. Orkwis and McLane (1998) suggest a variety of examples for incorporating multiple methods of presenting information and multiple methods of student response and engagement:

1. *Presenting Information* When presenting information in a lesson, plan to say, demonstrate, and write the information. This redundancy allows all students—those with visual and auditory impairments, learning disabilities, and those learning the English language—to access and benefit from the information. For example, when teaching the steps for dividing fractions, state the rule, "When dividing fractions, invert the divisor and multiply." Write the steps on the board. Then demonstrate by solving problems on an overhead transparency while stating the steps again and pointing to them on the board.

When you use visual supports in your lessons or activities, provide verbal descriptions to go with them. Provide written captions for audio materials. Whenever possible, use digital text so that it can be enlarged and changed in other ways to make it more accessible.

2. *Student Responses* When asking students to express their learning, include every student by offering alternatives, such as saying or recording the response, writing, typing, drawing, demonstrating, and so on. For example, students might respond to a math fact question— "What is 4 times 3?"—by writing the answer, saying the answer, or pointing to the answer on a number chart.

Word processing programs provide students with many supports, such as grammar and spelling checks. Students who are unable to make oral presentations may create multimedia presentations, or supply computer graphics as an alternative to hand drawing.

3. *Student Engagement* Keep students engaged in learning by offering alternatives in supports or scaffolds; these will help challenge individuals appropriately. For example, some students may use calculators while solving math word problems. Allow students to follow their individual interests by providing choices, such as copying popular music lyrics to practice handwriting. Also, reach students by allowing for flexibility in practice activities (working independently or with peers, for example).

Six Principles for Designing Instruction for Diverse Learners

Kame'enui et al. (2002) discuss six universal design principles for helping students gain cognitive access to the curriculum. The following principles were developed to guide the design of curricular materials, but many of the ideas can be applied as you develop lessons and activities:

1. *Big Ideas* are the fundamental concepts and principles in an academic area that help connect or "anchor" the smaller ideas. Big ideas help teachers decide what to teach, to select

and sequence objectives, to focus on important learning outcomes, and help students make connections and focus on the most important ideas. Consider big ideas as you prepare the content analysis and objective rationale. In the opening, use big ideas in advanced organizers. When presenting information, summarize and emphasize key points by referring to big ideas.

2. *Conspicuous Strategies* are the steps for solving a problem or accomplishing a task. When teaching strategies explicitly, they become clear and usable for students. While preparing the content (task) analysis, list the steps of the strategy; state, list, explain, and model the strategy by using "think alouds." In extended practice, provide opportunities to use the strategy in varied applications.

3. *Mediated Scaffolding* is the temporary support and assistance provided by the teacher, the materials, or the task during instruction. Provide varying levels of supports and gradually withdraw them. This allows each student to be successful during instruction and eventually become independent. Examples of mediated scaffolding include sequencing examples and tasks from easy to more complex; moving from the whole group, to partner, to individual practice; and providing varied materials (note-taking guides with more or less filled in, for example).

4. *Primed Background Knowledge* is the recalled prerequisite skills and knowledge needed for the new task. Having the necessary background knowledge and applying it to the new task is required for success. List prerequisites in the content analysis; assess prior knowledge; and remind, review, and reteach background knowledge as needed.

5. *Strategic Integration* involves putting together essential information and skills, which leads to higher-level thinking skills. As part of your long-term planning, be sure to plan lessons and activities in combinations that will lead to integration.

6. *Judicious Review* provides opportunities for students to review important learning. Carefully planned review will result in students remembering and being able to apply what they have learned. Include review in the openings and closings of lessons and activities, and build in extended practice and activities.

As you design lessons and activities, ask yourself if you are building in multiple methods of presentation, response, and engagement. Also ask yourself if you are incorporating big ideas, explicit strategies, scaffolding, primed background knowledge, integration, and review in such a way that the objectives can be achievable by all students.

Differentiated Instruction

Differentiated instruction is another approach or philosophy of teaching, with the goal that all children will learn. This type of instruction begins with the assumption that students in a class will vary in their readiness for a particular learning task, and in their personal interests and preferences. This approach emphasizes the importance of teaching toward important learning outcomes (that is, crucial concepts and principles, big ideas), assessing each student's prior knowledge and progress, maintaining high standards, and challenging each student. Teachers achieve differentiation by varying content, materials, pacing, activities, grouping, scaffolding, products, and so on, in various subject areas, units, or tasks for individuals or small groups, as needed (Tomlinson, 1999; Pettig, 2000). As you see, there are many similarities in the key concepts and recommended strategies of effective teaching, universal design, and differentiated instruction.

Built-Ins and Add-Ons

When you plan lessons and activities, make sure you always include critical teaching strategies and the principles of universal design. Include other differentiations, accommodations, and modifications depending on the makeup of your class. Build them in if they will benefit many. Add them on as individual accommodations if they will only benefit certain students and are not appropriate for the whole class.

Accommodations and Modifications

Accommodations are defined as changes in *how* you teach (providing more instruction, more practice, more time to complete tasks, highlighted textbooks, study guides, peer tutoring, and having students sit near the teacher, for example). Modifications are changes in *what* you teach. For example, you may teach the same subject matter but at a different level of difficulty, such as having one student work on locating named cities on a map while the rest of the class learns to predict the locations of cities based on natural features such as rivers. Other examples include reducing the criterion in an objective (accepting 75 percent rather than 100 percent accuracy on capitalizing), or teaching different content (functional academics, life skills).

Instructional accommodations for individuals are strategies that are intended to allow a student to meet the same goals as peers, such as providing a note-taker. When meeting the needs of individuals, teachers may need to apply temporary modifications to what a student is taught (for example, some students may be working on using periods and question marks at the ends of sentences, while other students are working on punctuating direct speech). The assumption is that the students will catch up with their peers. However, there may be potentially serious implications if students are learning less than their peers in the long run due to the modifications. Changing what students are taught can have an impact on their future success in school and employment. Teams that include parents should make these modifications very thoughtfully. Teachers should begin with the assumption that students, including students with disabilities, will learn the same content as their peers. However, if instructional accommodations do not allow the student to progress in the general curriculum and meet state standards, then changing the expected learning outcomes may be in the best interests of the student.

■ In This Chapter

This chapter is intended to provide a variety of strategies to consider as you plan lessons and activities for students in today's diverse classrooms. These strategies or suggestions are divided into four parts.

In Part 1, suggestions are categorized by the planning components described in Chapter 4 (Lesson Plans) and Chapter 5 (Activity Plans). These strategies will typically be built into initial planning. These suggestions will help:

a. Make teaching and management generally effective (everyone will benefit if active participation strategies are used).

b. Incorporate alternatives and flexibility into teaching and management to make it more likely that all students will be reached (by presenting information using multiple methods, for example).

c. Include strategies that may be essential for the success of some students, while being helpful to all of the students (the use of mnemonics, for example).

In Part 2, strategies are categorized by "problem" (for example, when students are having difficulty maintaining attention or beginning tasks). Dependent on the makeup of the class, these suggestions may be built into initial planning for the whole class or added on as individual accommodations or modifications for certain students. These suggestions focus on mild to moderate learning and behavioral problems and do not include accommodations necessary for complex, low-incidence disabilities. (For ease in locating ideas, strategies may be listed under more than one category in Part 1 and Part 2.)

Part 3 provides strategies that help plan for the cultural diversity of students. Suggestions about the content of lessons and activities and about methods of instruction and management are meant to help foster the involvement and success of students from diverse cultural backgrounds.

Finally, strategies are provided in Part 4 to help English-language learners be successful in your lessons and activities.

An Example of Planning for Diversity

The following example shows ways that teachers can build in and add on diversity strategies to help all students be successful.

Mrs. Hakim plans an activity in which her students are asked to create an ending to a story. The intention is to provide additional practice on predicting and making inferences, following reading comprehension lessons. After hearing or reading the first half of the story, students are asked to produce their own endings and justify them.

When Mrs. Hakim selects the story for which the students will create endings, she chooses a story by a Mexican-American author. She wants her students to identify with authors so she tries to promote this by choosing stories written by people with ethnic backgrounds similar to those of her students.

Mrs. Hakim helps students connect their prior knowledge and experience to this activity, an effective teaching strategy that she considers important for the learning of all students. She does this by helping students connect their use of inferences and predictions in everyday situations through asking questions such as, "You see pork, onions, green chiles, and tortillas on the grocery list. What do you think you'll have for supper? Why? What is another possibility?"

She plans to preteach key vocabulary using pictures and demonstrations. This is helpful to many of her students and very important for the English-language learners.

She plans to review the previously taught skill of predicting, based on finding clues in the story and making inferences. This is an effective teaching strategy.

Mrs. Hakim passes out a written copy of the first half of the story. She then reads the story out loud. Presenting information in these two ways (multiple methods of presenting) will allow more of her students to be successful.

During her initial planning of this activity, Mrs. Hakim automatically decides to provide both written and oral directions for producing the story endings. She knows that this effective teaching strategy is essential for several of her students and that many of them find it helpful. (She also finds that the process of writing directions results in clearer directions and saves instructional time.)

Many of Mrs. Hakim's students have difficulty completing tasks. Therefore, when planning the activity, Mrs. Hakim makes explicit the steps for completing this story ending assignment—finish ending, proofread ending, put name on paper, place in box on back table—and decides to list these on the blackboard. She has built this conspicuous strategy technique into her initial planning, rather than as a separate accommodation, because the makeup of her class makes this sensible.

Some of the students in Mrs. Hakim's class are more productive when they have the opportunity to work with peers; others prefer to work alone. This may be related to cultural background. Mrs. Hakim decides that the students may consult peers when writing their story endings, if they choose.

Two of Mrs. Hakim's students have very serious writing problems. The accommodation she plans for them is to dictate their story endings to a teaching assistant. The other students may choose to hand write or to type their assignments. She provides sentence patterns (for example, I think Carlos will _____ at the end because . . .) to several other students who need more support or scaffolding to be successful in writing.

She modifies the activity for one student. He is working on a different comprehension objective, recalling factual information. Mrs. Hakim creates questions that a parent volunteer asks him, recording his responses.

This chapter is a brief summary or review of some of the many strategies recommended in the literature for helping students learn (Algozzine, Ysseldyke, & Elliott, 2000; Cegelka & Berdine, 1995; Cummings, 1990; Evertson, Emmer, & Worsham, 2000; Fisher, Schumaker, & Deshler, 1995; Lovitt, 1995; Meltzer et al., 1996; Prater, 1992; and Sprick, Sprick, & Garrison, 1993, for example). It is essential to monitor the progress of individual students to assess whether the strategies are working, that is, to determine whether the student is learning. More specialized accommodations and modifications will be necessary for some students.

Note that a common concern of teachers these days is the number of students who have difficulties with inattention, impulsiveness, and overactivity, and who may or may not have the label of Attention Deficit Disorder (ADD) or Attention Deficit and Hyperactivity Disorder (ADHD). We are not going to include information on the use of medications nor deal with issues of labeling or over-diagnosis; instead, we have included suggestions for strategies that can help students pay attention, wait, and modulate activity levels. Some may be appropriate as part of whole class planning, and some as adaptations for individuals.

Part 1: Diversity Strategies by Planning Component

As you initially plan activities and lessons, consider the diversity strategies you can incorporate into each component of the plan to help all students succeed. These components include content, objective, model, signal for attention, behavior expectations, opening, body or middle, extended practice, closing, evaluation, management, and materials.

When Planning the Content

Consider the following when planning content in a diverse classroom:

■ Be sure that you are teaching important knowledge and skills. If students have fallen behind in the curriculum, there is no time for fluff and filler. Teach what is most generalizable.

■ Consider the possibility that you need to teach more lessons and fewer activities. Reexamine the rationale for the planned activities.

■ Select content based on the students' interests. Offer choices to students when possible. For example, allow students to read articles from the sports pages to practice reading skills.

■ Teach students to set and monitor their own learning goals.

■ Teach learning strategies along with teaching content areas, such as working on active reading strategies in the social studies textbook.

■ Teach school survival and task-related skills, such as social skills, study skills, test-taking skills, problem-solving skills, and organizational skills.

■ Teach students the skills they need to be successful in various teaching models and methods (discussion skills or peer interaction skills, for example).

■ Teach the behaviors you expect students to display in the classroom, such as procedures and routines for making transitions, asking for help, turning in homework, or cleaning up.

When Planning the Objective

Consider the following when writing the objective for a diverse classroom:

■ Be sure that your objective is connected to generalizations and big ideas, state standards, or Individualized Education Program (IEP) goals.

■ Pretest to make sure the objective is appropriate for the students.

■ Examine the criterion. Is it at the right level? Basic skills that are prerequisites for higher-level skills need high criterion levels. For example, 100 percent accuracy is necessary for letter recognition because that is an important basic skill needed for acquiring later skills. On the other hand, 100 percent accuracy in distinguishing reptiles from amphibians may not be necessary.

■ Examine the condition. Is it realistic? Students may be more motivated to reach objectives when they can see the "real-world" application.

■ After analyzing prerequisite skills, the objective for individual students may need to be altered. For example, could students who have poor writing skills demonstrate that they can recognize the key conflict in a short story by saying it rather than writing it? Could students who are inaccurate on multiplication facts demonstrate that they know how to find the area of a rectangle using a calculator? In other words, the purpose is to allow the student to go on learning, not to be held back by those writing or multiplication difficulties. On the other hand, in most cases the student continues to need instruction and practice on writing and multiplication.

Do not rush to make changes in the curriculum for students with learning problems. Changes may affect success in upper grades, or options for employment or further schooling in the long term. Having a student draw a picture or sing a song rather than write a paragraph may provide momentary success, but it is unlikely to be an option offered by future employers.

When Deciding on the Model and Methods

Consider these strategies when planning lesson models and methods for a diverse classroom:

Recognize that students with learning and behavioral problems often require very explicit instruction. This needs to be followed by focused, active practice with immediate feedback.

Evaluate the level of structure that the students need to be successful. Do not assume that all students learn best with, or even prefer, unstructured approaches.

If the students have fallen behind in the curriculum, use models and methods that are the most time-efficient.

Evaluate the amount of academic learning time that each student would have in the lesson or activity. For example, having groups of students work together to bake cookies may sound like a good way to practice measurement skills; however, when you look closely, you may see that, in an hour-long activity, Joanne spent 30 seconds measuring one tablespoon of cinnamon. Not much practice!

Be sure that students have the necessary skills to be successful in the methods you are using. For example, can they share materials or reach consensus if you are using small-group projects? These skills may need to be directly taught in advance. In addition, students may have to practice these skills on a simple level, such as having students work with one other student rather than in groups of five.

Small-group instruction may frequently be needed in a classroom of students with diverse achievement levels. Students should be carefully assessed on specific skills to form short-term skill groups. It is important to keep assessing and reforming groups as necessary.

When Planning the Signal for Attention

Consider the following suggestions when planning a signal for gaining the attention of your students:

Choose a strong signal, such as ringing a bell or turning off the lights.

Use fun or novel signals, such as playing Simon Says.

Change the signal periodically.

Let students design the signal.

Teach students to respond quickly to the signal. Have them practice.

Spend time teaching and reviewing how "attention" looks and sounds.

Strongly reinforce students for attending quickly.

Help students be prepared for the signal at the beginning of lessons or activities by having the daily schedule written on the board, by listing the materials needed for the next lesson or activity, and by providing reminders, such as, "In five minutes, we'll be starting math."

When Planning Behavior Expectations

Use the following suggestions when preparing your statement of behavior expectations:

Be absolutely clear and specific. Say, "Eyes on me, mouth closed, hands on desk, listen," rather than, "Pay attention while I read the story."

Consider using visual supports, such as a green flag that signals that talking is okay.

- Make sure expectations are realistic and important for learning. Decisions should be based on students' needs, not on the teacher's personal preferences. The goal should not be a classroom in which students never talk or move; however, students may learn best in a quiet, orderly, structured environment.

- Be brief; don't ramble.

- Be consistent in language. Use the same terms and phrases as when the rule, procedure, or expectation was originally taught.

- Evaluate whether you need to reteach lessons on asking for help, making transitions, or other instructional routines.

- Evaluate whether you need to develop more efficient routines and procedures.

- If students are not meeting expectations, evaluate the lesson or activity for difficulty level, pacing, clarity, and other areas. Look carefully at seatwork and small-group work.

- Write a specific behavior management plan for what will be done when students meet or do not meet behavior expectations. Involve students in this planning. Use strong and immediate reinforcers.

When Planning the Opening

The following suggestions will help you plan an opening that will engage students:

- Add drama, humor, novelty, or excitement to gain attention (use skits, puppets, music, video clips, jokes, riddles, or demonstrations, for example).

- Personalize by using the students' names and experiences. For example, open a writing lesson with a sentence, or a math lesson with a word problem, about the students ("If Mrs. Donahue's champion third graders win 16 games of four square . . .").

- In the opening, involve those students who are the most difficult to motivate or focus.

- Increase time spent on the review of earlier lessons or prerequisite skills and knowledge. Carefully plan ongoing daily, weekly, and monthly reviews.

- Involve everyone in active responses (for example, have all students write the definition of a term from yesterday's lesson rather than asking "Who remembers what ratio means?").

- Invite students to write or say everything they already know about a topic in three minutes.

- Use the opening to build up background knowledge. For example, if students will be reading a story that takes place on a subway and they have no experience with subways, preteach necessary information.

- Computer software is available that can help develop graphic organizers to show students connections in learning or to preview lessons.

When Planning the Lesson Body or Activity Middle

The following suggestions will help you plan a lesson body and activity middle that will allow for all students to learn:

Providing Directions, Procedures, and Rules

The following suggestions may help you to present information clearly:

- Shorten and simplify directions.

- Cue with numbers (for example, "first" or "second").

- Present orally and in writing, use picture directions, and provide demonstrations of what students are to do.

- Follow up by asking questions or by having students repeat or paraphrase what they are to do.

- Emphasize key words with intonations in your voice or by highlighting in written directions.

Presenting Information

The following suggestions will help you present information in an engaging and effective manner:

■ Repeat key ideas often, using the same wording.

■ Ask for frequent, active responses. For example, have students process, verbally or in writing, information just presented. Decrease the use of strategies that involve calling on a few students who raise their hands or asking several students to come up to the board and do a problem. Increase opportunities for all students to respond.

■ Break up the information. Teach a couple of steps and have the students practice; teach a couple more steps, and so on. Keep reminding the students of the whole task or big picture through demonstrations or by using graphic organizers.

■ Use analogies, metaphors, or vivid language.

■ Be sure that examples used are familiar to the students.

■ Increase the use of visual supports, such as photographs, videos, real objects, and computer multimedia presentations.

■ Cue note-taking (for example, "first," "second," or "This is important").

■ Provide partially filled in note-taking guides or graphic organizers that students can complete (outlines, concept maps, or webs, for example).

■ Stop often to summarize, review, and clarify how this information fits into the larger picture.

■ Provide mnemonic devices to help students remember information.

■ Adjust pacing; a brisker pace typically helps students attend and allows for more teaching.

Questioning

When asking students questions, the following suggestions may help you promote active participation:

■ If students are permitted to call out answers rather than required to raise hands, keep track of (or ask someone else to keep track of) whom is responding. If some students are consistently left out, rethink the use of this method.

■ Avoid calling only on the same few students who raise their hands quickly. Increase the wait-time. Develop a system for keeping track of whom you have called on (for example, use a seating chart or name sticks).

■ It is usually most effective to ask a question, pause, then call on a student by name, rather than saying, "Ben, what is the definition of . . . ?" This encourages all students to think of the definition, not just Ben. However, sometimes saying the name first may increase the involvement and success of particular students.

■ Call on nonvolunteers more often. Draw name cards at random or deliberately choose certain students to answer particular questions. The intention is not to embarrass students. Tell the class in advance that you will be calling on nonvolunteers and allow them to pass if they choose. The purpose is to keep all students attentive and to send the message that you want to hear from everyone—even those in the back row.

■ Ask frequent questions and use active participation strategies to get responses from all students. Make sure these strategies are varied. Make sure everyone really is participating during unison and signaled responses. Plan how to regain attention, or how to have students show they are ready to go on (for example, they will look at you or put their pencils down).

■ Questions can be used to keep students focused while they are listening or watching. For example, hand out a list of questions before the lecture or speech, video, story, or reading. Have each student take notes on the questions during the presentation. Divide the class into teams. Give each team time to go over the questions together, to write and compare responses, and to help each other learn the material. Make name cards for each team member. Pick a name card at random from each team's stack and call on that person to answer a question from the list. Team members cannot help each other at this point. Keep track of each team's correct answers. Teams that answer the questions correctly may be excused from the homework assignment.

Demonstrating

The following suggestions may help you when planning demonstrations:

- Increase the number of demonstrations.

- Emphasize or highlight important parts or steps in demonstrations.

- When demonstrating self-talk and self-questioning, be sure to use consistent terms and phrasing.

- Point to steps on a written list as they are demonstrated.

- Show videotaped demonstrations of real applications.

- In addition to showing a completed product, show partially completed products along the way.

Providing Supervised Practice

In providing supervised practice, consider the following suggestions:

- Increase the amount of initial practice with teacher support. For example, "Say it with me," or "Do it with me."

- Provide more structure and cues at first (an outline of a letter showing where to write the date, the greeting, and the other parts).

- Use similar examples for initial practice. Gradually change.

- Provide error drills.

- Increase the amount of initial practice with peer support by using more partner or small-group situations.

- Structure small-group and partner practice by teaching students how to work together. (See Chapter 12 for more information.)

- Increase the amount of individual supervised practice with immediate feedback.

- Build high levels of accuracy and fluency.

When Planning Extended Practice

Consider using the following strategies when preparing the extended practice section:

- Build in frequent review of basic skills (at the beginning of lessons, during end-of-day activities, and in learning centers).

- Reduce the length of each practice session, but provide more practice sessions.

- Change the task without changing the content to avoid boredom during a practice session. For example, have students say an answer versus writing an answer; have them write the answer on paper, the blackboard, or a transparency; or have them use computer practice programs.

- Make it fun; use a game format.

- Increase the amount of support during practice (study guides, peer tutors, and visual supports such as posters and desktop number lines, for example).

- When possible, provide practice in context as part of real tasks.

- When using homework, go over directions and begin during class. Be sure the task is the same or similar to supervised practice (Salend & Gajria, 1995).

When Planning the Closing

Consider the following when planning the closing:

■ Do not assume that students will automatically apply or generalize the new skill or knowledge. Be very direct about where and when to use it.

■ Actively involve students in summarizing at the end of the activity or lesson.

■ Use the closing as one more practice opportunity.

When Planning for Evaluation

The following suggestions will help you plan your evaluation (see also "When Planning the Objective").

■ Be sure you have taught what you are testing.

■ Keep the form of evaluation as direct and simple as possible so that you are not inadvertently testing skills irrelevant to the objective (testing reading skills in math word problems, for example).

■ Keep evaluating for retention and for improvement.

When Planning for Classroom Management

Consider the following when planning for classroom management:

■ Think about the planned lesson or activity. Has everything possible been done to make it interesting and motivating? Are students likely to be involved and successful? Effective instruction helps prevent behavioral problems.

■ Think about the room arrangement as related to the planned activity or lesson. Will students be able to see you, the blackboard, the poster, or whatever is necessary? Will you be able to see and get close to all students? Are desks or tables set up for class discussions, small-group work, or individual work? Who is sitting by whom? Who is sitting near you?

■ Consider the transitions within the activity or lesson. Are the directions planned for moving from desks to sitting on the rug; for moving chairs together for partner work; or for switching from large-group presentation to individual seatwork?

■ Plan for the efficient use of time. This will also help prevent behavioral problems. For example, consider needed materials and equipment. Does the VCR work? Are pens available for writing on the white board? Are the copies of the handout ready? Have you planned an efficient way to distribute materials? When will they be distributed so they are not a distraction? Are directions planned for how and how not to use them? Has safety been considered? Have you prepared directions for how to share materials and how to return them? (One of our practicum students wrote in her journal that she needed more practice in planning activities that involved the use of glue.)

■ Plan how and when students will be reminded of the various routines they have been taught that relate to this activity or lesson (for example, where to turn in assignments, how to get help, what to do when finished, how to set up for partner practice).

■ Many of the strategies listed under "When Planning the Lesson Body or Activity Middle" apply to the above content (give directions verbally, in writing, with pictures, or through demonstrations, for example).

■ Examine the plan and note those places where students may have difficulties, staying on task at learning centers, for example. Plan how to provide needed structure and support to avoid problems (for example, assign specific tasks to complete or provide the use of peer helpers).

■ Use stronger reinforcers, in addition to praise.

■ Be sure the reinforcers chosen are actually reinforcing to the students. Involve them in the selection and provide a menu of reinforcers from which to choose.

■ Clarify contingencies. Be very specific. For example, do not say "If everyone tries hard. . . ."

■ Use immediate reinforcers, not a popcorn party a week away.

■ Plan negative consequences for inappropriate behavior and make sure students are aware of them. Be fair and consistent, not arbitrary. Interrupt the activity or lesson as little as possible.

■ Look once again at your statement of behavior expectations. Communicating expectations very clearly is an important way to prevent management problems.

When Planning for the Provision of Materials and Equipment

In planning for the use of materials and equipment, consider the following suggestions:

■ Provide materials that support students (study guides, note-taking guides, graphic organizers, highlighted texts, or taped materials).

■ Highlight key words or features on worksheets and put less material on each page.

■ Include self-correcting materials and software, programmed materials, calculators, or video and audio tape recorders. These materials can be very useful in helping students work independently.

■ Provide students with laptop computers for note-taking or for doing assignments, along with software for checking spelling and grammar, for word prediction, and so on.

■ Use all levels of assistive technology.

■ Part 2: Diversity Strategies by Problem or Difficulty

As you are planning, you are not only thinking about the various components of your lessons and activities and how to make them most effective, you are also thinking specifically about your students. You may be thinking, "There is a long list of steps to follow in this lesson, and my class has trouble with that. What can I do to help them be successful?" Or you may be thinking, "Tim, Andrew, Bridget, and Anne are going to have a hard time sitting down long enough to finish this assignment. How can I help them?"

The following strategies may be built into the initial planning for the whole class or added as accommodations for individuals (Cohen & Lynch, 1991). Many of the ideas come from the literature on instructional recommendations for students with attention deficits, but will be helpful for many students (Bender & Mathes, 1995; Council for Exceptional Children, 1992; Dowdy, Patton, Smith, & Polloway, 1998; Kemp, Fister, & McLaughlin, 1995; Lerner, Lowenthal, & Lerner, 1995; Rooney, 1995; and Yehle & Wambold, 1998). Notice that these diversity strategies provide positive behavioral support for students as well as increasing academic learning.

You may need to plan for students who have difficulty with keeping still, waiting, selective attention, maintaining attention, routine tasks, memorizing, beginning tasks, completing tasks, following directions, organizing, reading, handwriting, messiness, taking tests, change, or self-control. The following sections offer suggestions on ways to help students with these difficulties.

Difficulty Keeping Still

When teaching students who have difficulty remaining still, consider the following strategies:

■ Let students stand or move when this does not disrupt learning. For example, let them stand at their desks to do independent work or walk around while doing oral practice.

■ Allow students to use various desks or work areas.

■ Let students use worry beads or doodle when this does not interfere with the task.

■ Build in movement for students in the daily schedule (hand out papers, run errands, clean up, or do stretching exercises).

- Build in movement in lessons and activities by using active physical responses (tell students to "stand up if you think this is the topic sentence" or "walk to the blackboard and write the definition").

- Teach students to signal when they need a break.

Difficulty Waiting or Impulsiveness

This may be a problem when students are standing in line, taking turns, responding on assignments or tests, during discussions, and so on. The following suggestions may help students with such difficulties:

- Use a cue that reminds students to remain quiet during the wait-time after questions.

- Tell students to discuss responses with their partners before saying or writing the answers.

- Teach students to highlight important words in test questions or in assignment directions.

- Cue the use of problem-solving steps.

- Teach students to outline essay test answers before writing.

- Teach students to think of the answer on their own before looking at multiple choices on a test.

- Teach students what to do while waiting for help (try another problem or task, ask a partner for help, or reread directions, for example).

- Cue the use of self-talk (for example, "I need to take a deep breath and . . .").

- Provide students with something to do while waiting in line or for a turn (play a game, sing a song, have something in their pockets to play with, for example).

- Teach students how to interrupt politely.

Difficulty with Selective Attention

Students who have difficulty with selective attention have trouble attending to the important aspects of a task or information. (For this problem, see Howell & Nolet, 2000, for suggestions to promote attention, memory, and motivation.) The following suggestions also help with this difficulty:

- Use color cues, highlight, or bold important details.

- Provide study guides and other comprehension supports, such as advance questions, to go with readings or presentations.

- Provide flash cards or cue cards that include key information and examples with no extraneous information.

- Use a consistent format for instruction and on worksheets.

Difficulty Maintaining Attention

Consider the following suggestions in classrooms with students who have difficulty staying focused:

- Provide preferential seating (sit the student near the teacher or another adult, near quiet peers, away from high-traffic areas, such as doors or windows, or at individual desks rather than at a table with other students).

- Teach the student to ignore distractions in the long run. Reduce distractions in the short run through preferential seating, the use of study carrels, screens, or headphones, or by reducing sounds and visual stimuli.

- Provide more frequent breaks or changes in tasks.

- Use more active participation strategies.

- Regain the student's attention frequently through proximity, touch, eye contact, or private signals.

- Teach students to self-monitor their own attention or on-task behaviors (Kaplan, 1995, see Chapter 9 in particular).

- Have a peer helper prompt students to pay attention.

Difficulty Sticking with Routine Tasks

The following methods may be effective when teaching students who find it difficult to complete tasks:

- Divide tasks into smaller segments, with brief breaks or reinforcement between segments, or spread tasks throughout the day or class.

- Remove anything unnecessary from tasks, such as copying sentences before correcting them.

- Analyze the amount of practice needed and remove unnecessary repetitions. Make sure the difficulty level is appropriate, and the objective is important.

- Alternate preferred tasks with less preferred ones.

- Alternate forms of practice and offer choices (for example, students can practice math problems on paper, the board, with a partner, or using a computer).

- Add novelty and interest with games, materials, personal interests, and so on.

- Teach on-task behaviors, including self-monitoring and self-reinforcement.

Difficulty with Tasks That Require Memory

To help students increase their ability to memorize, incorporate (and teach) memory strategies, such as mnemonics, visualizing, oral practice or rehearsal, and many repetitions. For example, teach students to make a word or sentence using the first letters of words in a list to be learned, or help students memorize new terms using picture clues and known words (Mastropieri & Scruggs, 1998).

Difficulty Beginning Tasks

When students find it difficult to begin tasks, consider the following suggestions:

- Provide cue cards on their desks, describing how to begin a task. Have students check off steps as completed. For example, (1) write name on paper, (2) read directions, and so on. (This is similar to reminders that appear on billing envelopes, such as "Have you written the account number on your check?")

- Go to the student quickly at the start of seatwork to help him start. Say that you will be back shortly to check.

- Provide a peer helper to prompt or to do the first step or problem together.

Difficulty Completing Tasks

To ensure that students finish tasks, consider the following methods:

- Assist students in setting goals for task completion within realistic time limits, and help them self-reinforce.

- Clarify what constitutes completion (answer all five questions in complete sentences, put name on paper, and place paper in assignment box on teacher's desk). Write this on the board or on cue cards on the student's desk.

- Establish routines—such as where and when—for turning in assignments.

- Provide peer help in reminding students to finish and turn in completed tasks.

- Help students list tasks to do and check them off as completed.

Difficulty Following Directions

If students find it difficult to follow directions, consider the following methods:

- Before giving directions, make sure you have the student's attention (for example, gain eye contact, say a name, or touch).

- Give only one or two directions at a time.

- Simplify the language and vocabulary.

- Emphasize key words.

- Ask the student to repeat the directions, at first to you and eventually to self.

- Give students their own copy of written directions.

- Have a peer read directions to the student.

- Teach the students to circle important words in written directions.

- Teach and follow consistent routines so directions do not have to be given too often.

Difficulty Organizing

The following suggestions may help students to organize:

- List assignments and materials needed on the board or a transparency.

- Teach students to use an assignment calendar or a checklist.

- Have students use notebooks with pockets or dividers.

- Provide places to put materials in desks or in the room (in boxes or trays).

- Help students to color code materials needed for various subjects.

- Provide time to gather materials at the beginning or end of each class or day.

- Teach a consistent routine for turning in or picking up assignments.

- Provide peer help.

- Help students divide assignments into steps or parts.

Difficulty Reading

When teaching reading is not the objective, the following suggestions may help students who experience difficulty in reading:

- Have a peer or other volunteer read to the student.

- Have a peer summarize information orally to the student.

- Provide highlighted text.

- Provide study guides, outlines, or graphic organizers to go with the reading to help with comprehension.

- Provide the necessary information in other forms, such as oral presentations, audio tapes, videotapes, or computer multimedia programs.

Slow or Poor Handwriting

When students exhibit poor handwriting, consider the following suggestions:

- Teach handwriting and provide for increased practice to build fluency. Provide practice that uses content of personal interest (for example, have students copy information about skateboarding).

When the objective of the lesson or activity is not to teach or practice handwriting, consider the following:

- Decrease nonessential writing. For example, do not require students to copy questions before writing the answers.
- Give students a copy of your notes or a copy of a peer's notes.
- Allow the use of other methods, such as using a word processor, giving oral presentations, having someone take dictation, or taping answers.
- Do not worry as long as it is readable.

Messiness

Use the following techniques to help students maintain neatness:

- Allow students to use a pencil and eraser, graph paper that helps organize writing on a page, or a word processor.

- Provide time and support for cleaning a desk or work area.

- Provide storage places (boxes, shelves, extra desks, or notebooks) and reminders of where to put things.

Difficulty with Taking Tests

When students find it difficult to take tests, consider the following options:

- Allow alternative forms of testing (oral rather than written, for example).

- Provide help with understanding directions for taking tests.

- Teach test-taking skills (for example, cross out incorrect answers on multiple choice tests or outline answers on essay tests).

Difficulty with Change

Some students become upset at changes in schedules and routines or in having different people in the classroom, and so on. The following suggestions may help you avoid surprises and help students adjust to changes:

- Maintain the same schedule of events, as much as possible, in the classroom. Post and discuss the schedule.

- Warn students of changes in advance (an assembly this afternoon or a parent visitor, for example).

- Support the students through any changes. For example, have them stay near you or a designated peer, give reminders of expected behavior, or provide words of comfort.

- Remind students to use previously taught relaxation techniques.

- Initially provide practice in dealing with change through role plays and controlled minor changes.

Difficulty with Behavioral Self-Control

The following suggestions may help avoid behavioral problems in the classroom (Kaplan, 1995; Rhode, Jenson, & Reavis, 1993):

- Be sure lessons and activities are appropriate for students.

- Teach self-management and social skills, such as problem solving, anger management, or stress management.

- Use precorrection plans (Walker, Colvin, & Ramsey, 1995).

- Be observant and intervene early.

- Provide structure and consistency.

- Spend time developing warm, personal relationships with students.

- Keep students busy (with entry tasks, with tasks to do when finished with assignments or while waiting for help, and during transitions).

- Carefully teach and provide practice on rules, procedures, and class routines.

- Develop a written behavior management plan that is clear and that includes positive and negative consequences.

- Seat students near you or selected peers.

- Arrange a time-out area.

- Use strong, frequent, and immediate reinforcers.

- Use behavior contracts.

- Use novel reinforcement systems.

- Involve parents.

- Use peer mediation.

Note that there are many more diversity strategies described in the professional literature. See the end of the chapter for suggested readings.

Part 3: Planning for Cultural Diversity

Cultural diversity needs to be considered when planning lessons and activities. It is important to be educated about cultures and cultural perspectives. It is also important to be aware of your own cultural background and how this affects beliefs, values, expectations, and in turn, the choice of subject matter, models, methods, management procedures, rules, and so on. There must be an awareness about the particular cultures of the students and how these affect the students' preferences and reactions to the methods and management used in the classroom. However, it is extremely important to see students first as individuals. The importance of cultural background must be recognized, but it is essential to avoid stereotyping. Understanding cultural diversity may make you a better decision maker or problem solver, by being able to generate more ideas or options when planning.

When planning, consider two general areas in which to provide for cultural diversity: *content* and *instruction or management* (Cartledge & Milburn, 1995; Grossman, 1991; Grossman, 1995; and Manning & Baruth, 1996). When planning content, incorporate subject matter, materials, and examples that reflect the contributions and perspectives of a variety of cultures and the personal experiences and interests of the students. The purpose is to help all students feel valued, represented, and motivated, and to help the students become knowledgeable and tolerant (or, more importantly, welcoming) of diversity.

In the selection of models and methods of instruction and management, consider the possible cultural preferences and experiences of the students. There is a real danger of stereotyping or overgeneralizing here, such as thinking that all African-American students learn best through cooperative learning. To avoid this, make a best guess as to which methods will work most successfully for particular students and then monitor their progress carefully, changing methods as needed. Because all students are not the same, plan a variety of models and methods for activities and lessons for the whole class, as well as individualizing for particular students.

Planning the Content

When planning multicultural content, consider both long-range and daily planning. The content of daily lessons and activities will be based on larger perspectives and units of instruction.

Long-Range Planning

There should be a multicultural perspective throughout the curriculum as well as specific units of instruction with multicultural content.

Even though long-range planning is beyond the scope of this book, it is important to mention that many options bring a multicultural focus to the content of units. For example, plan units on the contributions of particular cultural groups, on topics such as the history of the civil rights movement and immigration, and on themes such as conflict resolution, social justice, and stereotyping.

Daily Planning

A multicultural focus to activities and lessons that are not part of units on multicultural topics may also be included. For example, to provide practice on distinguishing between main ideas and details (the objective), read a story to the students. Have the students brainstorm a list of what they remember from the story and then sort main ideas and details (the activity). Because the topic of the story is irrelevant to the objective, select a story for a "cultural" purpose, such as a story about an individual with a disability, a homeless family, or an African folk tale. The "cultural" purpose may be to help individual students feel that their experiences or backgrounds are represented and valued in the classroom or to provide information about experiences or cultures unfamiliar to the students.

Another example might be the selection of an art activity to provide practice on the long-term objective of following directions. Perhaps select an art form of a particular culture. Many activities, especially in reading, writing, art, and music, may incorporate cultural information as an additional goal.

The same holds true for the selection of "carrier" content in lessons. For example, a teacher plans a lesson with the objective that students will identify nouns in sentences. Some students come from families who fish for a living and where fishing is an important aspect of their culture. The sentences used as examples or during practice could be about fishing. However, be very careful to avoid stereotyping with this technique, such as including sentences about sombreros or tepees.

It is also important to consider cultural diversity when planning activities and lessons on topics such as Thanksgiving, Columbus Day, and Mother's Day, to ensure that you represent various perspectives or "voices." Be sensitive to diversity when planning assignments such as designing a family tree or writing letters to Santa, and when planning social skills lessons, such as teaching assertiveness.

Note that teachers need to send a message of welcome and respect by learning the correct pronunciation and use of names. They should also learn the languages of their students (at least hello, goodbye, thank you, and so on.). Teachers may encourage the use of native languages, and include pictures and other materials that represent various cultures. Materials used in the classroom should reflect cultural diversity and must be examined to make sure they are free of bias.

Planning Instruction and Management

Cultural background can influence students' success with particular instructional and management methods. It is essential to see students as individuals and to make individual decisions, but knowledge of how culture contributes to variation can be helpful in thinking of instruction and management possibilities. For example, if a teacher has a student who does not ask for help on assignments when he needs it, knowledge of his cultural background may suggest trying a same-sex peer helper. The teacher must carefully monitor for the effectiveness of this strategy and be ready to try other methods if needed. However, this may be a sensible first try.

In the following sections, we have not categorized ideas by cultural group but, instead, have listed variables or possibilities to consider as you plan for instruction and management.

Instruction

The success of instruction is dependent on how well you meet the individual needs of your students. Consider the students in terms of the following variables as you plan the use of peer interactive instruction and practice:

■ Preference for learning from peers or from adults

■ Comfort with competition or cooperation

■ Preference for individual or group work

■ Valuing of generosity and sharing, and implications for helping each other on assignments, even tests

■ Expectations about interactions with the opposite sex (for example, there may be problems with having a boy and girl as learning partners)

■ Beliefs about excelling or standing out from peers

You may wish to try, for example, increasing or decreasing the amount of partner practice or the use of peer tutoring and various cooperative learning methods. You may consider these variables as you make decisions about the composition of groups and student roles, about using competitive game formats, and about publicly displaying accomplishments. Also, consider that one of the goals of using peer groups may be to promote cross-cultural interaction and friendships and to discourage segregation by race, social class, and so on.

Many variables also have implications for the selection of lesson models and the use or structuring of project- or center-based activities. As activities and lessons are planned, consider the teacher's role, the pacing of instruction, the amount of talk and movement, the specificity of directions, and other features. When selecting lessons and activities, consider the following about your students:

■ Comfort with making their own decisions, initiating their own projects, and choosing what or how to learn

■ Tolerance for structure or lack of structure

■ Experience with sitting quietly or with maintaining high activity levels

■ Comfort with the teacher as a co-learner or as an authority

- Desire for feedback or direction

- Independence or dependence on the teacher

- Beliefs about asking for help or questioning the teacher

Consider the following variables of your students as you plan discussions and brainstorming sessions, active participation strategies, and questioning techniques, such as calling on volunteers and nonvolunteers:

- Comfort with stating opinions, stating opinions passionately, disagreeing with others, including the teacher

- Comfort with volunteering to answer questions, or initiating their own questions or comments

- Experience with divergent or open-ended questions

- Beliefs as to what constitutes polite responses to questions or statements, and methods of interrupting

- Beliefs about how much talking is polite

Finally, consider the differences of your students in prior knowledge and personal experience when you plan topics, select readings, and plan openings. For example, ask yourself if you are assuming a familiarity with St. Patrick's Day, dairy farms, escalators, and other topics, as you plan activities and lessons.

Management

The responses to management techniques may also be influenced by cultural background. Consider the following when planning management techniques for your students:

- Expectations about relationships with adults having to do with respect, showing affection, and gender issues

- Preferences for close, warm, informal relationships or more distant, formal relationships with teachers

- Preferences about touching and being touched

- Beliefs about talking and conversations, considering the amount, who initiates, sharing personal information, and what is considered private

- Expectations about relationships with peers, considering age and gender issues, extended family, teasing, fighting, sharing, and excelling

- Differences in nonverbal communication, including the communication of motivation, interest, and listening

Consider these variables when analyzing your interactions with students and when evaluating the social climate in the classroom. Do not assume your students are just like you. They may be horrified if you sit on the floor with them or ask them to call you by your first name. If you do not hug them or ask about their families, they may believe you do not like them. Avoid making assumptions that you all agree on what is polite or respectful behavior.

Consider the following about your students before making assumptions:

- Expectations about rules and procedures, such as who develops them, what they are, and what level of strictness

- Beliefs about obedience, adult authority, arguing with or questioning adults, and providing rationale for rules or decisions

- Need for structure and organization, for a quiet environment, or for clear goals and expectations

- Valuing of conformity

- Expectations about asking permission or about functioning independently, such as borrowing materials or going to the restroom

- Changes in expectations by age or gender

These variables have clear implications for the development of classroom rules and procedures and for the behavior expectations component of activities and lessons.

Finally, consider the following variables that will clearly affect the planning of behavior consequences. Do not assume what will be reinforcing or punishing to individual students:

- Comfort with public or private recognition and punishment

- Comfort with individual versus group acknowledgment or reinforcement

- Preference for personal reinforcement, such as warm praise, rather than more impersonal reinforcement, such as prizes

- Valuing of praise or criticism from others, such as from peers or teachers

- Familiarity with different types of punishment, such as shaming, corporal, or discussions

Because each student is unique, the instructional and management methods and the decisions for individuals need to be varied. In some instances, students may need to be taught to become comfortable with approaches that they are not used to. In other cases, the teacher will need to adjust to the fact that certain behaviors are impermissible for some students for cultural or religious reasons.

We have suggested only a few of the many variations possible among cultures. You can see how important it is to become knowledgeable about cultural diversity in general, and with your own and your students' cultural backgrounds in particular (Cartledge & Milburn, 1995; Grossman, 1991; Grossman, 1995; and Manning & Baruth, 1996).

■ Part 4: Planning for English-Language Learners

As you plan activities and lessons, you need to consider your students' proficiency with the English language. You will want to include strategies that will help English-language learners be successful. (Assume in this section that the primary objective of the lessons or activities taught in English is content learning rather than teaching English.) Remember that a student's social or conversational English may be quite fluent, but her academic language proficiency in English may need a great deal of support.

We will discuss what you can do to help students understand what you say or present and what

you can do to provide opportunities for language use. (Many of these ideas are adapted from Gersten, Baker, & Marks, 1998.) These two categories of strategies are especially applicable to the planning of activities and lessons.

Make What You Present Understandable

Many authors call this "comprehensible input." Comprehensible input means that students are able to understand the sense or substance of what is said or presented, although they may not necessarily understand every word. The following strategies help promote comprehensible input:

1. *Teach vocabulary.* Selecting and defining key terms and vocabulary is an important part of content analysis (see Chapter 6). When teaching English-language learners, it is absolutely essential to consider the following suggestions:

   - Select a small number of words to introduce at a time. Gersten & Baker (2000) suggest seven or less.
   - Select important and useful words.
   - Preteach the vocabulary words at the beginning of lessons or activities or before reading.
   - Directly teach the words and meanings by saying them, writing them, and using visual supports and active participation strategies.
   - Help the students connect the words with prior knowledge and personal experience through discussions and semantic webs.
   - Provide various practice opportunities, such as acting out meanings, creating word banks, writing journal entries, or defining to partners.

2. *Use visual supports.* Visual supports are a very important method of scaffolding to help English-language learners understand vocabulary, concepts, principles, and procedures. The four types of visual supports described in Chapter 6 are helpful in various ways during instruction. For example, real objects, models, and pictures are very helpful in teaching vocabulary. Demonstrations and role plays make directions and procedures much more understandable. Writings are helpful for reinforcing verbal information in many parts of activities or lessons. Finally, graphic organizers can

improve comprehension, clarify abstractions, organize concepts, or demonstrate connections.

3. *Provide context and activate background knowledge.* New information is more easily understood when it is presented in a context than when it stands alone. At the beginning of a lesson, use the following methods to build background knowledge and provide a context:

   - Provide a familiar example (introduce fractions by saying, "Three friends have only one cookie and they want to share it . . .").
   - Ask questions (introduce a history unit on migrations by asking, "How many of you have sometime in your life moved to a new place? What did you take? How did you get there?").
   - Use group or individual brainstorming to create a web or map of what they already know about a topic.
   - Have the class, small groups, or individuals complete KWL charts (what I already **K**now about a topic, what I **W**ant to learn, and later, what I did **L**earn).
   - Connect an introduction of new concepts with the students' native languages.
   - Build background knowledge for the students by providing experiences, such as brief activities at the beginning of lessons ("I'm going to give one cookie to each group of three, and you need to share it fairly . . ."); activities that come before lessons (an activity involving experimenting with magnets before a lesson on how magnets work); or field trips, guest speakers, multimedia presentations, or stories that are relevant to the new learning).
   - Provide a context as you present by gesturing and demonstrating, showing examples of completed products, using graphic organizers, thinking aloud, or showing objects, pictures, videos, or audio recordings.

4. *Use consistent language.* Decide on the important words and phrases to be used in a lesson or activity, teach them, and then use those terms consistently. Avoid using synonyms at random; name the steps consistently when teaching procedures and strategies; remember that idioms, metaphors, and other figures of speech can be difficult to understand. Use

them carefully; and check for understanding frequently.

5. *Give explanations or directions in a variety of ways.* As you speak, use gestures and demonstrations; put information in writing; be explicit and explain step by step; give many examples; use "think alouds"; show completed products; and check for understanding.

Provide Opportunities for Language Use

In addition to providing comprehensible input, teachers need to help students process that input, and express and practice that learning. Gersten & Baker (2000) argue "that both extended discourse about academic topics and briefer responses to specific questions about content are cornerstones of academic growth for English-language learners" (p. 465). The following are some strategies for providing opportunities for language use in lessons and activities:

1. *Use active participation strategies* These strategies (discussed extensively in Chapter 6) are designed to keep students actively engaged in learning. As you select those strategies likely to be most valuable for English-language learners, look for strategies that require oral responses from students; provide opportunities for long, complex responses, instead of brief, one- or two-word responses; encourage discussions with peers (Think-Pair-Share, for example); and create nonthreatening opportunities to respond (unison responses).

2. *Use partner and small-group work* Having students work with partners or in small groups during lessons and activities provides many opportunities for language use. (Formal peer tutoring and cooperative learning programs are highly recommended as well.) Peers act as language models and can provide feedback. Their support can create a safe environment for using language. Chances to discuss new concepts or solve problems with other students, including those who speak the same native language, can be very beneficial. Teachers need to carefully monitor and structure partner and small-group

work to be most effective. (See Chapter 12 for more on this approach.)

Summary

The students you work with will be diverse in their success with various teaching and management methods. The key to planning is to make decisions based on the students' needs rather than your own preferences. The suggestions presented in this chapter are only a beginning. It is important to continue to add to your repertoire of diversity strategies.

References and Suggested Readings

Algozzine, B., Ysseldyke, J., & Elliott, J. (2000). *Strategies and Tactics for Effective Instruction* (2nd ed.). Longmont, CO: Sopris West, 1992.

Banikowski, S. K., & Mehring, T. A., (1999). Strategies to enhance memory based on brain research. *Focus on Exceptional Children, 32*(2), 1–16.

Bender, W. N., & Mathes, M. Y. (1995). Students with ADHD in the inclusive classroom: A hierarchical approach to strategy selection. *Intervention in School and Clinic, 30,* 226–234.

Cegelka, P. T., & Berdine, W. H., (1995). *Effective Instruction for Students with Learning Difficulties.* Needham Heights, MA: Allyn and Bacon.

Cohen, S. B., & Lynch, D. K. (1991). An instructional modification process. *Teaching Exceptional Children, 23,* 12–18.

Council for Exceptional Children (1992). *Children with ADD: A Shared Responsibility.* Reston, VA: Author.

Cox, P., & Dykes, M. (2001). Effective classroom adaptations for students with visual impairments. *Teaching Exceptional Children, 33*(6), 68–74.

Cummings, C. (1990). *Teaching Makes a Difference* (2nd ed.). Edmonds, WA: Teaching, Inc.

Dowdy, C., Patton, J., Smith, T., & Polloway, E. (1998). *Attention-Deficit/Hyperactivity Disorder in the Classroom.* Austin, TX: Pro-Ed.

Evertson, C. M., Emmer, E. T., & Worsham, M. E. (2000). *Classroom Management for Elementary Teachers* (5th ed.). Needham Heights, MA: Allyn and Bacon.

Fisher, J. B., Schumaker, J. B., & Deshler, D. D. (1995). Searching for validated inclusive practices: A review of the literature. *Focus on Exceptional Children, 28,* 1–20.

Howell, K. W., & Nolet, V. (2000). *Curriculum-Based Evaluation: Teaching and Decision Making* (3rd ed.). Belmont, CA: Wadsworth/Thomson Learning.

Kame'enui, E. J., Carnine, D. W., Dixon, R. C., Simmons, D. C., & Coyne, M. D. (2002). *Effective Teaching Strategies that Accommodate Diverse Learners* (2nd ed.). Upper Saddle River, NJ: Prentice-Hall.

Kaplan, J. S. (1995). *Beyond Behavior Modification* (3rd ed.). Austin, TX: Pro- Ed.

Kemp, K., Fister, S., & McLaughlin, P. J. (1995). Academic strategies for children with ADD. *Intervention in School and Clinic, 30,* 203–210.

Larkin, M. (2001). Providing support for student independence through scaffolded instruction. *Teaching Exceptional Children, 34*(1), 30–34.

Lerner, J. W., Lowenthal, B., & Lerner, S. R. (1995). *Attention Deficit Disorders.* Pacific Grove, CA: Brooks/Cole.

Lovitt, T. C. (1995). *Tactics for Teaching* (2nd ed.). Englewood Cliffs, NJ: Prentice Hall.

Mastropieri, M. A., & Scruggs, T. E. (1998). Enhancing school success with mnemonic strategies. *Intervention in School and Clinic, 33,* 201–208.

Mathews, R. (2000). Cultural patterns of south Asian and southeast Asian Americans. *Intervention in School and Clinic, 36*(2), 101–104.

Meltzer, L. J., Roditi, B. N., Haynes, D. P., Biddle, K. R., Paster, M., & Taber, S. E. (1996). *Strategies for Success: Classroom Teaching Techniques for Students with Learning Problems.* Austin, TX: Pro-Ed.

Orkwis, R., & McLane, K. (1998). A curriculum every student can use: Design principles for student access. *ERIC/OSEP Topical Brief.* Reston, VA: Council for Exceptional Children.

Ormsbee, C., & Finson, K. (2000). Modifying science activities and materials to enhance instruction for students with learning and behavioral problems. *Intervention in School and Clinic, 36*(1), 10–21.

Pettig, K. L. (2000). On the road to differentiated practice. *Educational Leadership, 58*(1), 14–18.

Prater, M. A. (1992). Increasing time on task in the classroom. *Intervention in School and Clinic, 28*, 22–27.

Reid, R. (1999) Attention deficit hyperactivity disorder: Effective methods for the classroom. *Focus on Exceptional Children, 32*(4), 1–20.

Rhode, G., Jenson, W., & Reavis, H. (1993). *The Tough Kid Book.* Longmont, CO: Sopris West.

Rooney, K. J. (1995). Teaching students with attention disorders. *Intervention in School and Clinic, 30*, 221–225.

Salend, S. J. (1998). *Effective Mainstreaming: Creating Inclusive Classrooms* (3rd ed.). Columbus, OH: Merrill.

Salend, S. J., & Gajria, M. (1995). Increasing the homework completion rates of students with mild disabilities. *Remedial and Special Education, 16*, 271–278.

Sprick, R., Sprick, M., & Garrison, M. (1993). *Interventions: Collaborative Planning for Students at Risk.* Longmont, CO: Sopris West.

Stormont-Spurgin, M. (1997). I lost my homework: Strategies for improving organization in students with ADHD. *Intervention in School and Clinic, 32*(5), 270–274.

Tomlinson, C. A. (1999). *The Differentiated Classroom: Responding to the Needs of All Learners.* Alexandria, VA: ASCD.

Walker, H., Colvin, G., & Ramsey, E. (1995). *Antisocial Behavior in School: Strategies and Best Practices.* Pacific Grove, CA: Brooks/Cole.

Welton, E. N. (1999). How to help inattentive students find success in school: Getting the homework back from the dog. *Teaching Exceptional Children, 31*(6), 12–18.

Williamson, R. D. (1997). Help me organize. *Intervention in School and Clinic, 33*(1), 36–39.

Yehle, A. K., & Wambold, C. (1998). An ADHD success story: Strategies for teachers and students. *Teaching Exceptional Children, 30*, 8–13.

 ## Cultural and Linguistic Diversity

Bigelow, B., Harvey, B., Karp, S., & Miller, L. (Eds.). (2001). *Rethinking Our Classrooms: Teaching for Equity and Justice* (vol. 2). Milwaukee, WI: Rethinking Schools.

Cartledge, G., & Milburn, J. (1995). *Teaching Social Skills to Children and Youth.* Needham Heights, MA: Allyn & Bacon.

Gersten, R., & Baker, S. (2000). What we know about effective instructional practices for English-language learners. *Exceptional Children, 66*(4), 454–470.

Gersten, R., Baker, S. K., & Marks, S. U. (1998). *Teaching English-Language Learners with Learning Difficulties.* Reston, VA: Council for Exceptional Children.

Grossman, H. (1991). Multicultural classroom management. *Contemporary Education, 62*, 161–166.

Grossman, H. (1995). *Classroom Behavior Management in a Diverse Society* (2nd ed.). Mountain View, CA: Mayfield.

Hagiwara, T. (1998). 20 ways to introduce multi-culturalism in your classroom. *Intervention in School and Clinic, 34*(1), 43–44.

Herrell, A. (2000). *Fifty Strategies for Teaching English-Language Learners.* Upper Saddle River, NJ: Prentice-Hall.

Kea, C. (1998, March). Focus on ethnic and minority concern: Critical teaching behaviors and instructional strategies for working with culturally diverse students. *CCBD Newsletter.* Reston, VA: The Council for Exceptional Children.

Manning, M. L., & Baruth, L. G. (1996). *Multicultural Education of Children and Adolescents* (2nd ed.). Needham Heights, MA: Allyn & Bacon.

Montgomery, W. (2001). Creating culturally responsive, inclusive classrooms. *Teaching Exceptional Children, 33*(4), 4–9.

Preface to the Lesson Models

Introduction

A lesson model is an overall teaching approach that is used to guide student learning in a specific way toward the attainment of a lesson objective (Arends, 2000). There are various lesson models for which lesson plans are written. In Chapters 8, 9, and 10, we provide information about three important models—direct instruction, informal presentation, and structured discovery. Chapter 11 features examples of how to use direct instruction and structured discovery to teach specialized content, such as concepts, social skills, and learning and study strategies.

These three models were selected for inclusion in this book because they are reasonably easy for teachers to implement, and they are very effective when used correctly. Additionally, they can be used to facilitate different types of learning.

A teacher needs to be able to successfully implement these three lesson models. Using various models and methods is essential because variety helps keep students motivated and interested. Variety also addresses the fact that not all students learn in the same way, and that certain content is best taught through certain models. It is also important to incorporate the use of peers into lessons and activities. This topic is covered in Chapter 12.

You may practice one model several times until you are comfortable with it; then begin practicing another model. A practicum student or student teacher has the opportunity to practice writing and teaching single lessons before teaching multiple lessons within one day. This allows you time to experiment with, and practice teaching various types of lessons.

Selecting a Model to Use

Students are guided toward a specific lesson objective in different ways, depending on the lesson model used. Some models, such as direct instruction and informal presentation, are best used to teach basic knowledge and skills. Some models, like structured discovery, may be used to promote inductive thinking and problem-solving skills. Therefore, a thorough understanding of the characteristics of various lesson models can help determine which particular model would benefit the students so they can master a particular objective.

A lesson model should always be selected after the lesson objective is written. Decide first where you want students to go (the lesson objective), and *then* decide how to help get them there (the lesson model). Once you have selected the model to use, it is necessary to be sure the written plan reflects the essential elements of the chosen model. For example, if you are writing a direct instruction lesson, the plan should detail how you will explain and demonstrate information; how you will check for understanding; and what types of practice opportunities will be provided. These are key elements of a direct instruction lesson. Although all lesson plans contain the same seven components, the content of the components will differ depending on the lesson model being used.

 ## Organization of Chapters 8-10

Similar information about direct instruction, informal presentation, and structured discovery models is presented. A basic model description introduces each model. Next, typical uses for the model are described. Some key elements of each model are discussed in "Key Planning Considerations." Finally, Figures 8.1–10.1 provide summaries of how to write the actual lesson plans.

Figures 8.1–10.1 are to be used as guides for writing lesson plans for specific lesson models. Our intent is for you to read carefully *all* of the information provided about each model and use it as a reference when you write your plans. The summaries can serve as reminders of the key information that needs to be included in the written plans. Refer to Chapter 4 for information about generic lesson components.

The content of each component included in each specific model is essential to defining the model. Certain component content may be added, rearranged, or omitted. However, if that is done, it is necessary to have a good rationale for doing so. Varying the critical elements of the model too much will result in something other than the model that was chosen. Changes must be carefully analyzed.

Note that before you select a specific lesson model to use, the following preplanning tasks must first be completed:

- Determine the specific content to be taught in the lesson and analyze that content.

- Write the lesson objective.

- Write the lesson rationale.

- Now, select the model and refer to the appropriate chapter for more information.

 ## References

Arends, R. I. (2000). *Learning to Teach* (5th ed.). Boston: McGraw-Hill.

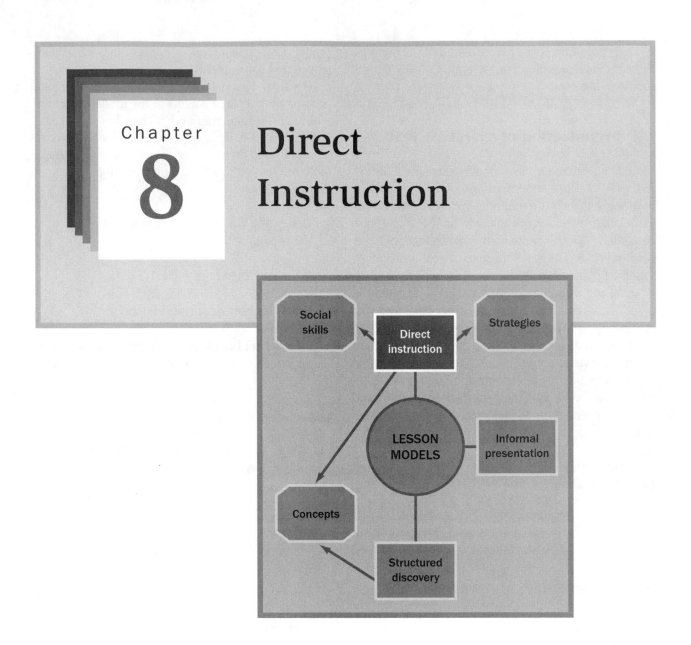

Chapter 8

Direct Instruction

 Introduction

Direct instruction is often summarized as "I do it, We do it, You do it," that is, the teacher demonstrates the skill, the teacher and students do the skill together, and the students do the skill by themselves. Another phrase used to describe direct instruction is "model-lead-test." It means the teacher shows and tells, the teacher leads the students in practicing, and the students are evaluated. Both phrases imply that the teacher is carefully guiding the learning of the students. This is precisely the intent of direct instruction. Direct instruction is explicit teaching.

Direct instruction lessons are teacher-directed, and the lesson events are focused on moving students toward a specific objective. Teachers begin by clearly stating the lesson objective and the lesson purpose to the students. They then explain and demonstrate the information or skill to be learned, using many examples. Students are given a variety of opportunities to practice the new knowledge or skill. Teachers carefully supervise the students' practice, which may occur within small groups or with a partner. The final supervised practice stage is always individual student practice. This allows teachers to see how each student is progressing.

Students are given feedback on their performance as teachers monitor the supervised practice opportunities. This helps ensure that students are accurately practicing the new information or skill. Careful monitoring also allows teachers to determine whether or not reteaching is needed and when evaluation should occur.

In the direct instruction approach information is presented in small steps so that one step can be mastered before moving to the next. The end result of the direct instruction lesson is that students demonstrate their new skill or knowledge independently, without help from anyone.

Note that there are two types of direct instruction. One type, often called "Big D.I.," refers to published programs that provide scripted lessons, such as Reading Mastery I and II Fast Cycle (Engelmann & Bruner, 1995). The other type, commonly referred to as "little d.i.," is the one described in this chapter. In both types of direct instruction, teachers explicitly guide students toward learning specific objectives. The individual writing the lesson plan creates the explanations, directions, and other material contained in "little d.i."

Uses of Direct Instruction

Direct instruction lessons play an important role in teaching basic skills, concepts, rules, strategies, procedures, and knowledge that lends itself to being presented in small, sequential steps. The following are some examples of content and topics that can be appropriately taught through direct instruction lessons:

- *Procedures* are a series of steps that lead to the completion of a task. Examples include how to measure in feet, read a map, serve in volleyball, convert fractions to whole numbers, initiate a conversation, react to teasing, resist peer pressure, complete make-up assignments due to absence, how to get help, or what to do with completed work.

- *Strategies* are a specific type of procedure. They are techniques that help students learn, study, or get organized. Examples include how to read text with comprehension, take notes from text reading, take multiple choice tests, proofread assignments, or create concept webs of main ideas. (See Chapter 11 for information on strategy instruction.)

- *Principles* are relational rules and are usually stated as cause–effect, if–then relationships. The following are examples of principles: If a sentence is a question, then it should end with a question mark; if $A(B+C) = D$, then $AB + AC = D$; when there is a silent *e* on the end of the *CVCe* word, it makes the previous vowel say its name; and when a sentence includes three or more related items, a comma belongs after each item.

- *Concepts* are categories of knowledge. Examples include triangle, peninsula, noun, socialism, migration, ecosystem, or plot.

Direct instruction lessons also play an important role in lessons that emphasize higher-level thinking. Higher-level thinking cannot occur without having basic facts and information about which to think. The content taught in direct instruction lessons may form the foundation for lessons that emphasize critical thinking and problem solving. The following are some examples of how higher-level thinking is dependent on knowledge of basic skills and information:

- Mr. Garcia wants his students to use the Internet as one resource for their country analysis. He first teaches them computer-access skills through direct instruction.

- Ms. Sparks wants her students to design their own science experiments to test certain hypotheses. She first teaches them steps in the scientific method through direct instruction.

Direct instruction lessons also play an important role in the use of certain teaching methods (Arends, 1997). For example, if you want to use cooperative learning groups or discussions in your lessons and activities, students will need to be directly taught skills such as reaching consensus, taking turns, active listening, and paraphrasing.

Key Planning Considerations

When writing the body of the direct instruction lesson, carefully consider and thoroughly plan in detail the presentation of information, the demonstration, and the supervised practice. The content analysis, which plays an important role in the lesson body, must be planned carefully as well.

Content Analysis

The content analysis of a direct instruction lesson varies according to the content you are teaching. When planning a "how-to" lesson, the content analysis will include a task analysis. When teaching a principle, you will write a clearly stated principle statement. Finally, when teaching a concept through direct instruction, include a concept analysis. Note that the task analysis, principle statement, or concept analysis will be presented and taught as part of the lesson body.

Presentation of Information

In the presentation of information section of the direct instruction lesson body, the teacher presents the information students need to know to meet the lesson objective. It should include a description of the content to be taught (the *what*) and how the new skill or knowledge will be explained (the *how*). It is important to present all of the information necessary for understanding the new knowledge or skill through explanations, descriptions, definitions, and specific examples and nonexamples.

Typically, the information in this section of the lesson is presented both in writing (on a transparency, a white board, a poster, or a handout) and orally. Any explanation that may be complex or have the potential to be confusing should be put in writing to help ensure it is complete, accurate, and clear. Also include descriptions of various visual supports that can add interest and help clarify information. Diversity and active participation strategies, as well as checks for understanding, are also very important parts of the presentation of information section, and should be planned out carefully. (See Chapter 6 for additional information on these topics.)

Appropriate parts of the content analysis, which were completed earlier, play a very important role in the instruction that occurs during the body of a direct instruction lesson. A task analysis, for instance, is directly shown, explained, and then demonstrated to the students. The same is true of a concept analysis or a principle statement. This is also the time and place where key terms may be introduced and taught. A well-planned content analysis can help the lesson body take shape.

When the body of the lesson is written, include enough detail to prevent being "caught off guard" during the lesson. Do *not* simply write in the plan, "I will explain the steps" or "I'll define each term." It is necessary to plan *how* you will explain—namely, by listing in the plan the key points or ideas you want to convey and the examples you want to include. Write out the definitions of key terms so that they are clear and complete. It is very difficult to spontaneously explain, describe, or define in a clear way. Often the ideas that seem most simple and obvious to the teacher are the most difficult to explain.

Remember that it is usually not appropriate to ask students to provide the initial explanations of the new information, because it is very important that initial explanations are accurate and clear. Students may be involved by asking them to review prerequisite knowledge or skills before the presentation of information. They could also be asked for their ideas and examples after the necessary information has been presented.

Carefully plan how you will check for understanding of the information. If there is a great deal of new information, incorporate checks for understanding and opportunities for student processing after each step or part of the information. Calling on one student to paraphrase or give an additional example will not reveal whether all of the students understand. Include active participation strategies that will allow you to check for understanding of all students.

Demonstration

Before, during, or after the presentation of information, teachers need to demonstrate—show or model—the new knowledge or skill. Demonstrating can mean showing a *product* (for example, "Here is an example of a paragraph that includes a topic sentence and supporting details"), or modeling a *process* ("Watch as I make this foul shot" or "Listen as I think out loud while developing my topic sentence"). A skit or role play can also be an effective method of demonstrating a new skill. Visual supports can be used during the demonstration to emphasize key points. During the presentation of information portion of the lesson body, teachers will probably show examples or demonstrate specific steps, but it is essential that they model the whole product or process as well.

Teachers or other experts should do the demonstrating so that a correct model is provided for students to follow. This reduces the chances that students incorrectly practice the new skill. Asking students to demonstrate will come later in the body of the lesson. (See supervised practice for further information.)

Again, it is important that teachers provide accurate and clear demonstrations before asking students to do so. It is important that teachers create a product or plan the demonstration in advance. Finally, do not forget to check for understanding.

Note that a common error is to forget to teach before asking students to practice. It is essential that teachers provide complete explanations, many examples, and many demonstrations. If you find this unnecessary, you are most likely planning a review or practice activity rather than a direct instruction lesson. Another common error is to ask students to do the initial teaching; this is done out of eagerness to promote active participation and involvement. If students can do the initial teaching, you most likely have planned an activity rather than a lesson. There are many ways of keeping students engaged without neglecting the responsibility of teaching clearly and accurately.

Supervised Practice

This portion of the lesson body is an extremely important one. After the teacher has presented and demonstrated information, it is time to provide opportunities for the students to practice under the guidance and supervision of the teacher.

Note that if the new knowledge or skill is complex, the teacher may choose to provide formal supervised practice after each step or part. It is very important that the teacher controls and monitors this practice, so students are not practicing errors. The teacher leads, prompts, and gives corrective feedback immediately.

The following are three levels of supervised practice:

1. *Whole group practice* The teacher may begin by demonstrating the skill again, but this time involving the class ("Let's do a problem together; what should I do first?" or "What's the first decision I must make . . . everyone?").

2. *Small-group or partner practice* The second level involves asking students to practice with the support of peers while the teacher monitors and provides feedback. Students must be told exactly how to work together ("Partner 1 will circle the errors, and Partner 2 will correct the errors; then switch roles for the second sentence").

3. *Individual practice* The final and essential level involves asking each student to practice alone while the teacher monitors and corrects.

The first two levels provide a bridge between teacher demonstration and individual practice, so that initial attempts have peer, as well as teacher, support. This is a form of scaffolding.

During the presentation and demonstration section of the lesson, if the teacher checked everyone's understanding and believed they "got it," then he may go right to supervised *individual* practice.

The three levels of supervised practice allow for flexibility in planning the rehearsal of new information. The essential individual supervised practice portion gives all students an opportunity to receive feedback on their own progress. When the new knowledge or skill is especially difficult or complex, or if prior checks for understanding show that students are struggling, the teacher will probably want to use whole class, small-group, or partner practice prior to individual practice.

The practice activities during the supervised practice portion of the lesson must be congruent with or match what was taught during the presentation of information and demonstration sections. All parts of the lesson must be congruent with the lesson objective. (See Chapter 4 for more information on congruence.)

Note that individual supervised practice is *not* the formal evaluation. This practice is designed as an opportunity for each student to receive performance feedback from the teacher. It is a step toward meeting the objective. During the evaluation portion of the lesson, however, students must again perform the objective individually and independently, without the help of peers or the teacher. The evaluation follows instruction.

Figure 8.1   Writing a Direct Instruction Lesson

When preparing direct instruction lessons, you will typically include the following content within the different components:

COMPONENT 1: PREPLANNING TASKS

The preplanning tasks section is a cover sheet for the rest of the lesson plan. Include the following:

- *Connection analysis*   Identify the generalization or big idea, the IEP goal, and the state standard addressed in the plan.
- *Content analysis*   May include a task analysis, a concept analysis, or a principle statement, key terms and vocabulary, and a list of prerequisite skills or knowledge.
- *Objective*   Possible objectives for a direct instruction lesson could be for students to demonstrate, list, rewrite, give an example, identify, state reasons, label, use a strategy, or compute.
- *Objective rationale*   To help clarify the value of the objective.

COMPONENT 2: LESSON SETUP

The lesson setup is the first component of the lesson plan that is actually presented to students. Include the following in the lesson setup:

- *Signal for attention*   Examples of signals include playing music, flicking lights, or saying, "Let's get started."
- *Statement of behavior expectations*   An example would be to say, "If you need help, you may ask your partner."

COMPONENT 3: LESSON OPENING

The lesson opening should effectively prepare the students for new learning. Include the following in the lesson opening:

- A strategy designed to generate interest in the lesson and to relate new learning to prior knowledge.
- A way to state the objective so students know what they will learn. In a direct instruction lesson, students are told directly what they will be expected to do or know following the lesson.
- A statement of the objective purpose, so students know why the new learning is valuable and useful.

COMPONENT 4: LESSON BODY

The lesson body looks like a series of repeated steps. First, teachers "show and tell"; next, check for understanding; next, conduct supervised practice with feedback; then, provide more "show and tell"; and so on. For less complex lessons, teachers will "show and tell" all steps and then provide supervised practice. Provide the

continued on next page

| **Figure 8.1** | Writing a Direct Instruction Lesson (continued) |

following in the lesson body:

- Teacher "show and tell." The *presentation of information* and an accompanying *demonstration* that is necessary to enable the students to learn the content or perform the skills being taught (or the first step in a sequence). This should include many, varied examples. Do not forget to include visual supports.

- Strategies that will be used to promote *active participation.* For example, students may compare answers with a partner, write answers on a piece of scratch paper and hold it up for you to see, or respond in unison.

- Techniques that will be used to *check for understanding.* These should involve overt responses on the part of the students (that is, they do or say something) so you can determine if students are progressing toward the objective. For example, students may use thumbs up or thumbs down to signify they agree or disagree.

- *Supervised practice* opportunities. You will always include individual supervised practice, but you may choose to include whole-group, partner, or small-group practice as well. For example, you may first provide practice for the whole group ("Let's do one more problem together"). Next, students work with a partner ("You will practice the next six problems with your partner. Each of you take turns working three problems while thinking out loud, and your partner will check for accuracy"). Finally, students work alone ("Try the next two problems by yourself, and I will come around and check your answers").

- *Diversity strategies.* Decide which strategies you will build in or add on to help all students be successful. For example, use an elaborate opening to build background knowledge, individual behavior contracts, large print worksheet, picture directions, or expanded partner practice.

COMPONENT 5: EXTENDED PRACTICE

Extended practice is one of the key elements in the direct instruction lesson. (See Chapter 4 for further information.) Students will need additional practice to develop the accuracy and fluency necessary for the application and generalization of the new skill or knowledge. Seatwork and homework are types of assignments that provide extended practice opportunities, and they should match the individual supervised practice in the body of the lesson. Checking these assignments carefully will let you know when formal evaluation should occur. Long-term extended practice is typically provided in the form of activities. (See Chapter 5 for detail.) Include the following in writing the extended practice:

- A list of additional practice opportunities, including assignments and homework, to be provided. Be sure that final practice activities provide students with an opportunity to practice alone. One diversity strategy to consider in this component is variation of extended practice opportunities. Some students will need a great deal of extended practice, while others will need far less. Application and generalization should be emphasized.

- A list of lessons and activities, if appropriate, that will build on this objective and additional opportunities for students to generalize, integrate, and extend the information.

COMPONENT 6: LESSON CLOSING

The lesson closing in a direct instruction lesson will occur in one of two places, following supervised practice. If

continued on next page

| **Figure 8.1** | Writing a Direct Instruction Lesson (continued) |

extended practice is assigned as in-class work, the teacher may close the lesson after the assignment has been completed. If extended practice is assigned as homework, the lesson closing will occur immediately following the lesson body. When preparing the lesson closing, include the following:

■ A strategy for closing the lesson.   Frequently selected strategies for closing the direct instruction lesson are a review of key points of the lesson, a description of where or when students would use their new skills or knowledge, a time for students to show their work, or a reference to the opening. Plans that involve students in the closing are especially effective.

COMPONENT 7: EVALUATION

The evaluation component of the direct instruction lesson is planned when the measurable lesson objective is written. Evaluation is designed to determine individual student progress in relation to the lesson objective, which means the student does not receive help from peers or teachers during the evaluation. Careful monitoring of progress during supervised and extended practice activities will help determine when students are ready to be evaluated. When preparing the evaluation, include the following:

■ A description of the evaluation.   You may want to include a sample in the case of a paper and pencil test, and may want to tell when and how the evaluation will occur if not immediately following the lesson. An example would be to write, "Later in the day, during other activities, I will ask each student individually to draw an example of a right triangle for me, and I'll check them off on my class list if they do it correctly."

Remember to use editing tasks to evaluate your plan!

References and Suggested Readings

Arends, R. I. (1997). *Classroom Instruction and Management.* New York: McGraw-Hill. (See Chapter 2 in particular.)

Borich, G. (2000). *Effective Teaching Methods* (4th ed.). Columbus, OH: Merrill, an imprint of Prentice Hall. (See Chapter 5 in particular.)

Carnine, D., Silbert, J., & Kame'enui, E. J., (1997). *Direct Instruction Reading* (3rd ed.). Upper Saddle River, NJ: Merrill.

Engelmann, S., & Bruner, E. (1995). *Reading Mastery 1/11 Fast Cycle.* Columbus, OH: Macmillan/McGraw-Hill.

Lasley II, T. J., Matczynski, T. J., & Rowley, J. B. (2002). *Instructional Models: Strategies for Teaching in a Diverse Society* (2nd ed.). Belmont, CA: Wadsworth/Thomson Learning.

O'Brien, J. (2000). Enabling all students to learn in the laboratory of democracy. *Intervention in School and Clinic, 35*(4), 195–205.

Rosenberg, M. S., O'Shea, L., & O'Shea, D. J. (2002). *Student Teacher to Master Teacher: A Practical Guide for Educating Students with Special Needs* (3rd ed.). Columbus, OH: Merrill, an imprint of Prentice Hall. (See Chapter 6 in particular.)

Smith, P. L., & Ragan, T. J. (1999). *Instructional Design* (2nd ed.). Columbus, OH: Merrill, an imprint of Prentice Hall. (See Chapters 10 and 11 in particular.)

Summarizing What You Read

This is a direct instruction lesson for a small reading group.

I. PREPLANNING TASKS

A. Connection analysis: *State Reading Standard #2:* The student understands the meaning of what is read. *Component 2.1:* comprehend important ideas and details. *Benchmark 1 (Grade 4):* demonstrate comprehension of the main idea and supporting details; students summarize ideas in their own words.

B. Content analysis

   1. Task analysis: How to Summarize What is Read

      a. Read the passage.

      b. State the main idea in a few words or a sentence.

      c. State the supporting details in a few words or sentences.

      d. Tips: Use your own words, and as few words as possible.

   2. Prerequisite skills: Know how to identify the main idea and supporting details, and how to paraphrase.

   3. Key terms or vocabulary: **Summarize**—to tell about something in as few words as possible.

C. Objective: Given a task analysis of how to summarize and three paragraphs of grade-level reading material, students will summarize each paragraph in their own words (say the main idea and two supporting details in no more than two to three sentences).

D. Objective rationale: Summarizing helps comprehension, and puts material read into manageable form for future use.

E. Materials: *Three transparencies* (one for reviewing terms, two that include the task analysis at the top and reading passages about insects that we have been studying in science on the bottom), and an *evaluation handout* for each student.

II. LESSON SETUP

A. Signal for attention: Play music (tape recorder).

B. Behavioral expectations: Eyes on me; participate (point to T chart: "What does participating look like and sound like?").

III. LESSON OPENING

A. Activate background knowledge: "Has anyone told you about a TV show or a movie they saw? What did they say? Did they tell you every single word that was said and everything that happened? Or, did they summarize?"

B. Statement of objective; objective purpose:

   1. "Today you will learn how to summarize what you read."

   2. "This will help you better understand what you read and make it easier to use what you read (for a book report, for example)."

C.   Review prior learning: "To summarize, you must know the main idea and supporting details."

   1.   Show transparency #1. Review definitions: **main idea** and **supporting details**

AP = Choral read definitions

   2.   Show sample paragraph. Have students find the main idea and details.

AP = Tell a partner, call on nonvolunteers

IV. LESSON BODY

A.   Presentation of information

   1.   Show transparency #2 (task analysis and paragraphs).

   2.   Explain that summarizing involves following a series of steps; give examples and nonexamples of the tips in the task analysis.

   3.   CFU and AP: "State steps in your own words to your partner"; call on nonvolunteers.

B.   Demonstration

   1.   Do a think-aloud of the task analysis (using Paragraph 1): "First I read the passage. Then . . . ."

AP = Choral reading

   2.   Draw a graphic organizer while thinking aloud, such as a concept map of insects and body parts.

   3.   End with, "My summary is: Insects have three body parts. They are the head, thorax, and abdomen."

   4.   Repeat the think aloud with Paragraph 2.

C.   CFU

   1.   Do another think aloud using Paragraphs 3 and 4.

AP = Choral reading

   2.   At the same time, ask students specific questions, such as "What do I do first?" "What is the main idea?" and so on.

AP = Call on nonvolunteers

D.   Supervised practice

   1.   Show transparency #3 (task analysis and paragraphs).

   2.   "Work with a partner on the next four paragraphs."

      a.   "The first person reads and summarizes, while the second person checks. Switch after each paragraph."

      b.   CFU: "What does the first person do? And then . . . ?"

      c.   Remind students of the rule about giving feedback politely.

   3.   I monitor and give feedback.

   4.   "Summarize the next three by yourself" (individual supervised practice).

   5.   Monitor and give feedback. Make sure I hear each student summarize at least one paragraph.

V. LESSON CLOSING

A. Review the importance of the skill by asking students to explain the value of summarizing.

B. Review steps. Students say the steps to a partner.

AP = Call on nonvolunteers

VI. EXTENDED PRACTICE

A. Form cooperative learning groups for science.

    1. Each member has three paragraphs of written material on a different insect.

    2. Members will orally summarize paragraphs to the group.

    3. I monitor and provide feedback.

VII. EVALUATION

Throughout the day, I'll have individual students summarize three paragraphs of appropriate grade-level reading material to me. The topic of the paragraphs is Martin Luther King, Jr. This fits in with our unit on famous Americans. I will check students off if they can do it without prompting.

How to Write a Cover Letter

This is a direct instruction lesson for secondary students.

I. PREPLANNING TASKS

A. Connection analysis: *State Standard, Writing 2.2*: Write for a broad range of purposes including to apply for jobs.

B. Content analysis

    1. Task analysis: *Components of a Cover Letter* (see lesson body).

    2. Prerequisite skills: Writing paragraphs and letters; prior practice with writing about their education and accomplishments.

    3. Key terms or vocabulary: **Cover letter**—a letter that accompanies a resume.

C. Objective: Given a personal fact sheet and a job description, students will write a cover letter that includes two addresses, an opening, a body with at least one paragraph, and a closing, and provides a convincing argument for being hired.

D. Objective rationale: This lesson will help students learn the basics of writing cover letters to send along with resumes, which will in turn help them in their search for a summer job.

E. Materials: *Transparencies:* (1) graphic organizer of unit, (2) cover letter/purpose of cover letter, (3) components and samples of cover letters, (4) blank cover letter template; posters. Student handout packets: copies of transparencies, templates, job descriptions; and students' fact sheets from last week's lesson.

F. Reference: http://www.naz.edu/dept/career_services/coverletters.html

II. LESSON SETUP

A. Signal for attention: Turn on overhead projector.

B. Behavior expectations: Follow along and participate; raise your hand and wait to be called on before speaking; and show respect (listen when others speak).

III. LESSON OPENING

A. Review prior learning.

    1. Say, "This lesson is part of the job search unit."

    2. Show a graphic organizer of the unit (transparency #1) with "writing cover letter" highlighted.

    3. Remind them of last week's lesson on how to write a resume.

B. Statement of objective; objective purpose.

    1. Say, "Today we will learn how to write a basic cover letter to accompany a resume."

    2. Say, "A well-written cover letter will increase your chance of getting a job."

C. Preview the goal of a cover letter.

   1. Show transparency #2 with Part 1: Robby's cover letter, and Part 2: "Purpose of a Cover Letter."

   2. Read Robby's cover letter (applying for a construction job).

   3. Explain "Purposes of a Cover Letter"—to introduce yourself, summarize your qualifications, and so on.

   4. Think aloud how the letter matches the purposes. Ask students to find other examples, such as "Where does the writer summarize his qualifications?"

> *AP = Talk to partner, call on nonvolunteers*

IV. LESSON BODY

A. Presentation of information and demonstration (of product)

   1. Pass out the packet of handouts. Students will follow along and take notes as I present information and assign practice.

   2. Show transparency #3 (Part 1: Components of a Cover Letter; Part 2: Sample cover letter).

   3. Read "Components of a Cover Letter" and explain each, using examples from the sample cover letter at the bottom of the transparency.

> *AP = Call on nonvolunteers to read; students follow along on their own copies*

    I. Addresses

        A. Writer's address (including city, state, zip) in the upper right corner

        B. Company or organization's address in the left margin

    II. Opening paragraph

        A. State what you are seeking (your objective), and match it to their needs.

        B. Say something positive or flattering about the business.

    III. Body of the letter is one or two paragraphs describing your education, skills, accomplishments.

        A. Emphasize how you can help the organization. Use any important "buzz words."

        B. Highlight skills you have that match their needs.

    IV. Closing paragraph

        A. State a plan of action, such as they call you or you call them, to arrange a meeting.

        B. Thank them for their consideration and note enclosures or attachments, such as a resume.

   4. CFU: Ask specific questions about parts of the letter ("What goes in the opening?") and where parts of the task analysis are found ("Where do you talk about your accomplishments?").

> *AP = Talk to partner, call on nonvolunteers*

   5. Repeat with another example if needed (Gail's cover letter).

B. Demonstration (of process)

   1. Show transparency #4 (blank cover letter template) and posters of job descriptions and personal fact sheet.

2.   Using my fact sheet and job description do a think aloud of each component while filling in the template ("Next, I write the opening . . . I need to state the job I'm interested in, . . . " and so on). They copy what I write on their partially completed template.

AP = Note-taking, fill in own partially completed template

3.   CFU: Ask specific questions about parts of the letter ("What did I put in my opening?").

AP = Talk to partner, call on nonvolunteers

C.   Individual supervised practice

1.   Hand out the personal fact sheet of an imaginary person.

2.   Pass out a job description (superhero, rock star).

3.   Have students write a cover letter using a template.

4.   I monitor and give feedback to each student.

V. EXTENDED PRACTICE

A.   Have students select sample cover letters from my file and label the components.

VI. LESSON CLOSING

A.   Group review of practice

1.   Have students share successes and trouble spots of writing cover letters.

B.   Preview tomorrow's evaluation: "Tomorrow we will write our own, personal cover letters using our own information and a realistic job description."

VII. EVALUATION

Tomorrow, students will write their own, personal cover letter (as described in the objective).

How to Get Help on In-Class Tasks

This is a direct instruction lesson for teaching a classroom procedure.

I. PREPLANNING TASKS

A. Connection analysis: This is part of a series of lessons focused on the general rule "Use your time wisely." IEP goal: Ken will seek help appropriately when frustrated with assignments.

B. Content (task) analysis: See presentation of information.

C. Objective: Students will correctly follow the procedure for getting help when they encounter difficulty on an in-class task in three out of three observations.

D. Rationale: This procedure will prevent wasted time and help students be more independent and efficient in getting help.

E. Materials: Poster, handouts of steps, worksheets, class list and clipboard.

F. Rehearsal: Practice skit with assistant and practice demonstration with Ken and Rich before class.

II. LESSON SETUP

A. Signal for attention: Eyes up here, let's get started.

B. Behavior expectations: Follow the active listening guidelines (point to poster).

III. LESSON OPENING

A. Attention getter: Do skit with teaching assistant. She has arm up in air, obviously for a long time. Just when she puts arm down to rest, teacher looks up and helps someone else with hand raised.

B. Objective and purpose: Has this happened to you? Today you'll learn a better procedure to get help. This procedure is important because your time won't be wasted, it's more fair, and you'll learn to help each other and yourselves. It's part of our rule "Use your time wisely."

C. Application: Use this procedure when doing assignments in class independently or in groups.

IV. LESSON BODY

A. Presentation of information

  1. Show steps of task analysis on poster.

  2. Explain and give examples of each step.

  3. CFU: Ask students to paraphrase each step to partner before going to next one.

  4. Task analysis: How to get help on in-class tasks.

    a. If you run into difficulty, try helping yourself:
      (1) Look at examples or reread directions or use resources such as glossary.
      (2) Try again.

    b. If you still need help:
      (1) Ask peers (if allowed).
      (2) Use signal to teacher (stand book up on desk or write group name on board).

      c. While waiting for help:

         (1) Plan question to ask (not just "I don't get it").

         (2) Skip problem and go on if possible.

B. Demonstration

    1. Hand out copies of steps and tell students to check off the steps as they see me demonstrate them (AP).

    2. Sitting in student desk with math worksheet, I think out loud the steps ("I'm stuck on this one. Let's see, is there an example like this at the top of the page . . ." and so on). Call on students at random to describe each step I followed (CFU and AP).

    3. Demonstrate incorrectly with social studies questions (don't reread directions, call out "I can't do this" in whiny voice). Have students tell partner errors and call on students at random to correct me (CFU and AP).

    4. Demonstrate correctly with Ken and Rich (who often have trouble with this). We pretend to be working on a group project. Include the steps of asking peers for help and writing group name on board. Ask class which steps they checked off.

C. Supervised practice

    1. Leave up poster.

    2. Give students very challenging worksheets with unfamiliar format and no oral directions.

    3. Tell them to use the procedure when they need help.

    4. Provide positive and corrective feedback on following the steps, to each student.

V. LESSON CLOSING

A. Refer back to opening skit: What could I do differently? Would I feel different?

B. Application: Ask students to think of a time when they are likely to need this procedure and visualize themselves using it.

C. Review: Read steps in unison from poster.

VI. EXTENDED PRACTICE

A. Leave poster up. Ask students to review steps before each period for which they'll be needed the next three days.

B. Occasionally give computer time points to students who follow steps. (Try to catch Ken and Rich doing it right the first day.)

C. Don't help students until they follow the steps—point to poster as reminder.

D. Reteach individuals and provide cards with steps to check off, to put on their desks, as needed.

E. Ask class for feedback after the third day. Are they getting help faster? Are they helping themselves or each other more often?

VII. EVALUATION

During the following week, observe students as they work on tasks and check them off as they follow the procedure without prompting at least three times.

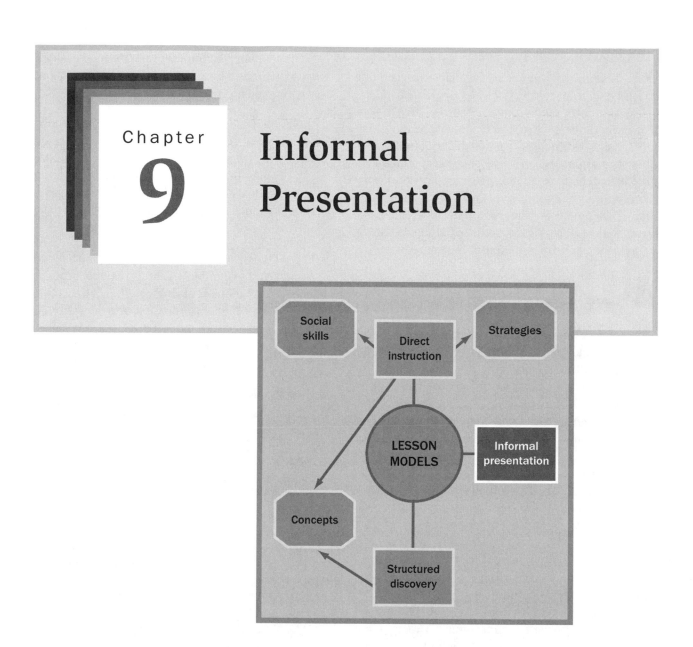

Chapter 9

Informal Presentation

Introduction

The purpose of the informal presentation model is to deliver information to students in a clear and concise manner. Arends (2000) suggests that this teacher-directed model is the most popular one used in schools today. He also suggests that its popularity is no surprise, because it provides a very effective way to help students acquire the array of information they are expected to learn. The main idea of this model is that the teacher first tells the students what they are going to be told, then tells them, and finally tells them what they were told (Moore, 1999). Careful planning can make these lessons effective in all subject areas with either large groups or small groups of students who are of varying ages and abilities (Arends, 2000).

An effective informal presentation lesson is designed to lead students to a specific objective. The lesson content is delivered in a clear, interesting manner and the main ideas of the lesson are emphasized through the use of an advance organizer (Ausubel, 1960), graphic organizers, visual supports, and so on. A key characteristic of this model is that students are kept actively involved in the lesson and in rehearsing the new information in a variety of ways, such as asking questions, summarizing concepts, discussing key ideas with a partner, or stating examples. At the end of this type of lesson, students will be able to explain, compare and contrast, define, or describe the new information.

This lesson model provides several advantages. For one, students who have reading or reading comprehension problems can benefit significantly, as this type of lesson can serve as an accommodation for them. They are able to gain necessary information without having to rely solely on written material. This model is also very time efficient. Large groups as well as small groups of students can be taught the same information at the same time.

Uses of Informal Presentation

The informal presentation model is generally used to teach declarative information, that is, knowledge about something or knowing that something is the case, rather than how to do something (Arends, 2000; Smith & Ragan, 1999). A subject matter outline prepared by the teacher is the organizational framework for the presentation. This framework provides the teacher with a mechanism by which to evaluate what information should be included. This can help ensure that content to be presented is related and relevant.

Principles can also be taught using informal presentation. Plan a clear principle statement in advance and communicate it to the students during the lesson. Many supporting examples accompany the thorough explanation of the principle.

The informal presentation model is appropriately used to present a wide range of topics. Here are some examples of specific content topics organized into the two general categories of knowledge:

■ *Declarative Knowledge.* This category of knowledge includes such topics as the history of the stock market, community helpers, differences between poetry and prose, the story of Anne Frank, and mammals.

■ *Principles.* This type of knowledge includes ideas like drinking alcohol can cause alcoholism; when the economy is sluggish, interest rates generally go down; birds migrate when there is a change in the weather; and when a company's profit margin is high, its stock price usually is high.

The following examples illustrate the variety of purposes that can be addressed by the informal presentation model:

■ Mrs. McBride includes content about sexually transmitted diseases (STDs) in a unit she teaches as part of her health class curriculum. She begins the unit with an informal presentation lesson on types of STDs and criteria used to classify them. In this case, Mrs. McBride is using this lesson to *present new information.*

■ Ms. Wines uses an informal presentation lesson to teach her students about various types of cloud formations. This information is to be used as background information for a series of lessons on causes of weather. Ms. Wines is using an informal presentation lesson to *teach background information* for future lessons.

■ Mrs. Davis follows a student reading assignment about the causes of the Civil War with an informal presentation lesson. The purpose of the lesson is to *help clarify previously studied information.* She clarifies the information her students gained from the reading assignment.

■ Mr. Chin prepares an informal presentation lesson to *conclude a series of lessons* on the civil rights movement. He plans to summarize a number of key points and generalizations for which his students are held responsible.

■ Mrs. Brown uses an informal presentation lesson about volcanoes—complete with a working model—as an introductory lesson to a unit on land forms. The purpose of the lesson is to teach specific content and to *help create interest* in the upcoming unit.

■ Ms. Bishop teaches informal presentation lessons on several aspects of computer technology. The computer content changes far more rapidly than student textbooks are replaced, so the information in her textbooks is often outdated. Ms. Bishop reads extensively to stay current in her field, but the written material she reads is not appropriate for her students. In this case, Ms. Bishop uses informal presentation lessons to *present information not readily available in other sources,* such as textbooks.

▇ Key Planning Considerations

Informal presentation lessons are not difficult to plan if the teacher begins with a thorough understanding of the content to present. When planning the lesson, give special consideration to the following elements:

Content Analysis

The content analysis for an informal presentation lesson will most often include a subject matter outline. Whenever the goal is to teach about something (rather than to teach how to do something), a subject matter outline is an effective way to organize the information to be presented. A well-planned subject matter outline will be used in the lesson body, where it will be called a presentation outline.

Careful preparation of the subject matter outline can be of great benefit. First, it can help ensure that you select content that directly relates to the objective to be accomplished, as well as the knowledge structure of the discipline. (See content knowledge.) It can also help prevent errors in accuracy and, hopefully, ensure that the information to be presented is clear. Finally, the outline simplifies the planning of the lesson body because it is used to guide the presentation delivery portion. Various active participation and diversity strategies, visual supports, and presentation techniques will become the main focus of the lesson body planning rather than organization of the content.

A carefully written subject matter outline (presentation outline) can be an excellent resource for your students as well. You may choose to show the outline to the students during the actual presentation, or you may give them a copy, or partial copy, to use as a note-taking guide. Another option would be to give them the outline to use as a study guide. They can add more information to it from readings, interviews, videos, Internet sites, or other sources.

There is no set rule about the amount of detail to include in the outline. Provide enough detail to ensure a clear presentation, but not so much detail that the presentation loses focus. Strive to prepare an outline that is detailed, yet brief. Single words and short phrases should serve as cues for information that has been committed to memory. These are preferred to lengthy sentences or narrative (Esler & Sciortino, 1991). The outline, which should not be read, should serve as a reminder of what will be said.

Include a principle statement in the content analysis when you are going to teach a principle. Remember that principles are relational rules that prescribe the relationship between two or more concepts. When teaching principles using the informal presentation model, a principle statement serves as the organizer for the presentation.

Be sure that you plan in advance how to explain the principle to your students. Begin by writing out the complete principle statement, including the condition and the result or the action that needs to be taken. It can be difficult to correctly or accurately explain the principle spontaneously during the lesson or activity. Next, carefully consider which words are best used as part of your explanation. Finally, be sure that you plan many, varied examples to illustrate the principle. It is important that your students can *apply* the principle to unknown examples, not just state it (Smith & Ragan, 1999).

Content Knowledge

All teachers find themselves in the position of needing to teach lessons on topics they have never taught before. When this happens to you, be prepared to spend some time learning the content before you begin planning how you will teach it. It would be difficult, if not impossible, to prepare a complete, accurate presentation outline for use in the lesson if you do not fully understand the subject matter. Your study of the content will help you in choosing interesting and meaningful examples, making relevant comparisons, and connecting information to real-life applications. When using the informal presentation model, thorough content knowledge is absolutely essential. The time you spend learning will be time well spent as it will likely result in increased student learning.

Using this model also makes it important to understand how the current content fits into the knowledge structure of the discipline from which it comes, because all disciplines have key concepts, information, generalizations, or "big ideas" that define them as distinct from other disciplines. These concepts form a knowledge structure—perhaps best conceptualized as one enormous subject matter outline—that provides an organized way to think about and study the information within the discipline, such as categorizing it and showing relationships among categories (Arends, 2000). When teaching content from a particular discipline, students learn best if they can see how it fits into the big picture.

Advance Organizer

Use advance organizers to orient students to a new learning task—to focus attention and organize student thinking (Schmidt & Harriman, 1998; Arends, 2000). The organizer can be a picture, diagram, or statement made by the teacher. For example, use oral introductions to a lesson, written questions presented at the beginning of a chapter in a text, study guides, or graphic organizers as advance organizers (Schmidt & Harriman, 1998). Use various visual supports, such as photographs, to help further clarify, explain, or demonstrate the content of the advance organizer, as needed.

Advance organizers play an important role in providing students with cognitive scaffolding. First, they help students see how the content they will learn fits into the big picture. Explanations about how the content is organized and how it will be presented further assist students to understand. The preview that the advance organizer provides is a valuable aid to comprehension.

The advance organizer may be seen as the equivalent of the chapter introduction in a textbook. It is generally more abstract than the content of the current lesson (it contains an overriding organizational idea into which the information to come will fit). An example of a verbal advance organizer is, "There are many types of families, but they all have in common the caring for and support of individual members." Designing the organizer can help you plan a presentation that is aligned with this important big idea.

The lesson opening is generally where the advance organizer will be presented. The teacher may begin by using one strategy to address prior knowledge, such as a review of previous related lessons, followed by the presentation of an advance organizer. This way, the information to come is linked to prior knowledge. An advance organizer may help students utilize their prior knowledge, but it should also be designed to relate directly to the information that follows it.

The following are examples of advance organizers:

- Mrs. Dyson explains to her students that opera themes reflect the composer's interpretation of the social climate of the time.

- Mrs. Garcia opens her presentation on the westward movement by stating, "Human migration follows new economic opportunities and/or political upheavals."

- Mr. Lundquist explains the commonalities among sonatas, prior to playing recordings by various composers.

- Ms. Thomas shows a diagram of drugs classified into six types—stimulants, depressants, hallucinogens, inhalants, narcotics, and cannabis products—before providing information about specific drugs.

Checks for Understanding and Active Participation

A variety of techniques can be used to check for understanding. These checks should occur throughout the presentation and just prior to moving to extended practice or other activities. Many active participation strategies are appropriate for this purpose. For example, you could periodically stop during the presentation and ask students to write summary statements, review their notes with a partner, or use response cards to signal agreement or disagreement. The important thing is to make sure that students do not leave the presentation with misinformation or misunderstandings.

Presentation Delivery

Clarity of presentation is a must in this model. The following suggestions will help you to present information clearly:

- Use cues in the delivery to help students identify key ideas or important points ("Write down this definition in your notes," or "The first three . . . are . . .").

- Stop at certain points during the presentation and give students an opportunity to review their notes and ask questions.

- Repeat key points.

- Use visual supports to help clarify information (video clips, CD segments, slides, posters, charts, and so on).

The delivery of this lesson is unique because the teacher is "on stage." A good way to prepare for this type of lesson is to practice the delivery before presenting it to the students. You could practice in front of a mirror or teach the lesson to the empty classroom after school. Strive for movement around the room, as well as varied voice inflections, facial expressions, and gestures (R. Keiper, personal communication, October 2001).

The length of the presentation will depend on the students. Two factors to consider are age and attention span. In a primary classroom, the limit for this type of lesson may be five minutes, while in a high school classroom the teacher's presentation may last 15 minutes (Ornstein, 1990).

Extended Practice

The informal presentation lesson is always followed by extended practice opportunities. The information presented in the lesson body is explored, applied, emphasized, and enriched in the extended practice component of this lesson. Students may study or practice the information in more depth, or they may have an opportunity to synthesize various skills with the knowledge learned in the current lesson. During this portion of the lesson, check individual student progress and decide when the students are ready for evaluation. Carefully select, plan, and monitor extended practice activities. Here are some examples of extended practice tasks:

- Ms. Reed delivers a presentation on genetic engineering that is followed by small-group discussions of ethical considerations.

- Mrs. Bedell first presents basic information about different types of families around the world. Students then complete various "center" activities where they read, write, draw, and interview peers about their families.

- Mrs. Cline presents information about cell division. Students then go to their lab stations to perform experiments.

- Mr. Springer teaches an informal presentation lesson about parts of a research paper. Students then go to the library to begin collecting resources for their own papers.

- Cooperative groups brainstorm scenarios about emergencies prior to Mrs. Wood's presentation on using 911.

Figure 9.1   Writing an Informal Presentation Lesson

The following list describes what is typically included in each component in an informal presentation lesson plan.

COMPONENT 1: PREPLANNING TASKS

The preplanning tasks section is a cover sheet for the rest of the lesson plan. Include the following in this section:

- *Connection analysis*   Identify the generalization or big idea, the IEP goal, and the state standard addressed in the plan.
- *Content analysis*   Include a *subject matter outline* (which will become the presentation outline) or principle statement, key terms and vocabulary, and necessary prerequisite skills or knowledge.

continued on next page

Figure 9.1   **Writing an Informal Presentation Lesson (continued)**

- *Objective*   In addition to the content objective, a learning strategy objective may be included (such as taking notes from a lecture).
- *Objective rationale*   To help students know why the lesson is valuable.

COMPONENT 2: LESSON SETUP

Include the following in the lesson setup:

- *Signal for attention:* Turn on overhead projector, ring a bell, or raise your hand, for example.
- *Statement of behavior expectations:* "Please raise your hand before speaking."

COMPONENT 3: LESSON OPENING

A lesson opening should be planned carefully, so it will effectively prepare the students for the new learning. An advance organizer is an integral part of the lesson opening in this model. Include the following in preparing a lesson opening:

- A strategy designed to generate interest in the lesson and to relate new learning to prior knowledge.
- A way to state the *objective,* so students know exactly what they will be expected to know and do.
- A statement of the *objective purpose,* so students know why the new learning is valuable.
- An *advance organizer* and a plan for presenting it. Another visual support may also be included.

COMPONENT 4: LESSON BODY

The lesson body is the detailed presentation outline (the subject matter outline prepared as a preplanning task), along with questions, active participation and diversity strategies, and checks for understanding. Include the following when preparing the lesson body:

- *Presentation outline* (use the subject matter outline).
- A plan for making the presentation delivery smooth and interesting (use of voice variations, humor, interesting examples and analogies, summaries, and so on).
- *Active participation* strategies that will be used to keep students involved, such as giving opportunities to discuss content with peers.
- Techniques that will be used to *check for understanding.* Plan relevant and stimulating questions in advance.
- *Diversity strategies* for use throughout the lesson body. You may provide *graphic organizers* such as study guides or presentation outlines (complete or partial). You may also provide support for note-taking by teaching note-taking skills or providing peer note-takers.

continued on next page

| Figure 9.1 | Writing an Informal Presentation Lesson (continued) |

COMPONENT 5: EXTENDED PRACTICE

The informal presentation lesson always includes relevant extended practice activities, such as following a presentation with a discussion or writing assignment. All extended practice opportunities must relate directly to the lesson objective and the information presented in the lesson body. Provide individual practice during this component because students will be evaluated on their individual performance in relation to the lesson objective. You will need to monitor these assignments or activities carefully so you will know when formal evaluation should occur. Include the following when preparing this component:

■   A plan for providing extended practice immediately following the presentation or within a day or two. Some extended practice options include reading related materials, watching a video about the topic presented, gathering additional information by doing library research, conducting experiments in the lab, developing questions from the information presented to be used in a team game, and participating in a debate.

COMPONENT 6: LESSON CLOSING

The lesson closing generally follows the lesson body if the extended practice activity is a homework assignment. The closing could also occur after extended practice if practice opportunities are to be completed in class immediately following the lesson body. The closing would then follow the in-class practice. Consider the following when preparing the lesson closing:

■   A strategy for closing the lesson. Selected closing strategies for the presentation lesson frequently refer back to the opening (the advance organizer), and provide review of the key points of the lesson. The closing may also provide an opportunity to preview future learning, describe where or when students should use the new knowledge, give students one last chance to ask questions, or have students compare their notes with a partner.

COMPONENT 7: EVALUATION

Teachers may conduct a lesson evaluation immediately after the presentation with a paper and pencil test. More commonly, teachers evaluate after providing extended practice opportunities. By carefully monitoring activities that occur after the actual informal presentation, you will be able to tell when students are ready for the lesson evaluation. The evaluation specified in the lesson objective is used to "test" whether individual students have attained the specific objective. When preparing a plan, include a description of the evaluation.

Remember to use editing tasks to evaluate your plan, and practice, practice, practice the delivery before presenting it to the students!

References and Suggested Readings

Arends, R. I. (2000). *Learning to Teach* (5th ed.). Boston: McGraw-Hill. (See Chapter 7 in particular.)

Ausubel, D. P. (1960). The use of advance organizers in the learning and retention of meaningful verbal material. *Journal of Educational Psychology, 51,* 267–272.

Callahan, J. F., Clark, L. H., & Kellough, R. D. (2002). *Teaching in the Middle and Secondary Schools, Part 11, Module 9* (7th ed.). Upper Saddle River, NJ: Merrill.

Eggen, P. D., & Kauchak, D. P. (2001). *Strategies for Teaching: Teaching Content and Thinking Skills* (4th ed.). Boston: Allyn & Bacon. (See Chapter 9 in particular.)

Esler, W. K., & Sciortino, P. (1991). *Methods for Teaching: An Overview of Current Practices* (2nd ed.). Raleigh, NC: Contemporary Publishing Company.

Herrell, A. L. (2000). *Fifty Strategies for Teaching English Language Learners.* Columbus, OH: Merrill, an imprint of Prentice Hall. (See Chapter 2 in particular.)

Joyce, B., Weil, M, with Calhoun, E. (2000). *Models of Teaching* (6th ed.). Boston: Allyn & Bacon. (See Chapter 13 in particular.)

Kame'enui, E. J., Carnine, D. W., Dixon, R. C., Simmons, D. C., & Coyne, M. D. (2002). *Effective Teaching Strategies that Accommodate Diverse Learners* (2nd ed.). Columbus, OH: Merrill, an imprint of Prentice Hall.

Moore, K. D. (1999). *Middle and Secondary School Instructional Methods.* Boston: McGraw-Hill College.

Ornstein, A. C. (1990). *Strategies for Effective Teaching.* New York: Harper & Row. (See Chapter 6 in particular.)

Schmidt, M. W., & Harriman, N. E. (1998). *Teaching Strategies for Inclusive Classrooms: Schools, Students, Strategies, and Success.* San Diego, CA: Harcourt Brace College Publishers.

Smith, P. L., & Ragan, T. J. (1999). *Instructional Design* (2nd ed.). Columbus, OH: Merrill, an imprint of Prentice Hall. (See Chapter 9 in particular.)

Rosa Parks and the Civil Rights Movement

This is an informal presentation for a large group of students.

I. PREPLANNING TASKS

A. Connection analysis:

    1. Primary state standard: *History:* Identify and analyze major issues, movements, people, and events in U.S. history from 1870 to the present with particular emphasis on growth and conflict (for example, industrialization, the civil rights movement, and the information age).

    2. Additional standards:

        a. *Writing standard:* Produce a legible, professional-looking final product.

        b. *Social studies:* Investigate a topic using electronic technology, library resources, and human resources from the community.

    3. *Big Idea:* Problem/Solution/Effect (Kame'enui, Carnine, Dixon, Simmons, & Coyne, 2002)

B. Content analysis: *Subject matter outline* (see presentation outline).

C. Objective(s): In a five-paragraph written report, students will explain three or more facts about Rosa Parks (education, birth date, and so on), the events that led to the Montgomery, Ala., bus strike, and the results of the boycott. (A prepared rubric given to the students will provide more specific detail; for example, include an introduction, conclusion, and so on in the report.)

    1. They will work toward this objective for several days (the first few days will involve fact finding, and the second few days will involve report writing). The students will also practice word-processing skills and Internet search skills.

D. Objective rationale: Knowing about Americans who have had a significant impact on events in the United States contributes to overall general knowledge. It is also important for students to see how activists can inspire change without violence.

E. Materials: Report rubric, presentation outline, transparencies of newspaper articles and photographs, and note-taking guides.

II. LESSON SETUP

A. Signal for attention: Turn on overhead projector.

B. Behavioral expectations: "Keep eyes on work, participate (ask and answer questions, take notes)."

III. LESSON OPENING

A. Review prior learning: Yesterday, we began to talk about America prior to the civil rights movement; talked about segregation and the treatment of African-American people . . . .

B. Preview:

    1. Today, we will begin to study the civil rights movement, how it began, and why it was so important.

    2. We will start by learning about one individual whose bravery made a big difference for African-Americans.

C. Objective and purpose.

1. You will learn about the Montgomery, Ala. bus boycott, an important event in the civil rights movement. You will also learn about the remarkable woman who inspired it.

2. You will gather information about this woman from a variety of resources and write a five-paragraph report about her and the boycott. The report will be graded, both on the content of the report and the quality of the product. (Show transparency of rubric.)

3. The purpose of the lesson is to teach the history of race relations and to learn how one person can make a difference.

D. Advance organizer: There are many important events that played a role in changing the relationships between African-Americans and white citizens of the United States.

IV. LESSON BODY

A. Prepare for presentation.

1. Pass out two variations of the note-taking guide (one blank with only headings and subheadings, and one completed outline for Jeffrey who has writing problems).

2. Say, "During my presentation, listen for and write down the key ideas and facts that I present. You will add to those ideas later on when you do some additional research. For now, the goal is to gather some basic information."

B. Show the presentation outline.

- Event leading to the Montgomery, Ala. bus boycott (show photographs #1–2).

| *AP = Take notes throughout* |

  - Who and When? Rosa Parks was riding home from work on December 1, 1955 (show photo #1, on bus).
  - Where? Cleveland Avenue bus line in Montgomery, Ala.
  - What happened? Rosa Parks refused to give up her seat in the front row of the "colored section" to a white man who could find no seat in the section reserved for whites.
    - The event defied local ordinances and Alabama state statutes requiring segregation in transportation.
    - Parks was arrested, jailed, and eventually convicted of violating segregation laws. She was fined $10, plus $4 in court costs (show photo #2, in court).
    - The black community in Montgomery was outraged.

CFU = What happened on the bus? When did it happen? How do you think she felt? Has anything like this happened to you? and so on.

| *AP = Have students turn to partners, call on nonvolunteers, for all CFUs* |

- The Montgomery, Ala. bus boycott (show photos #3–4 and newspaper article #1).
  - Protesters formed the Montgomery Improvement Association (MIA) (show photo #3 of MLK).
    - MIA was formed under the leadership of Dr. Martin Luther King, Jr., a minister who recently moved to the city.
    - MIA urged sympathizers not to ride segregated buses and helped them find other transportation.
  - The boycott (show photo #4 of empty buses and people walking), which lasted 381 days, began as a one-day demonstration on Dec. 5, 1955 (show article #1 about the boycott).

CFU = What organization was formed by protestors? Who gave leadership to the group? How is this protest similar to and different from protests during the American Revolution?

- Result of the boycott (newspaper articles #2–4).

  - In November 1956, a federal court ordered the Montgomery buses to be desegregated (article #2).
  - On Dec. 20, 1956, federal injunctions served on city and bus officials forced them to comply (#3).
  - On Dec. 21, 1956, Dr. King and Rev. Glen Smiley, a white minister, shared the front seat of a public bus; the boycott was a success (#4).

> *AP = Pause, and have students compare notes*

CFU = What were the results of the boycott? Was it successful? Do protesters use boycotts today?

C. Tomorrow we'll focus on Rosa Parks. Who was this brave woman? What brought her to that day on the bus in Montgomery?

V. EXTENDED PRACTICE

A. Explain today's activity.

1. With your reading partner, generate a list of questions about Rosa Parks and the boycott about which you would like more information.
2. Look for answers in books and on the Internet.
3. Partner #1 records; Partner #2 is On-Task Supervisor. (Pair Gail with Leon.)

VI. LESSON CLOSING

A. Summarize: The boycott was the first large-scale, organized protest against segregation that used nonviolent tactics. Rosa Parks's personal act of defiance helped start something good.

B. Preview: Tomorrow we will see a video and learn more about Rosa Parks, beginning with her early life.

VII. EVALUATION

A. Check Point #1: Collect and check their notes for accuracy after the videotape tomorrow.

B. Check Point #2: Collect and grade the five-paragraph report.

C. Check Point #3: Students will be asked about information stated in the objective on the unit test.

REFERENCE

Parks, Rosa Louise, Microsoft® Encarta® Online Encyclopedia 2001 (http://encarta.msn.com). (c) 1997–2001 Microsoft Corporation. (Information contributed by Paul Finkelman, B.A., M.A., Ph.D. Professor of Law, University of Akron School of Law. Author of *Slavery and the Founders: Race and Liberty in the Age of Jefferson.* Coeditor of The Macmillan Encyclopedia of World Slavery.)

Note that excellent examples of documents (such as photographs of newspaper articles written during the boycott) are available at the following site: http://www.archives.state.al.us/teacher/rights/rights1.html.

Portion Distortion: Americans' Love Affair with Food

This is an informal presentation lesson for a large group of students.

I. PREPLANNING TASKS

A.   Connection analysis: *State Standard Health & Fitness:* Develop and monitor progress on personal nutrition goals based on national dietary guidelines and individual needs.

B.   Content analysis

   1.   Subject matter outline: Portion Distortion and Standard Serving Size (see lesson body).

   2.   Prerequisite skills: Knows the terms *USDA Food Pyramid, food product label information,* and *serving size.*

   3.   Key terms and vocabulary: **Portion distortion**—misjudging standard portion size, believing standard portions are larger than those recommended by USDA.

C.   Objective: On an in-class test, students will list examples of standard serving sizes for five foods, each from a different part of the USDA Food Pyramid, and a common object that approximates the standard serving (for example, three oz. of meat is about the size of a deck of cards).

D.   Objective rationale: Knowing what standard serving sizes look like can help students better judge the amount of calories they are taking in when eating meals or snacks. This can help with weight management.

E.   Materials: Presentation outlines, transparencies, recording sheets, foods.

II. LESSON SETUP

A.   Signal for attention: "Attention please."

B.   Behavioral expectations: Participate (answer questions, take notes) and be respectful (eyes on speaker, listening).

III. LESSON OPENING

A.   Generate interest.

   1.   Think about weight control for a minute. Which is more important— to watch what you eat or how much you eat? (78 percent of Americans believe that what they eat is more important in managing their weight than the amount of food they eat.)

   > *AP* = Cover, then ask for a show of hands

   2.   Both are important: It is possible to gain weight by eating small portions of foods that are high in calories, and also possible to gain weight by eating large portions of foods that are low in calories. For example, a 1/2 cup serving of pasta may contain the same calories as four cups of green beans.

B.   Objective and purpose:

    1.   The purpose of this lesson is to help you make better choices for selecting the amounts of food you eat.

    2.   Today you will learn standard serving sizes and how to determine portion sizes for foods you eat so you can adjust your own eating habits. (Too little food can be just as serious a health problem as too much.)

C.   Advance organizer: People tend to eat the portions they are given or what is on the plate. This tendency can lead to overweight or obesity and health problems. Knowledge of serving size can help prevent this problem.

IV. LESSON BODY

A.   Delivery reminders.

    1.   Move around the room; make eye contact with *all* students.

    2.   Use verbal cues such as "First . . . , next . . ." to help students focus on important points.

    3.   Stop after each section for a brief summary.

B.   Pass out note-taking guides.

    1.   Provide Jan with an outline that also includes some detail.

    2.   Partner John with Ada for the review of notes.

C.   Show presentation outline (on transparency).

> *AP = Note-taking*

- The Problem With Too Much Food.
  - Problems of obesity
    - Heart disease, stroke
    - Diabetes, increased risk of cancer
  - Statistics
    - 55 percent of Americans are clinically overweight
    - 1 in 4 Americans are obese
  - Factors that contribute to obesity (American Institute for Cancer Research)
    - Eating out (poster of fast food restaurant logos, such as the golden arches)
    - Concept of portion distortion

D.   Pause and have students compare notes with a partner. (AP)

E.   CFU: Review key points by asking specific questions, such as, "What problems are caused by being overweight or obese?"

> *AP = Call on nonvolunteers at each CFU*

- The Food We Eat (portion sizes).
  - Standard serving size (show transparency #2).
    - The *USDA Food Guide Pyramid shows:*
      - Approximate number of servings to eat per day
      - Various categories of food
      - That number of servings (and therefore calories) varies by body size and level of exercise (key idea)

- How to find out the *standard serving size*:
  - Look at containers (show cans of soup, box of scalloped potatoes)
  - Estimate with fresh foods and fast foods.
- *Portion Distortion*—the American Dietetic Association (show transparency #3).
  - Definition (people are either unaware of or have a distorted guess of the standard serving size).
  - The American Dietetic Association Survey.
    - People were asked to estimate standard serving sizes of eight different foods, including pasta, green salad, beans, and mashed potatoes.
    - The results revealed that 1 percent answered all questions correctly, 63 percent missed five or more questions, and 31 percent estimated only *one* serving size correctly.
  - Results of portion distortion (larger and larger portions, with more and more people becoming overweight).

F. Pause: compare notes.

G. CFU: What are standard serving sizes? What is portion distortion? How does portion distortion contribute to weight gain?

- How to Avoid Portion Distortion (transparency #4).
  - Measure foods as possible
    - Read labels.
    - Count foods (e.g., potato chips) or measure (milk).
  - Estimate portions when measuring is not possible
    - Explain portion sizes as compared to common objects (for example, 3 oz. of meat is approximately the same size as a deck of cards or a computer mouse, and serving of cheese is about the size of an adult thumb).
    - Demonstrate with *real objects*.

H. Pause: compare notes.

I. CFU = What are 2 ways to avoid portion distortion?

V. EXTENDED PRACTICE

A. In-class activity stations. There are five stations with different foods at each. (The goal is to have students see that "eye-balling" something is often not accurate. Measuring out and learning which common object represents the serving size is better.)

1. Distribute recording sheets.

2. Explain the directions.

   a. Read the standard serving size.

   b. Estimate the amount of food that constitutes a standard size by pouring it into bowl (how much cereal is 1/2 cup, for example).

   c. Measure out the portion accurately.

   d. Think of a common object of similar size.

   e. Record it on a recording sheet.

   f. Group 1 begins at Station 1 and so on. (Show transparency of group membership.)

3. Explain group roles (written on board).

    a. Member #1 reads and estimates, Member #2 measures, Member #3 thinks of a common object of similar size, and Member #4 records.

    b. The roles switch at each new station (Member #1 becomes #2 and so on).

4. CFU by asking specific questions about directions and group roles.

B. Homework assignment: Identify 10 of your favorite foods—including fast foods—that cannot be easily measured. Determine portions and come up with common objects about the same size.

VI. LESSON CLOSING

A. Explain that portion size in the United States is a cultural phenomenon and is not representative of the world.

B. Assign homework (see extended practice).

VII. EVALUATION

On the Nutrition Unit Test to be given next week , students will list examples of standard serving sizes for five foods, each from a different part of the USDA Food Pyramid, and a common object that approximates the standard serving.

REFERENCES

American Dietetic Association (1999). Are you a portion size dropout? ADA offers visual aids to cure portion distortion. http://www.eatright.org (December 22, 1999).

Grieger, L. (June 12, 2001). What is a serving size anyway? http://parentsplace.com

Medical College of Wisconsin Health Link (March 30, 2000). Americans ignore importance of food portion sizes. http://healthlink.mcw.edu/article/954384501.html

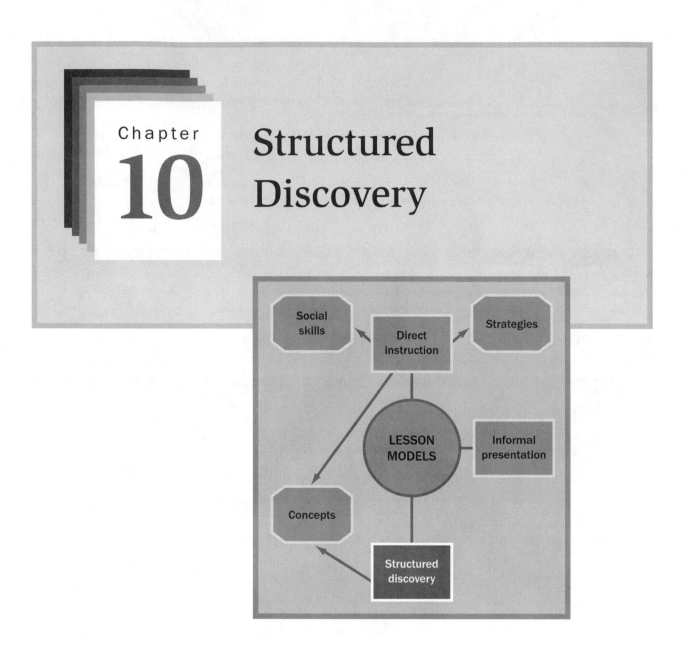

Chapter 10

Structured Discovery

Introduction

The structured discovery model is one in which students "discover" information rather than having it told to them. The discovery from the lesson is a planned one (that is, students discover a correct answer). What they discover is the lesson objective that is predetermined by the teacher. Students are led to the specific objective in a convergent rather than divergent manner. Structured discovery utilizes an inductive rather than deductive approach to learning. This model will help round out the repertoire of beginning skills needed to plan lessons.

Structured discovery lessons have a number of similarities to direct instruction lessons. The purpose of both lesson models is for students to reach a specific academic objective. The major difference between them is the route that students take to reach the objective. The lesson body is where the most significant differences between the two models are found. In the structured discovery lesson, the teacher prepares the students for the discovery by presenting examples and perhaps nonexamples for them to explore. In a direct instruction lesson, the teacher is telling and showing the information that the students need to know to reach the objective. The rest of the lesson body is quite similar in both types of lessons. The teacher follows the students' discovery by summarizing, reviewing, and providing additional practice with the new learning (supervised practice). The same methods also follow the show and tell portion of the body in a direct instruction lesson.

Structured discovery is often confused with the inquiry method or model of instruction. Students "discover" in both models, but the purpose and outcome of the discovery vary significantly. The major goal of structured discovery is for students to learn academic content, while the major goal of inquiry is for students to experience and practice the actual process of making a discovery (Arends, 2000). For example, students may do air pressure experiments to discover facts about air pressure. On the other hand, the goal may be for students to practice making accurate scientific observations. In this case, magnetism, or some topic other than air pressure, might have been selected because the topic is solely a vehicle for having students practice observing. In the first example, an objective would be written that focuses on knowledge of air pressure. In the second case, the objective would be written for the skill of making observations and would be a long-term objective. Therefore, inquiry fits our definition of an activity rather than a lesson.

Understanding the intent of the structured discovery model lays the foundation for using it successfully. The previous paragraphs have described what structured discovery *is* and how it compares to other models. The following tells what structured discovery is *not*. It is *not* a lesson without purpose or focus. It does *not* create a setting where students randomly experiment with materials or information. It also is *not* a time when students are encouraged to come up with any "creative" idea or conclusion that comes to mind. A teacher would *not* be successful if students had a great deal of fun "discovering," but did not discover the information needed for the next day's science lesson. Structured discovery is a model to be selected when content knowledge is to be taught. The lesson process is an added benefit—a secondary objective—not the major one.

■ Uses of Structured Discovery

The primary objective in a structured discovery lesson is always an academic one. Teachers may choose to use this model for teaching principles or concepts in any content area. Some examples of specific topics that could be taught using structured discovery are the definition of a noun, rules for punctuation, what magnets will pick up, when you should call 911, and typical locations of cities.

There are several reasons why a structured discovery lesson may be selected to teach particular academic content. One reason is increased student motivation. The challenge of "making the discovery" can create an exciting situation for the students and, therefore, may hold their attention more readily. When preparing to teach a topic that students may consider to be uninteresting (for example, a grammar rule), consider using a structured discovery lesson. It might provide just the right motivation.

Structured discovery lessons may also be selected because they promote higher-level thinking skills. Most educators agree that all students need opportunities to develop their ability to reason and solve problems. Structured discovery lessons are one way to provide this practice. Older students or highly capable students may need even more of these opportunities and will likely be especially excited and challenged by structured discovery lessons.

Note that, in addition to the primary short-term academic objective, you may wish to include a long-term objective that addresses "thinking," such as problem solving, analysis, asking relevant questions, or drawing conclusions, in the lesson plan.

A third reason to use a structured discovery lesson is to enhance retention. Students may be more apt to recall what they have learned when they have been given the opportunity to figure out something for themselves.

Structured discovery lessons are a valuable teaching tool, but they are not always appropriate. This type of lesson should obviously never be used when the safety of students is an issue. It would not make sense, for instance, to have students discover how to use a Bunsen burner safely or how to effectively break a fall from a balance beam. Additionally, this type of lesson would not be used when damage to materials or equipment may result. For example, it would be inappropriate for students to discover how to turn off a computer.

A structured discovery lesson should also not be used when it is likely that a student will fail. It would not make much sense, for example, to have students discover how to solve long division problems. It is fairly predictable they would flounder in failure as they repeatedly practiced the wrong way to compute long division problems. It may make sense, however, to have them discover math concepts such as "division."

A structured discovery lesson also would not be a good choice when the time involved in making the discovery outweighs the benefit of the discovery itself. It may be possible, for instance, for students to eventually discover how to solve long division problems. However, the time it would take to make such a discovery would most likely decrease the value of making the discovery.

A thorough content analysis can help determine when a structured discovery lesson would be a good choice. Using some good common sense will help here as well.

Key Planning Considerations

Structured discovery lessons require very careful planning to help ensure that students will learn information accurately. These lessons have a high probability of resulting in student confusion. It is especially important to consider the following areas.

Content Analysis

Structured discovery lessons can be used to teach a variety of types of content. Therefore, the content analysis of this lesson will vary. If the objective is for students to discover a concept, write a concept analysis. If students are to discover a principle, include a clearly stated principle statement.

Assessing Prerequisite Skills and Knowledge

Lesson readiness can be determined in two steps. First, it is necessary to analyze what one needs to know, that is prerequisite skills or knowledge, to be successful in the current lesson. Secondly, there must be an assessment as to whether or not the students know it. For example, you plan a structured discovery lesson on adjectives. You know that students must be able to identify nouns to understand adjectives. Therefore, you test your students on noun identification.

Gathering assessment information can be either fairly simple (correcting papers from yesterday's assignment), or more complicated (writing and administering a formal pretest). However, individual students must be assessed regardless of the level of difficulty.

Writing the Objective

The short-term academic objective written for the structured discovery lesson is no different from an objective written for lessons using other models. The important thing to remember about structured discovery objectives is how they should *not* be written. They should not, for example, say something like, "Students will discover . . . ." Objectives for all lessons must state what the students will know or do at the end of the lesson. The means to the end is not stated in the objective. (See Chapter 3 for more detail.)

Stating the Objective to Students

While you will not begin the structured discovery lesson by telling the students the outcome of the learning because that would spoil the discovery, it is important they understand what they will learn. During the lesson opening for example, students could be told they are going to learn about a scientific law or a grammar rule. Any specifics about the law or rule will be saved for later.

Setting Up the Discovery

The lesson body component of the structured discovery lesson usually begins by presenting examples and nonexamples of the content to be learned. Next, the discovery is "set up" by telling students directly what they are to discover (for example, "The underlined words in these sentences are adjectives. See if you can write a definition for adjective").

Selecting Examples and Nonexamples

Examples and nonexamples for these lessons must be carefully selected because of the potential for confusion during the discovery phase. It is best to start with the clearest, purest examples and nonexamples. Successive examples can be more abstract, more difficult to discriminate. Examples and nonexamples can be in the form of individual problems, words or scenarios, pictures, demonstrations, and so on.

Sometimes it is not necessary to include nonexamples. For instance, if you plan a lesson in which students are to discover the relationship between adjectives and nouns, nonexamples are not needed because students are not being taught to distinguish between an adjective and other parts of speech. A careful content analysis will help you determine whether or not nonexamples are needed.

Planning Questions and Prompts

It is a good idea to plan in advance how to guide the discovery. What will be done, for example, if students seem completely baffled by the initial explanation and examples? Writing down specific questions, statements, or clues will be beneficial, as they will serve to prompt students' thinking. Visual cues may also be planned.

Supervised Practice

One of the tricky parts of a structured discovery lesson is determining whether or not all of the students have really "discovered." The teacher must take an active role in helping students draw correct conclusions before the end of the discovery part of the lesson.

Follow this by having students practice the new learning under the teacher's supervision. It is very important to remember that the part of the lesson where the students "discover" is *not* supervised practice. For example, after the students have discovered principles of air pressure, you would want to provide new problems or demonstrations that would allow them to apply the principles they have learned. As students practice, you must monitor to be sure they are using the "discovered" information accurately.

Behavior Expectations

Students often work together in partners or in small groups during the "discovery" portion of the structured discovery lesson. Remember that students may need to be taught or reminded of specific behaviors necessary for working successfully with others. When lessons involve manipulating or sharing materials or equipment, behavioral expectations need to be addressed as well. You may also need to consider students' tolerance for working through feelings of frustration and confusion, as the probability of this happening is greater in this type of lesson.

Figure 10.1   Writing a Structured Discovery Lesson

The following list describes what is typically included in each component in a structured discovery lesson plan.

COMPONENT 1: PREPLANNING TASKS

The preplanning tasks section is a cover sheet for the rest of the lesson plan. Include the following when preparing the preplanning tasks:

- *Connection analysis*   Identify the generalization or big idea, the IEP goal, and the state standard addressed in the plan.

- *Content analysis*   This may be a concept analysis or principle statement, key terms and vocabulary, or necessary prerequisite skills and knowledge.

continued on next page

Figure 10.1 **Writing a Structured Discovery Lesson (continued)**

■ *Objective* Remember that the objective represents the learning outcome, not the learning activities or process. For example, you would not write, "Students will discover . . . ." Possible objectives for a structured discovery lesson could be for students to describe, state a principle, identify, define, or give examples.

■ *Objective rationale* To help you clarify the value of the objective.

COMPONENT 2: LESSON SETUP

The lesson setup is the first component of the lesson plan that is actually presented to students. Include the following when preparing the lesson setup:

■ *Signal for attention:* Use a hand signal, or say, "Listen, please."

■ *Statement of behavior expectations:* Have eyes on me; follow directions; take turns with your partner.

COMPONENT 3: LESSON OPENING

The lesson opening should effectively prepare the students for the new learning. Include the following when writing the lesson opening:

■ A strategy designed to generate interest in the lesson and to relate new learning to prior knowledge.

■ A way to state the objective so students know what they will learn. Be careful not to give away the discovery, however.

■ A statement of the objective purpose, so students know why the new learning is valuable.

COMPONENT 4: LESSON BODY

The lesson body is a detailed, step-by-step description of the actual teaching to the objective that will be done (that is, what the teacher and the students will be doing). Include the following:

■ *Examples and nonexamples* that lead students to discover the definition, principle, and so on, that you are teaching. Be sure to repeat, review, and *check for understanding* of the essential learning to ensure that all students "discovered" the correct information. Include *supervised practice* with feedback as well.

■ *Active participation* strategies, such as partner work, to keep students learning.

■ *Diversity strategies* throughout the lesson body that, for example, (1) provide more structure in the initial presentation of examples (in the use of cues, concrete objects, leading questions), (2) give explicit directions and demonstrate how students should share tasks in partner or group work, and (3) increase the amount and types of extended practice. (See Component 5.)

continued on next page

Figure 10.1 Writing a Structured Discovery Lesson (continued)

COMPONENT 5: EXTENDED PRACTICE

Extended practice opportunities help students develop levels of accuracy and fluency high enough to ensure they can generalize the skill or knowledge. Some students may need a great deal of extended practice, while others may need enrichment activities. Include the following when writing extended practice:

- A plan for providing extended practice immediately following the lesson or soon thereafter.
- A list of lessons or activities that will build on this objective. Any additional opportunities students will have to generalize and extend the information should be included as appropriate. You may have planned a structured discovery lesson to teach information that students will need in a lesson to follow (for example, "Today's structured discovery lesson, designed to teach the definition of a noun, provides the background information necessary for tomorrow's direct instruction lesson on common and proper nouns").

COMPONENT 6: LESSON CLOSING

The lesson closing may follow the body of the lesson or it may follow extended practice. Include the following within the lesson closing:

- A strategy for closing the lesson. You may wish to include a variety of activities in your lesson closing, including (a) a review of key points of the lesson, (b) opportunities for students to draw conclusions, (c) a description of where or when students should use their new skills or knowledge, and (d) a reference to the lesson opening.

COMPONENT 7: EVALUATION

The lesson evaluation is planned when the objective is written, so the evaluation must match exactly what is stated in the objective. Remember that evaluation is not necessarily a paper and pencil test. Also, remember that its purpose is to determine how individual students are progressing toward the lesson objective, which means the student does not receive help—from peers or the teacher—during the evaluation. Do not forget to test with new examples. Careful monitoring during supervised and extended practice activities will help you decide when evaluation should occur.

Remember to use editing tasks to evaluate your plan!

References and Suggested Readings

Arends, R. I. (2000). *Learning to Teach* (5th ed.). New York: McGraw-Hill. (See Chapter 11 in particular.)

Cruickshank, D. R., Bainer, D. L., & Metcalf, K. K. (1999). *The Act of Teaching* (2nd ed.). Boston: McGraw-Hill College. (See Chapter 7 in particular.)

Guillaume, A. M. (2000). *Classroom Teaching: A Primer for New Professionals.* Columbus, OH: Merrill.

Jacobsen, D. A., Eggen, P., & Kauchak, D. (2002). *Methods for Teaching* (6th ed.). Columbus, OH: Merrill Prentice Hall. (See Chapter 7 in particular.)

Joyce, B., Weil, M., with Calhoun, E. (2000). *Models of Teaching* (6th ed.). Boston: Allyn & Bacon. (See Chapter 10 in particular.)

Kame'enui, E. J., Carnine, D. W., Dixon, R. C., Simmons, D. C., & Coyne, M. D. (2002). *Effective Teaching Strategies that Accommodate Diverse Learners* (2nd ed.). Columbus, OH: Merrill Prentice Hall.

Kellough, R. D. (2000). *A Resource Guide for Teaching: K–12* (3rd ed.). Columbus, OH: Merrill.

Orlich, D. C., Harder, R. J., Callahan, R. C., & Gibson, H. W. (2001). *Teaching Strategies: A Guide to Better Instruction* (6th ed.). Boston: Houghton Mifflin Co.

Rosenberg, M. S., O'Shea, L., & O'Shea, D. J. (1998). *Student Teacher to Master Teacher: A Practical Guide for Educating Students with Special Needs* (3rd ed.). Columbus, OH: Merrill, an imprint of Prentice Hall. (See Chapter 6 in particular.)

Magnetic Attraction

This is a large- or small-group, structured discovery science lesson.

I. PREPLANNING TASKS

A. Connection analysis: *State Science Standard, Science 2.2:* Think logically, analytically, and creatively. *Benchmark 1:* Examine data to verify a conclusion in a simple investigation. *Big Idea:* the scientific method of forming and testing a hypothesis.

B. Content analysis

   1. Principle: Magnets pull objects made of iron or steel.

   2. Prerequisite skills and knowledge: Use a recording sheet.

   3. Key terms and vocabulary: **Attract, repel.**

C. Objective: Given a list of 10 objects, students will underline the six objects that would be pulled by a magnet, and write the reason next to each (for example, "made of steel"). (An additional objective is that students will infer a principle from available data.)

D. Objective rationale

   1. Knowing how magnets work can help students appreciate the various uses of magnets, such as to sort materials (scrap yard), find direction (compass), hold items in place (electric can opener), pick things up (sewing pins).

   2. Knowing how to draw conclusions from examining data is a skill that can be applied to many situations. This is an application of the scientific method.

E. Materials and equipment: Small box of pins; 10 bags of small objects for five groups of four students, with two bags per group (note that objects have been selected carefully and the only thing the examples have in common is that they are made of steel or iron or not); 10 magnets (two per group); and 20 copies each of two worksheets (#1 is double-sided and consists of three parts: Part 1 includes the activity directions, group member roles, and space for listing groups of objects—"pulled," and "not pulled"; Part 2 includes pictures and descriptions of six new objects and it includes Part 3, the evaluation).

II. LESSON SETUP

A. Signal for attention: "Let's get started."

B. Behavior expectations: Sit in seats, eyes on me, listening.

III. LESSON OPENING

A. Motivate, get students to focus on lesson topic.

   1. Demonstrate magnetic puppets moving on stage.

2. Ask, "How do you think the puppets are moving?" (Puppets have thumbtacks or paperclips on their feet, and the magnet moving underneath them makes them move).

> *AP = Tell a partner, then call on nonvolunteers*

3. After the answer is discovered, ask, "Have you ever played with a magnet? What were you able to do with it?"

> *AP = Call on nonvolunteers*

B. State the objective and purpose.

1. Say, "Today we are going to discover a rule about which objects magnets can attract (pull). This will help you understand how magnets help us." (Demonstrate by spilling a small box of pins and picking them up with a magnet.)

IV. LESSON BODY

A. Set up the discovery.

1. Show transparency (activity directions, roles, and discovery goal), and explain and demonstrate.

2. Directions for using the materials and testing objects.

> *AP = Choral read steps*

   a. Take objects from the bag.

   b. Touch your magnet to each object.

   c. Sort. Which objects are pulled by the magnets? Put these in a group. Which objects are not pulled by the magnet? Put these in another group.

   d. Record findings on worksheet provided (demonstrate on transparency).

   e. Write a rule about what magnets pull.

3. CFU: Ask, "What do you do first, everyone . . . ? Second, everyone . . . ?" and so on.

4. Directions for group roles (they know these roles): recorder, on-task supervisor, reporter, and sorter.

5. CFU: Ask, "What does the recorder do?" and so on (leave transparency up).

> *AP = Call on nonvolunteers*

6. Distribute bags and worksheets.

B. Monitor the discovery. Have early finishers write predictions about which other objects magnets would pull or not pull.

C. Review the discovery.

1. Ask, "What did you find out about your magnet and objects?"

> *AP = Call on nonvolunteers*

2. Ask, "How are the objects in the 'pulled' group alike?" (same color? shape? size?).

3. Ask, "What rule did you make about which objects your magnets pulled?"

> *AP = Table Groups, then call on each Reporter*

4. Write rule on board (if the rule is incorrect, demonstrate by testing it).

D.   Individual supervised practice.

   1.   Test the discovery.

      a.   Pass out new bags of objects, magnets to each student (eight objects and one magnet).

      b.   Read directions for Part 2 on worksheet. Sort objects using a written description of the object property (aluminum, steel). Write a rationale, such as made of steel; then "test" to see if you are right.

> *AP = Choral read directions*

      c.   CFU: What do you do first? Where do you explain why you put an object in a certain pile? and so on.

> *AP = Call on nonvolunteers*

      d.   Have students complete worksheets individually. I monitor, prompt, and provide feedback.

      e.   When finished, collect materials and have students get back together as a large group.

V. LESSON CLOSING

A.   Review: Today you discovered what magnets attract. What do they attract? What is the rule about what magnets attract?

B.   Preview: Tomorrow you will learn about the force field surrounding magnets.

> *AP = Turn to partner, then call on nonvolunteers*

VI. EVALUATION

A.   Pass out worksheet which is a list of 10 objects, including a description of their properties, of which six objects will be "pulled" by a magnet. Tell students completion of worksheet is their "ticket to recess."

VII. EXTENDED PRACTICE

A.   Explain that they will have more practice tomorrow in centers (with new objects) if needed.

How to Punctuate a Series

This is a structured discovery lesson for a large or small group.

I. PREPLANNING TASKS

A. Connection analysis: *State Writing Standard*: The student writes clearly and effectively, applies capitalization and punctuation rules correctly. *IEP Goal*: Trish will use correct punctuation (commas, periods, quotation marks) in writing samples. *Big Idea*: the writing process (Kameenui, Carnine, Dixon, Simmons, & Coyne, 2002).

B. Content analysis

　　1. Principle statement or rule: When a series occurs in a sentence, commas are placed after each item except the last.

　　2. Prerequisite skills: Recognize commas

　　3. Key terms:

　　　　a. **series**—three or more related items listed consecutively in the same sentence

　　　　b. **punctuate**—using marks or characters to make the meaning clear

C. Objective: Given 10 sentences, each of which contain a series, SW place all commas correctly.

D. Objective rationale: Knowing basic punctuation marks helps students produce written products that are accurate and clear.

E. Materials: one transparency and two worksheets

II. LESSON SETUP

A. Signal for attention: "Let's begin."

B. Behavioral expectations: Eyes on me, raise hand, and wait to be called on.

III. LESSON OPENING

A. Review prior learning: Review already learned punctuation marks: period, question mark, semicolon, apostrophe.

B. Statement of objective, objective purpose: Today you will learn one of the uses for the comma—a basic punctuation rule—knowing this rule helps make your writing clear.

IV. LESSON BODY

Reminder to myself: As I monitor seatwork, be sure to mark points on Garth's behavior chart.

A. Set up the discovery

1. Show transparency: 10 correctly punctuated series and five sentences that need punctuation and the discovery goals. Show only sentences #1–10 for now. (Leave transparency up on overhead during discovery phase.) Example sentences include:

   a. Tammy, Larry, Johnny, and Sherry are members of my family.

   b. My horses' names are Josie, Thunder, and Lucky.

   c. Mt. Baker, Mt. Rainier, and Mt. St. Helens are volcanoes in Washington state.

2. Say, "Look carefully at the commas in these sentences. They are used to punctuate a series. Your job is to make two discoveries. See if you can figure out (1) a definition for a series and (2) a rule for how to use commas to punctuate a series."

3. Explain partner work expectations for making the discoveries:

   a. Work with Study Buddy (Review what on-task looks like and sounds like for buddy work.)

   b. Roles: one person recorder for task 1, then switch; both contribute ideas

B. Monitor the discovery

1. While students work, circulate and listen to their discussions. Ask what they are finding or thinking. (Check in with Alice and Mary frequently.)

2. Prompt, if necessary, by asking questions such as: "How many words make up the series?" "What words are related?" "What words make up the series?" "Where is the first comma? second?"

3. Stop when all or most partner groups seem to have made the discoveries.

C. Review the discovery

1. Ask students to tell their discoveries. I write them on the board.

   a. Definition of series

   b. Rule for punctuating a series

   > *AP = Students write definition and principle in their language notebooks*

2. CFU: Uncover sentences #11–15 on transparency.

   a. Work through sentences and have students talk me through where to put commas.

   b. Ask specific questions such as "Which words make up the series in this sentence?" "The first comma goes after what word, everyone . . .?"

   > *AP = Turn to partner, unison responses*

D. Supervised practice

1. Pass out worksheet #1 (give Lidia a large print version) which includes 15 sentences such as:

   a. Katherine Michael and Robby are the children of Gail and Leon.

   b. Trigger Fury Flicka and Blaze are the names of famous horses.

2. Direct students to add commas to the first five sentences.

3. I will move around the room and make sure each student is accurate in placing commas, and will give feedback to everyone.

V. EXTENDED PRACTICE

Seatwork assignment: Assign last 10 sentences on worksheet #1 as more practice, if students are not yet fluent. I'll grade and pass back tomorrow prior to evaluation.

VI. LESSON CLOSING

A. Final review: Students explain how to use commas in a series.

B. Preview tomorrow's lesson: They will learn another use for commas.

> *AP = Tell a partner*

VII. EVALUATION

A. Evaluation time: After supervised practice today or after extended practice.

B. Evaluation task: Worksheet #2 with 10 sentences, each containing a series of items to be punctuated. (Use sentences about topics that are of high interest.)

    1. Examples of some of the sentences are:

        a. Sea otters whales starfish and barnacles are found at the beach.

        b. Our school has a gym a music room and a lunchroom.

        c. Pizzas made with sausage peppers olives pepperoni and mushrooms are delicious.

Chapter 11

Concepts, Social Skills, and Strategies

Introduction

This chapter is about how to teach concepts, social skills, and learning and study strategies. We have included this information in a separate chapter because this content requires somewhat specialized planning. Effective instruction for concepts, social skills, and learning and study strategies is not qualitatively different than teaching other content. It is really more of a difference in instructional emphasis. For example, when planning to teach about concepts, you emphasize using examples and nonexamples; when planning social skill and strategy lessons, you emphasize demonstrating processes and using think alouds. We have included basic information about each type of content as well as key planning considerations for each.

Teaching Concepts

Regardless of the content area you teach, you will find yourself teaching concepts. Sometimes concepts are taught within a lesson or activity; other times they are taught in separate lessons or activities. For example, the concept of "main idea" would most likely be taught in a series of lessons and activities. The concept of peninsula, on the other hand, might be taught within another lesson.

Concepts Defined

Concepts are categories of knowledge. For example, "island" is a concept. There are many specific examples of islands, such as Lopez, Barbados, and Greenland. They all belong to the category of island because they have certain attributes in common, that is, they are all land masses completely surrounded by water. Teaching concepts is much more efficient than solely teaching specific examples (Cummings, 1990). A geography teacher does not need to teach every island in the world separately, because learning concepts allows us to generalize. If the concept of island is understood, new places can be recognized as being islands if they have the necessary traits.

To check your understanding of "concept," consider the following examples and nonexamples:

Examples	Nonexamples
President	Harry Truman
Rocking chair	My grandma's black rocker
Impressionist art	Van Gogh's "Starry Night"
Planet	Mars

To determine if something is a concept, ask if you can think of more than one example of it. In other words, lake is a concept because there are many examples of it—Michigan, Samish, Placid, Geneva, Victoria, and others. Mars is not a concept because there is only one Mars. Other examples of concepts are friendship, soft rock, fairness, appropriate spectator behavior, on-task, tessellation, mammal, and tiny.

Types of Concepts

Concepts vary according to how concrete or abstract they are, how broad or narrow they are, and the type of definition they have. It is important to think about the type of concept to be taught when deciding how to teach it.

Some concepts are very concrete, such as table or flower. Some are very abstract, such as truth or love. Many fall in between, like polygon, family, or adverb. The more concrete a concept is, the easier it is to learn and to teach.

Some concepts are very broad, such as living things. Some are very narrow, such as elephants. Between these two extremes, there are a series of concepts in a hierarchy, as in the following example: living things, animals, mammals, land mammals, large land mammals, large land mammals living today, elephants.

When teaching a particular concept, it is important to fit it into a hierarchy of broader and narrower concepts. For example, "We have been learning about geometric shapes. Today we are going to learn about one type of geometric shape—the triangle. In later lessons we will learn about different kinds of triangles, such as equilateral triangles."

Typically, a very narrow concept, such as "elephant," should not be taught through a formal concept lesson (unless, perhaps, the students are training to be wildlife biologists). Of the many, many concepts, it is necessary to select those that are most important and useful for the students to learn.

Concepts also vary according to how they are defined. For example, "table" is defined in terms of one set of attributes, that is, a table has a flat surface and at least one leg. This is called a conjunctive concept. Other concepts—called disjunctive—are defined in terms of alternative sets of attributes. For example, a citizen is a native or naturalized member of a nation (Martorella, 1994, p. 161). A strike in baseball is a swing and a miss, a pitch in the strike zone, or a foul ball (Arends, 2000, p. 281). A third type of concept—relational—is defined in terms of a comparison, such as "big." A mouse is big in comparison with an ant, but it is not big compared to a dog. The concept "big" has no meaning except in relation to something else.

As you analyze a concept and select examples or nonexamples in preparation for teaching, it is important to recognize whether you are teaching a conjunctive, disjunctive, or relational concept.

Concepts may be taught using the direct instruction model or the structured discovery model. The direct instruction model uses a deductive approach, while the structured discovery model uses an inductive approach. Each model requires different steps initially. However, the last two steps are the same in both models.

Direct Instruction Model

The following steps illustrate how concepts are taught using the direct instruction model:

■ Teacher (T) names and defines the concept.

■ T states the critical and noncritical attributes of the concept while showing examples and nonexamples of the concept.

■ T provides new examples and nonexamples and asks students to discriminate between them.

■ T asks students to explain their answers, that is, to refer to critical attributes present or absent.

Structured Discovery Model

The following steps illustrate how instructors teach concepts using the structured discovery model:

■ Teacher (T) names (usually) the concept.

■ T shows examples and nonexamples.

■ T asks students to examine the examples and nonexamples and to identify critical and noncritical attributes.

■ T asks students to define the concept or explain the concept rule.

■ T provides new examples and nonexamples and asks students to discriminate between them.

■ T asks students to explain their answers, that is, to refer to critical attributes, present or absent.

Teaching concepts using the direct instruction model provides less opportunity for confusion or misconceptions and is more time efficient. This model is useful when students have little prior knowledge of the concept.

Teaching concepts using the structured discovery model may provide an approach that is more interesting or motivating to students, and that provides practice in inductive thinking skills. This model is useful in helping students refine their understanding of familiar concepts.

Students typically have some prior knowledge and experience of a concept before it is taught. It is helpful to assess and to build on each student's knowledge. Also, it is important to ascertain whether the student has formed inaccurate concepts because of limited experience, such as thinking that all people who speak Spanish are from Mexico, all fruits are edible, or all islands have people living on them.

Both direct instruction and structured discovery models are effective for teaching concepts. Each model has advantages. First, determine the concept to teach, and write the objective. Then, weigh the advantages of both models. Select the one that best meets the needs of the students.

Key Planning Considerations

Concept Analysis

A careful concept analysis is essential for effective concept teaching. A concept analysis includes a definition, critical and noncritical attributes, and examples and nonexamples of the concept.

Developing a definition at an appropriate level for the students is important. Dictionary definitions are not always the best to use. A better source may be the glossary of content area textbooks. The language and complexity of the definition must be suitable for the students. For example, the definition of "mammal" or "square" would be stated differently for first-grade students than for tenth-grade students.

When a concept is analyzed, list the critical and noncritical attributes that will be most helpful in distinguishing that concept from similar ones. Critical attributes are essential characteristics of a concept. For example, "four sides" is a critical attribute of a square. However, when defining a

concept, any one critical attribute is necessary but not sufficient to defining the concept. A square must have four sides, but the sides must also be of equal length. Noncritical attributes of a concept are those that are not necessary. Whether the length of those equal sides is 3 miles or 3 inches is unimportant. Size is a noncritical attribute of a square. A square is a square whether it is big or small.

Carefully select examples and nonexamples to bring out all of the critical and noncritical attributes of the concept. It is important to begin with the "best" examples, the examples that are the clearest and least ambiguous. Gradually introduce examples and nonexamples that are more difficult to differentiate. For example, do not begin with a platypus as an example of a mammal, or with a rhombus as a nonexample of a square (Howell & Nolet, 2000).

Many examples and nonexamples are needed. That is because different sets must be used for the initial presentation, the practice, and the evaluation. This is to ensure that students have not merely memorized the examples and that they understand the concept and its attributes.

When presenting examples and nonexamples, use cues such as underlining, colors, and arrows to emphasize critical attributes. Gradually fade the cues.

Objective

Think carefully about what your students need to learn to understand and use the concept you are teaching. Possible objectives for concept lessons include defining the concept, listing critical attributes of the concept, recognizing examples and nonexamples of the concept, stating why something is an example or nonexample, producing examples, stating similarities and differences between related concepts, using the concept in a novel way, or producing a graphic organizer of the concept.

Opening

When opening concept lessons, it is very important to assess what students already know about the concept and to find out if students have any misconceptions about the concept. It may be useful to brainstorm or conduct "think to writes" (writing down everything you know about reptiles in two minutes). These strategies can also be used to help students connect the new learning with prior knowledge. When possible, help students make connections to personal experience. For example, if you are going to teach the concept "democracy," ask about the students' experiences in electing the class president. It is also best to use some type of organizer that shows the relationship of the concept being taught to broader and narrower concepts or to related concepts, such as islands and peninsulas. Remember that you would not state a specific objective that includes the definition of the concept at the beginning of a discovery lesson.

Closing

Some options for closing a concept lesson include reviewing the concept definition, critical attributes, and best examples, discussing related concepts or previewing future lessons on related concepts, reviewing the purpose of learning the concept, describing how students can use their knowledge of the concept in the future, asking students to show their graphic organizers or new examples, and asking students to expand or correct their "think to writes."

To summarize, concepts are categories of information found in all content areas. They can be taught using direct instruction or structured discovery lesson models. A carefully designed concept analysis can help students develop a clear understanding of the concept they are studying.

■ Teaching Social Skills

What are social skills? The term *social skills* encompasses many categories and examples. The term includes very broad cognitive-behavioral skills, such as interpersonal problem solving, anger management, and empathy, and narrow, specific interpersonal skills such as accepting compliments or greeting others. Teachers may need to teach social skills required for classroom success, such as listening, following directions, asking for help, or waiting for help; cooperative social skills for working in groups, such as taking turns, sharing, or disagreeing appropriately; social skills for employment, such as asking for directions or sharing tasks; social skills needed for making friends, such as starting conversations or joining activities; and skills for dealing with conflict, such as responding to teasing or an accusation, accepting no, staying out of fights, negotiating, or accepting consequences.

Why teach social skills? Some students come to school skilled at making friends, getting along with adults, expressing feelings, and understanding the feelings of others. But some could use help in learning to work or play with others, to resolve conflicts, and to manage feelings. A few students are already rejected by others, are dangerously aggressive or withdrawn, and are in desperate need of help in developing social skills. Because social competence is essential for success in school and in life, many schools are beginning to take a proactive approach by making social skills instruction a regular part of the curriculum, as well as providing more intense instruction for those individuals who need it. You will likely need to teach social skills to at least some of your students.

Choosing the Lesson Model to Use

Teaching social skills is similar to teaching other procedures or how-to lessons. You begin with a task analysis of the skill and then teach the steps using direct instruction. As in all direct instruction lessons, you will include a presentation of information component in which you explain and give examples for each step. You will demonstrate the use of the social skill and you will ask the students to practice the social skill by acting it out in a role play. You will evaluate whether each student has met the lesson objective by having the student demonstrate the skill in another role play.

Note that when teaching social skills it is critical to attend to generalization. For this reason, it is very important to follow initial direct instruction lessons with planned activities (see Chapter 5). This gives students the opportunity to apply the skill in a variety of contexts. You may plan an activity to practice a social skill, such as a reading and discussion of a controversial topic to practice disagreeing politely. You may also teach social skills as an objective in activities with other purposes. For example, you could use the sample activity plan, "Tic-Tac-Toe Spelling" at the end of Chapter 5, to practice the social skills of taking turns, giving compliments, or accepting being corrected, in addition to practicing spelling. In this case you would review the social skill in the activity opening and include directions for how and when to use the skill in the activity middle.

Key Planning Considerations

Content Analysis

The content analysis for a social skills lesson includes a task analysis. List the steps for using the social skill, including the steps that involve stopping to think and making decisions. For example, you may plan to teach students to accept "no" for an answer and list the steps as (1) stop and take a deep breath; (2) look at the person; (3) say "ok"; and (4) do not argue. Published social skills programs are good sources of task analyses.

Demonstration

In social skill lessons, demonstration means acting out or modeling the social skill in a scenario that is meaningful to the students. For example, demonstrate the skill of "accepting no" in a scenario, in which a teacher refuses to allow a student to sit by a friend in math class.

GUIDELINES FOR DEMONSTRATING (MODELING)

Each step needs to be modeled clearly and correctly, so be sure you and your assistants rehearse in advance. The following guidelines are provided by McGinnis and Goldstein (1997) and Sheridan (1995):

■ As you act and talk, point to the steps written on a poster.

■ Be sure to think aloud.

■ Keep it simple. Teach one skill at a time, each step in sequence, without a lot of extra detail.

■ Check for understanding by assigning students to watch for different steps and asking them to describe how the step was demonstrated following the modeling.

■ You may choose to show a nonexample as well, for clarity.

■ Be sure you model the skill working, that is, having a positive outcome: "Thanks for accepting no so calmly. You may sit by Ichiro later during lunch."

■ Generalization will be encouraged if you select scenarios relevant to your students and model a variety of scenarios showing different applications, such as accepting no at home and at school, from peers and adults, and for major and minor requests.

Supervised Practice

The students practice the skill by role-playing and receiving feedback. You may begin by having them brainstorm scenarios when they will need to use the skill. Then select the first student to take the lead and choose other students for supporting roles.

GUIDELINES FOR SUPERVISED PRACTICE
(ROLE-PLAYING)

Each student should have multiple opportunities to play the lead role and to receive feedback. Each student demonstrates asking permission and accepts no as an answer, for example. This may mean scheduling the supervised practice over several days. McGinnis and Goldstein (1997) and Sheridan (1995) provide the following guidelines:

■ Some students may need scaffolding. They may need to discuss how they will demonstrate each step, or have the opportunity to rehearse with peers first. You may provide support by pointing to the steps on a poster and prompting as they role-play.

■ If a student makes an error during the role play, stop him right away, correct the error, and have him redo the role play. You can correct the error through prompting, modeling, or directly telling the student the correct step.

■ Other students can be assigned steps to observe and on which to give feedback (active participation).

■ Promote generalization by having students provide ideas for scenarios, and by observing them in a variety of settings for scenario ideas. When possible, go to the actual settings to role-play, such as going to the playground to practice joining games.

■ To prepare students for the real world, include scenarios where the skill does not work, such as when the teasing does not stop, they do not get to join the game, or they do not receive permission. Teach alternatives.

■ Provide for cultural diversity by role-playing options and varying scenarios. For example, some students when practicing "dealing with teasing" will be more comfortable with passive responses such as ignoring the teasing or getting help. Others will be more comfortable with more assertive responses such as telling the person to stop.

Extended Practice

This component is key in promoting generalization. It is essential to provide a great deal of additional practice in real-world applications. Extended practice often takes two forms, homework and follow-up practice at school.

Students may be given homework assignments to use the social skill. Provide a form with a place for the students to list the steps in the skill, to describe where, when, and with whom they used the skill, and to describe the results. The form can also include a place for students to self-evaluate their use of the skill, and a place for others (parents, coaches, day care providers, or peers) to initial that they saw the student use the skill. Homework can incorporate goal setting or be written in the form of a behavior contract. The purpose is for the student to practice using the skill in a variety of situations.

The teacher can also plan follow-up practice for students to use the skill immediately following the body of the lesson. Depending on the skill, this practice may occur during free time, partner or small-group work, class discussions, centers, recess, lunch, or planned activities in the form of games or projects. Tell the students ahead of time to use the skill ("Remember to practice taking turns while using the computers for your projects"). Coach and prompt the students during the practice situation, and debrief following. Also watch for those unplanned teachable moments.

To summarize, social skills are important for success in school as well as in all other parts of a student's life. Social skills can be taught directly

through modeling and role plays. Promoting generalization through well-planned extended practice is very important.

Teaching Learning and Study Strategies

Why teach learning and study strategies? Knowing the academic expectations for students described in the state standards helps teachers plan what they will teach. Simply knowing the expectations, however, is not very helpful in planning for students who have difficulty learning, remembering, and using information. Students who have effective strategies for learning and studying definitely have an increased chance of performing well on tasks necessary for school success. The learner with missing or ineffective strategies is often at risk for school failure. This is really what strategy instruction is all about, helping students learn and study in more efficient ways so they may be more successful in school.

What are strategies? A strategy is a special kind of procedure, one that is designed to help students become more effective learners. Learning strategies (sometimes called cognitive strategies) and study strategies (sometimes called study skills) are the two basic strategy types.

Learning and study strategies differ in their focus. A learning strategy facilitates the use of higher-level thinking behaviors, such as decision making, self-motivation, and self-monitoring (Deshler, Ellis, & Lenz, 1996). For example, using a strategy for finding the main idea requires students to make decisions about what they are reading by asking themselves questions such as "Does this idea encompass all of the important details in this paragraph?" Therefore, a strategy to find the main idea is an example of a learning strategy.

A study strategy, on the other hand, is more similar to a standard procedure, as described in Chapter 6. The students work through an ordered series of steps that requires limited use of higher-level thinking skills such as decision making or self-monitoring. For example, a proofreading strategy in which students are to complete steps such as "Check to see that each sentence begins with a capital letter" would be considered a study strategy. The strategy steps can be completed without the use of higher-level thinking skills. Deciding whether a letter is upper or lower case is pretty cut and dried. Learning strategies achieve cognitive goals (Arends, 2000), whereas study strategies achieve procedural goals, and both are important.

Strategy Purposes

All kinds of strategies can be taught to help students study and learn. Thinking about their purposes can help teachers select appropriate ones. Some strategies are designed to help students gather information from texts and presentations (for example, strategies that teach students how to take notes from a lecture or read for comprehension). Other strategies help students retain information for later use (for example, learning how to use mnemonic strategies or construct concept maps). Still other strategies help students show what they know (learning how to proofread assignments or take multiple-choice tests, for example). One additional group of strategies helps students develop personal organizational habits (learning how to maintain an assignment calendar or complete assignments, for example).

You can decide which strategies to teach your students, by carefully analyzing the trouble spots they encounter when trying to perform school tasks. Information about specific strategies is readily available in journals and texts. (See the resources listed at the end of this chapter for more information.)

Choosing the Lesson Model to Use

Direct instruction is an effective model to use for teaching strategies. The strategy lesson begins with the teacher clearly establishing the value of the strategy and what the students will be expected to know and do. This is followed by the presentation of the strategy steps (developed through a task analysis). Next, the teacher explains and demonstrates each step, and finally, the students practice with feedback from the teacher. These are key elements for use in teaching strategies.

Key Planning Considerations

Content Analysis

A task analysis is used to organize the content of a strategy. Because strategies are usually written as a series of steps or subskills, the task analysis is already written for you. In addition, the strategy steps almost always include a built-in remembering technique (usually a first-letter mnemonic device), which is very helpful for students when trying to recall the steps. For example, the letters in the RCRC memorization strategy stand for *R*ead, *C*over, *R*ecite, and *C*heck (Archer & Gleason, 1990). Each letter represents a step of the task analysis needed to complete the strategy. Note that the task analysis and remembering technique will be used during the presentation of information and demonstration portions of the lesson body.

Opening

The opening of a strategy lesson is a good time to establish the importance of the strategy and the effect its use can have. You could begin by using a technique designed to motivate students, such as by asking a question that describes a problem caused by not using the strategy. You might ask, "How many of you have ever lost points on a writing assignment because it was not complete?" Another important part of the opening is to tell the students the objective ("Today you will learn a technique for checking your written work before you turn it in so that you can be sure that it is complete"). Complete the opening by stating the objective purpose, such as saying, "Using this strategy can help ensure that you receive full credit for your work and can help increase your grade."

Presentation of Information

During the presentation of information section of the lesson body, it is important to explain, tell about, and describe the strategy steps to the students. This is most effective when you show the task analysis (use a transparency or a poster) to the students, and then explain it and give examples of each step. Pointing out and referring to the mnemonic device in the strategy throughout the lesson helps students focus on the key steps or subskills.

At some point, students need to memorize the steps of the strategy, so they can be more automatic in their use of the steps. However, you will need to decide in advance of your lesson whether memorization will be part of the initial lesson or not. If you do not plan for your students to memorize the steps at this point, be sure to provide a visual support of the strategy (a poster of steps, for example) during all phases of your lesson. If you do want your students to memorize the steps, plan ample practice opportunities so students can learn them.

Demonstration

It is very important to demonstrate or model the use of the strategy. This takes place after or during the presentation of information portion of the lesson. Using the think aloud technique is very effective as it allows students to see the steps being used (demonstration) and hear the thinking that is necessary to complete the steps. For example, in the COPS (C = capitalization; O = overall appearance; P = punctuation; S = spelled) error monitoring strategy (Schumaker, Deshler, Nolan, Clark, Alley, & Warner, 1981), the teacher would say, "Let's see, 'C' stands for capitalization. Have I capitalized the first word in every sentence? Yes . . . I capitalized 'The' in the first sentence," and so on.

Be sure that your actions and thoughts during this component of the lesson are obvious (exaggerate if needed), and that students can easily see and recognize what you are doing. Depending on the complexity of the strategy, you may need to model it numerous times before students are ready to try it. In some cases, you may wish to model a number of times over several days.

Extended Practice

The extended practice portion of the strategy lesson is meant to provide opportunities that help students become fluent in their strategy use and to facilitate generalization. These opportunities are often organized as in-class practices, although carefully structured homework assignments can be effective also.

Use in-class practice activities if your goal is to provide frequent, varied practice opportunities so that the use of the strategy will become a habit. As you work through various content areas, point out when it would be appropriate to use the strategy and then have students practice it. Over time, your role in this area can decrease.

Use carefully organized homework assignments for students to effectively practice the learned strategies at home. For example, include a check-off

sheet with a strategy homework practice assignment. A parent or sibling could check off the steps finished as the student completes them.

Generalization of strategy use requires special attention. Even though a student may know how to use a strategy, this does not guarantee that the student will use the strategy in various settings. You can increase the likelihood that students will generalize strategy use if practice sessions take place in a variety of settings, with varied materials, and with prompts to use the strategy. For example, if you have taught a reading comprehension strategy, plan for students to practice the strategy with science, social studies, and other subject matter. In all cases, use interesting materials for practice sessions to help increase a student's interest in using the strategy.

To summarize, strategy instruction provides students with a valuable tool to use in school. The use of effective strategies can increase the possibility that students will experience success with school tasks. When strategies become habits, students become more independent, effective learners.

 ## References and Suggested Readings for Concepts

Arends, R. I. (2000). *Learning to Teach* (5th ed.). New York: McGraw-Hill. (See Chapter 9 in particular.)

Cummings, C. (1990). *Teaching Makes a Difference* (2nd ed.). Edmonds, WA: Teaching. (See Chapter 11 in particular.)

Eggen, P. D., & Kauchak, D. P. (2001). *Strategies for Teaching: Teaching Content and Thinking Skills.* Boston: Allyn & Bacon.

Howell, K. W., & Nolet, V. (2000). *Curriculum-Based Evaluation: Teaching and Decision Making* (3rd ed.). Belmont, CA: Wadsworth/Thomson Learning.

Martorella, P. H. (1994). Concept learning and higher-level thinking. In J. M. Cooper (Ed.), *Classroom Teaching Skills* (5th ed.), 153–188. Lexington, MA: D.C. Heath.

Smith, P. L., & Ragan, T. J. (1999). *Instructional Design.* Columbus, OH: Merrill, an imprint of Prentice Hall. (See Chapter 10 in particular.)

References and Suggested Readings for Social Skills

Allsopp, D., Santos, K., & Linn, R. (2000). Collaborating to teach prosocial skills. *Intervention in School and Clinic, 35*(3), 141–146.

Elksnin, L., & Elksnin, N. (1998). Teaching social skills to students with learning and behavior problems. *Intervention in School and Clinic, 33*(3), 131–140.

Goldstein, A., & McGinnis, E. (1997). *Skillstreaming the Adolescent: New Strategies and Perspectives for Teaching Prosocial Skills* (rev. ed.). Champaign, IL: Research Press.

McGinnis, E., & Goldstein, A. (1997). *Skillstreaming the Elementary School Child: New Strategies and Perspectives for Teaching Prosocial Skills* (rev. ed.). Champaign, IL: Research Press.

Sargent, L. (1998). *Social Skills for School and Community*. Reston, VA: Council for Exceptional Children.

Sheridan, S. (1995). *The Tough Kid Social Skills Book*. Longmont, CO: Sopris West.

Sugai, G., & Lewis, T. (1996). Preferred and promising practices for social skills instruction. *Focus on Exceptional Children, 29*(4), 1–16.

References and Suggested Readings for Strategies

Arends, R. I. (2000). *Learning to Teach* (4th ed.). Boston: McGraw-Hill. (See Chapter 13, "Learning and Study Strategies," in particular.)

Archer, A., & Gleason, M. (1990). *Skills for School Success*. North Billerica, MA: Curriculum Associates.

Ashton, T. (I999). Spell checking: making writing meaningful in the inclusive classroom. *Teaching Exceptional Children, 32*(2), 24–27. (This title provides a strategy for the effective use of a spell checker.)

Boyle, J. R. (2001). Enhancing the note-taking skills of students with mild disabilities. *Intervention in School and Clinic, 36*(4), 221–224.

Bryant, D. P., Ugel, N., Thompson, S., & Hamff, A. (1999). Instructional strategies for content-area reading instruction. *Intervention in School and Clinic, 34*(5), 293–302. (This title provides strategies for word identification, vocabulary, and comprehension skills.)

Casteel, C. P., Isom, B. A., & Jordan, K. F. (2000). Creating confident and competent readers: transactional strategies instruction. *Intervention in School and Clinic, 36*(2), 67–74.

Cegelka, P. T., & Berdine, W. H. (1995). *Effective Instruction for Students with Learning Difficulties.* Boston: Allyn & Bacon.

Czarnecki, E., Rosko, D., & Fine, E. (1998). How to call up note-taking skills. *Teaching Exceptional Children, 30*(6), 14–19.

DeLaPaz, S. (2001). STOP and DARE: A persuasive writing strategy. *Intervention in School and Clinic, 36*(4), 234–243. (This title provides a strategy for writing persuasive essays.)

Deshler, D. D., Ellis, E. S., & Lenz, B. K. (1996). *Teaching Adolescents with Learning Disabilities: Strategies and Methods* (2nd ed.). Denver: Love Publishing. (See Chapters 3–9 for strategies in reading, writing, test-taking, note-taking, math, and social skills.)

Ellis, E. S., Deshler, D. D., Lenz, B. K., Schumaker, J. B., & Clark, F. L. (1991). An instructional model for teaching learning strategies. *Focus on Exceptional Children, 23*, 1–24.

Gauthier, L. R. (2001). Coop-Dis-Q: A reading comprehension strategy. *Intervention in School and Clinic, 36*(4), 217–220. (This article provides a reading comprehension strategy.)

Gleason, M. M., Colvin, G., & Archer, A. L. (1991). Interventions for improving study skills. In Stoner, G., Shinn, M. R., & Walker, H. M., (Eds.). *Interventions for Achievement and Behavior Problems*, 137–160. Silver Spring, MD: National Association of School Psychologists.

James, L. A., Abbott, M., & Greenwood, C. R. (2001). How Adam became a writer: Winning writing strategies for low-achieving students. *Teaching Exceptional Children, 33*(3), 30–37.

Landi, M. (2001). Helping students with learning disabilities make sense of word problems. *Intervention in School and Clinic, 37*(1), 13–18.

(This article provides a strategy for solving math word problems.)

Lebzelter, S., & Nowacek, E. (1999). Reading strategies for secondary students with mild disabilities. *Intervention in School and Clinic, 34*(4), 212–219 (This article provides decoding, vocabulary, and comprehension strategies.)

Lovitt, T. C. (2000). *Preventing School Failure: Tactics for Teaching Adolescents* (2nd ed.). Austin, TX: Pro-Ed. (See Chapter 3, on study skills, in particular.)

Lovitt, T. C. (1995). *Tactics for Teaching* (2nd ed.). Columbus, OH: Merrill, an imprint of Prentice Hall.

Mastropieri, M. A., & Scruggs, T. E. (1998). Enhancing school success with mnemonic strategies. *Intervention in School and Clinic, 33*(4), 201–207.

Mastropieri, M. A., & Scruggs, T. E. (2000). *The Inclusive Classroom: Strategies for Effective Instruction.* Columbus, OH: Merrill, an imprint of Prentice Hall. (See Chapter 11 on teaching study skills.)

Meltzer, L. J., Roditi, B. N., Haynes, D. P., Biddle, K. R., Paster, M., & Taber, S. E. (1996). *Strategies for Success: Classroom Teaching Techniques for Students with Learning Problems.* Austin, TX: Pro-Ed. (See Chapters 3–6 on strategies for spelling, reading comprehension, written language, and math.)

Olson, J. L., & Platt, J. M. (2000). *Teaching Children and Adolescents with Special Needs* (3rd ed.). Columbus, OH: Merrill, an imprint of Prentice Hall. (See Chapters 8 and 9 in particular.)

Polloway, E. A., & Patton, J. R., (1997). *Strategies for Teaching Learners with Special Needs* (6th ed.). Columbus, OH: Merrill, an imprint of Prentice Hall. (See Chapter 14 on study skills.)

Reithaug, D. (1998). *Orchestrating Academic Success by Adapting and Modifying Programs.* West Vancouver, BC: Stirling Head Enterprises. (This title provides strategies for reading, writing, spelling, and math.)

Schumaker, J. B., Deshler, D. D., Nolan, S., Clark, F. L., Alley, G. R., & Warner, M. M. (1981). *Error Monitoring: A Learning Strategy for Improving Academic Performance of LD Adolescents* (Research Report No. 32). Lawrence, KS: University of Kansas Institute on Learning Disabilities.

Vaughn, S., & Klinger, J. K. (1999). Teaching reading comprehension through collaborative strategic reading. *Intervention in School and Clinic, 34*(5), 284–292.

Wood, D. & Frank, A. (2000). Using memory-enhancing strategies to learn multiplication facts. *Teaching Exceptional Children, 32*(5), 78–82.

Polygon: A Direct Instruction Concept Lesson

This is for a large group of students.

I. PREPLANNING TASKS

A. Connection analysis: *State Standard, Mathematics 1.3:* Understand and apply concepts and procedures from geometric sense. *Benchmark 2:* Use multiple attributes to describe geometric shapes.

B. Content analysis

    1. Concept analysis

        a. Concept name: Polygon

        b. Definition: A polygon is a two-dimensional, closed figure of three or more sides made by joining line segments, where each line segment intersects with exactly two others at its endpoints.

        c. Critical attributes: Two-dimensional, closed figure with three or more sides, made of joined line segments, each line segment intersects with exactly two others at its endpoints

        d. Noncritical attributes: Size, shape, color, patterns inside or out

        e. Examples: Triangle (three sides), quadrilateral (four sides), pentagon (five sides), or hexagon (six sides). Both regular and irregular polygons need to be included in examples.

        f. Nonexamples:

    _____

    2. Prerequisite Skills or Knowledge: Know how to identify when the endpoints of line segments intersect.

    3. Key terms and vocabulary: **Line segment, endpoint, intersect.**

C. Objective: Given 12 geometric figures on a worksheet, student will circle (or point to) the seven polygons.

D. Objective rationale: Polygons are basic geometrical shapes and recognizing them is a prerequisite skill for other geometrical concepts, such as regular and irregular polygons.

E. Materials or equipment: 3 transparencies, math workbooks, worksheet for evaluation.

II. LESSON SETUP

A. Signal for attention: Play musical chords (tape recorder).

B. Behavior expectations: Raise hands to contribute, listen to explanations and comments of teacher and peers, and keep eyes on the speaker.

III. LESSON OPENING

A. Review prior geometry lessons.

 1. Discuss the various shapes ("What are they?") in the current geometry unit.

 > *AP = Brainstorm*

B. State objective and objective purpose.

 1. Say, "Today you are going to learn how to identify our new shape, polygons. You will learn a definition and the characteristics that make a polygon."

 2. "This lesson will help prepare you for future lessons, such as learning about various types of polygons."

IV. LESSON BODY

A. Presentation of information

 1. Show transparency #1 (concept analysis with polygon definition, list of critical and noncritical attributes, and examples and nonexamples of polygons).

 2. Read the definitions (with students), discuss critical and noncritical attributes, pointing out attributes in the examples, and then point out noncritical attributes.

 > *AP = Choral read*

B. Demonstration

 1. Show transparency #2 (with a list of questions to ask to help decide if shapes are polygons, and more examples and nonexamples).

 2. Think aloud with the first two examples to show how to use questions to analyze shapes (a poster of questions will remain on the white board tray).

    a. Is it two-dimensional?

    b. Is it made of line segments?

    c. Is it a closed shape?

    d. Does each line segment intersect with exactly two others at its endpoints?

    e. Are there at least three sides?

    f. If the answer to all of these questions is yes, the shape is a polygon.

 3. CFU: Repeat questions with the next four examples and nonexamples. Ask the students if they agree with my conclusions (have some incorrect ones).

 > *AP = Thumbs up/down*

C. Supervised practice. (Have students take out their yes and no response cards.)

 1. Partner practice.

    a. Show transparency #3 (list of questions and new examples and nonexamples).

    b. Have students determine whether or not each shape is a polygon (first five shapes). Prompt the use of the five questions.

    c. Turn to partner; then use response cards.

2.   Individual practice.

   a.   Point to each of the last five shapes and have students signal. (Have Leah help Molly with reading the questions if needed.)

V. EXTENDED PRACTICE

A.   Provide a seatwork assignment. Have students circle the polygons on math workbook page 55, which shows 25 shapes with 15 polygons.

VI. LESSON CLOSING

A.   Final review of information learned.

   1.   Say, "Today we learned . . . ."

   2.   Quickly review the concept analysis (transparency #1).

B.   Pass out and explain the evaluation.

   1.   Say, "Your ticket to lunch is finding the polygons on the worksheet."

   2.   CFU: Ask questions, such as, "How do you show which are polygons?"

VII. EVALUATION

A.   Provide a worksheet of 12 geometric figures, seven of which are polygons. Students complete worksheets individually and independently. (Parent volunteer will evaluate Stephan. He will point to the polygons.)

Polygon: A Structured Discovery Concept Lesson

This is for a large group of students.

I. PREPLANNING TASKS

A. Connection analysis: *State Standard, Mathematics 1.3:* Understand and apply concepts and procedures from geometric sense. *Benchmark 2:* Use multiple attributes to describe geometric shapes.

B. Content analysis

    1. Concept analysis

        a. Concept name: Polygon

        b. Definition: A polygon is a two-dimensional, closed figure of three or more sides made by joining line segments, where each line segment intersects with exactly two others at its endpoints

        c. Critical attributes: Two-dimensional, closed figure, with three or more sides, made of joined line segments, each line segment intersects with exactly two others at its endpoints

        d. Noncritical attributes: Size, shape, color, patterns inside or out

        e. Examples: Triangle (three sides), quadrilateral (four sides), pentagon (five sides), or hexagon (six sides). Both regular and irregular polygons need to be included in examples.

        f. Nonexamples

    2. Prerequisite skills or knowledge: Know how to identify when the endpoints of line segments intersect.

    3. Key terms and vocabulary: **Line segment, endpoint, intersect**

C. Objective: Given 12 geometric figures on a worksheet, student will circle (or point to) the seven polygons.

D. Objective rationale: Polygons are basic geometrical shapes and recognizing them is a prerequisite skill for other geometrical concepts, such as regular and irregular polygons.

E. Materials or equipment: 4 transparencies, math workbooks, worksheet for evaluation.

II. LESSON SETUP

A. Signal for attention: Play musical chords (tape recorder).

B. Behavior expectations: Raise hands to contribute, listen to the explanations and comments of the teacher and peers, and keep eyes on the speaker.

III. LESSON OPENING

A. Review prior geometry lessons.

    1. Discuss the various shapes ("What are they?") in the current geometry unit.

> *AP = Brainstorm*

B. State objective and objective purpose.

    1. Say, "Today you are going to learn how to identify our new shape, polygons. You will learn a definition and the characteristics that make a polygon."

    2. "This lesson will help prepare you for future lessons, such as learning about various types of polygons."

IV. LESSON BODY

A. Set up the discovery.

    1. Show transparency #1 (examples and nonexamples of polygons).

    2. Say, "Some of these shapes are polygons. Watch me as I circle them" (circle them).

    3. Say, "You have five minutes to see if you can figure out how all of the circled shapes are the same."

B. Monitor the discovery.

    1. Walk around and prompt as needed, such as, "Are all of the shapes the same color?" "Are the shapes closed?" and so on. Ask questions about both critical and noncritical attributes.

C. Review the discovery.

    1. Construct a concept analysis together on transparency #2.

        a. Ask, "In what ways are the circled shapes the same?" (write critical attributes).

        b. Ask, "Can you think of a way to write a definition for a polygon?" (write definition).

> *AP = Turn to partner, and then call on nonvolunteers*

    2. CFU: Read definition and critical attributes.

        a. Ask, "If this is a complete definition, put thumbs up. If not, put thumbs down."

        b. Repeat the procedure with each critical attribute, having students give thumbs up or down.

    3. Show transparency #3 (list of questions to ask to help decide if the shape is a polygon and examples and nonexamples of polygons). Explain how to use questions to analyze shapes.

        a. Is it two-dimensional?

        b. Is it made of line segments?

        c. Is it a closed shape?

        d. Does each line segment intersect with exactly two others at its endpoints?

        e. Are there at least three sides?

        f. If the answer to all of these questions is yes, it is a polygon.

> *AP = Choral read*

D. Supervised practice—Have students take out their yes or no response cards.

   1. Partner practice

      a. Show transparency #4 (list of questions and new examples and nonexamples).

      b. Have students determine whether or not each shape is a polygon (first five shapes). Prompt the use of the five questions.

      c. Turn to partner; then use response cards.

   2. Individual practice.

      a. Point to each of the last five shapes and have students signal. (Have Leah help Molly with reading the questions if needed.)

V. EXTENDED PRACTICE

A. Provide a seatwork assignment. Have students circle the polygons, on math workbook page 55, which shows 25 shapes with 15 polygons.

VI. LESSON CLOSING

A. Final review of information learned.

   1. Say, "Today we learned . . . ."

   2. Quickly review the concept analysis put together as a class (transparency #2).

   > *AP = Choral read*

B. Pass out and explain the evaluation.

   1. Say, "Your ticket to lunch is finding the polygons on the worksheet."

   2. CFU: Ask questions, such as "How do you show which are polygons?"

   > *AP = Call on nonvolunteers*

EVALUATION

A. Provide a worksheet of 12 geometric figures, seven of which are polygons. Students complete worksheets individually and independently. (Parent volunteer will evaluate Stephan. He will point to the polygons.)

Social Skills Lesson: Standing Up for Someone

A direct instruction lesson for a small group

I. PREPLANNING TASKS

A. Connection analysis: This lesson is part of an anti-bullying program. Related state standard in civics: Understand individual rights and their accompanying responsibilities, explain why democracy requires citizens to exercise their own rights and to respect the rights of others.

B. Content (task) analysis for "standing up for someone" (steps adapted from Goldstein & McGinnis, 1997):

   1.   Decide if the person is not being treated right by others.

   2.   Decide if the person wants you to stand up for him or her.

   3.   Decide how to stand up for the person.

   4.   Do it.

C. Lesson objective: In a given role play, students will correctly think aloud and demonstrate each step in standing up for someone.

D. Objective rationale: Standing up for someone who is being treated unfairly or unkindly is an important part of friendship and community building and helps prevent bullying at school.

E. Materials: Graphic organizer; poster with steps; homework forms; and backup and evaluation scenarios.

II. LESSON SETUP

A. Signal for attention: "Let's get started."

B. Behavior expectations: Listen when others are speaking; contribute ideas; give feedback politely (refer to the behavior, not the person).

III. LESSON OPENING

A. Show graphic organizer of components of the anti-bullying program.

B. Remind students of an earlier lesson on standing up for yourself. Ask for key points: using "I" statements, and humor, examples of when to get help.

> *AP = First say to partner*

C. With parent helpers, do a skit in which someone is not being treated right (called a "retard" and excluded from a game), and a bystander does not know how to help.

D. Ask students for examples of when they have needed this skill in their lives.

E. State the objective and rationale (both written on board).

IV. LESSON BODY

A. Presentation of information

1. Show steps written on a big poster. Talk through and add definitions, examples, and questions.

   a. Decide if the person is not being treated right by others. Ask yourself, Is this person (friend, classmate, stranger) not being treated right (disrespectfully, unfairly, unequally, unkindly) by others (child, adult, group)?

   b. Decide if the person wants you to stand up for him or her. Ask yourself, Does this person want my help? How can I find out? (Ask directly, read body language, or think how you would feel.)

   c. Decide how to stand up for the person. Ask yourself, What shall I do to help? (Remember the rules: Do not get hurt and do not make it worse.) Consider the options of telling the other person to stop; explaining why it is unfair; saying something nice to the person not being treated right or walking away with him; and getting help (always use the last two in dangerous situations).

   d. Do it. Use "I" statements in a calm voice. Do not be unkind back.

2. AP and CFU after each step. Call on students at random to paraphrase, repeat, or add examples; or write a definition or example on the white board and hold it up, or have students discuss with their partners.

B. Demonstration

1. AP: Select students to watch for each step (change for each scenario).

2. With parent volunteers, model three scenarios (demonstrate a student at recess being taunted and pushed around by older kids, the class laughing when a student struggles during oral reading, and a sibling being unfairly accused of breaking a dish and lying). Model each step including think alouds.

3. CFU: After each modeling, call on selected students to describe how each step was used.

C. Supervised practice

1. Have the group brainstorm other scenarios that they have seen (be sure to get at least one from each student).

2. Select Edgar to role-play first, allowing him to choose the scenario. (Parent volunteers will play the roles of "person" and "others.") Leave the poster up for role players to refer to.

3. Ask questions of Edgar to set the scene, such as, Where is this happening?

4. Assign steps to watch for to other students.

5. Stop, correct, and redo if errors.

6. Then ask for feedback from peers and adults.

7. Continue until each student has done a role play. (Select Jareese to go second.)

V. LESSON CLOSING

A. Redo skit from the opening; using think/pair/share, ask the students what they think the bystander should do.

VI. CONTINUATION

A. The next day, model a scenario of a student having his lunch taken and being made fun of for being "foreign", while pointing to each step on poster (review).

B. Then each student will role-play another scenario (continued supervised practice).

VII. EVALUATION

A. The following day, pull students aside, one at a time, to role-play the skill using a new scenario that I provide.

B. Use parent volunteers as "others" and "persons."

VIII. EXTENDED PRACTICE FOR GENERALIZATION

A. Provide homework. "Write the steps on a homework form, noting each time you use the skill this week and how well you do."

B. Have parents initial that they read the homework form.

C. Conduct a follow-up activity, having students videotape themselves role-playing a scenario they create, and then having the class critique.

D. I will explain the skill to the recess supervisor and she will give good-citizen awards to those who use the skill this month. I will do the same in the classroom.

E. Hold a review session in two weeks.

Strategy Lesson: Designing Mnemonic Devices

This is a direct instruction lesson for a large group.

I. PREPLANNING TASKS

A.   Connection analysis: This strategy helps students progress successfully toward many state standards, as many require that students have mastered large quantities of information. *IEP objective:* Molly will use memorization strategies as appropriate when preparing for content tests.

B.   Content (task) analysis: See lesson body for Designing Mnemonic Devices (steps adapted from Archer & Gleason, 1990)

C.   Prerequisites: Know the RCRC strategy (Archer & Gleason, 1990).

D.   Key terms and vocabulary: **Strategy**—a plan or method; **Mnemonic Devices**—tricks for memorizing.

E.   Objective and rationale

   1.   Given three lists of related items, students will design a word or sentence mnemonic device for each that makes sense.

   2.   This will help students organize information to be memorized in preparation for tests and increase scores on tests.

F.   Materials and equipment: Transparencies with the last test results, task analysis, lists of related information, and an evaluation worksheet.

II. LESSON SETUP

A.   Signal for attention: Ring bell.

B.   Behavior expectations: Students will look and listen, answer questions, raise hands, and wait to be called on.

III. LESSON OPENING

A.   Motivator: Show and explain transparency #1 (shows groups of facts that students needed to know for their last social studies test and examples of incomplete answers from the actual test).

B.   Objective and purpose: If this has ever happened to you, then you will be happy to know that today you are going to learn a trick to help you memorize information better and in less time.

C.   Review RCRC by having students call out the words in unison.

IV. LESSON BODY

A.   Presentation of information and demonstration

   1.   Define mnemonic device and strategy.

2. Explain the steps of the strategies.

   a. Talk through transparency #2, which shows the task analysis below, *and* point out poster of task analysis.

   b. Provide an enlarged version on a handout for Leah.

3. Designing mnemonic devices (task analysis)

   a. Using the word strategy:

     (1) Underline the first letter of each item to be memorized (list of words, task parts, steps, and so on). For example: <u>S</u>uperior, <u>H</u>uron, <u>E</u>rie, <u>M</u>ichigan, <u>O</u>ntario.

     (2) Determine whether a word can be made from the first letters (reorder the letters if necessary): *HOMES.* If the word strategy works, go to (3). If not, go to (4).

     (3) Memorize the word and item that goes with each letter of the word using RCRC.

   b. Using the sentence strategy:

     (4) Reorder the first letters of the words and create a sentence (*fruit, meat, vegetable* = the phrase, *very funny man*).

     (5) Memorize the sentence and item that goes with each word in the sentence using RCRC.

4. CFU: Ask for definitions, paraphrases of steps, and purpose of strategies. (Think–Pair–Share)

5. Do a think aloud of the steps using the following lists of subject matter, which include both word and sentence strategy (five food groups: fruits, vegetables, meat and poultry, dairy, fats/oils/sweets; parts of an insect: head, thorax, abdomen).

   a. Pass out white boards.

   b. Have students work steps along with me.

> *AP = White boards*

   c. Emphasize that there is more than one answer.

6. CFU: Provide new content (types of rocks: sedimentary, igneous, metamorphic).

   a. Students will work each step on white boards ("Do step one, show me," and so on).

   b. If more instruction needed, use these examples: primary colors, exports from California.

B. Supervised practice: Monitor and give feedback.

1. Partner practice

   a. Give partners two more examples and a checklist of strategy steps.

   b. Have Partner 1 do the first example, while Partner 2 checks it off, and then reverse the roles.

   c. Use the following examples of tap roots: carrots, radishes, beets, turnips, and parsnips; parts of a plant: roots, stem, leaves, and sometimes flowers.

   d. Partner Darin with Kristin to help with reading.

2. Individual supervised practice

   a. Have individuals work two more examples (parts of a volcano: parasitic cone, base, summit, crater, and magma reserve; colors of the rainbow).

V. LESSON CLOSING

A. Go back to transparency #1 of test items. Have partners create mnemonic devices for missed groups of facts. Share with class.

> **AP** = *Use partner work*

VI. EXTENDED PRACTICE

A. Conduct in-class practice activities (seatwork).

1. During the next two days, we will look for examples of information in various content areas. Students will need to memorize these and develop a mnemonic device for each one, such as the states in the Pacific Northwest region or examples of foods that are low in fat.

VII. EVALUATION

A. Worksheet with three lists of related pieces of information. Students will develop a mnemonic device for each one.

Chapter 12 Using Peers in Instruction

▮ Introduction

This chapter is about planning for how students will work and learn together. This is another important aspect of preparing activities and lessons for a diverse classroom.

Why Use Peers in Instruction?

Throughout this book, the emphasis has been on the importance of active student participation in the diverse classroom. Teachers must carefully and imaginatively plan and work hard to ensure that all students are involved and can obtain success. As teachers cannot be everywhere at the same time, an abundant source of help can come from students. Having students work with their peers can increase opportunities for active responses and practice with immediate feedback. Using peers may also be motivating, provide practice in social skills, increase social integration, and offer more variety in methods. All of this helps satisfy individual differences and preferences, as well as results in more engaged time.

Examples of Using Peers in Instruction

Teachers can have peers work together in any of the following ways:

- *Active participation strategies* During informal presentation and direct instruction lessons, students may be encouraged to process new information with peers through techniques such as "tell your neighbor."

- *Diversity strategies* Peer helpers may provide assistance with paying attention, reading directions, homework, and so on, to students with learning or behavior problems.

- *Activities* An activity plan may incorporate the use of groups or teams of students for working on projects, solving problems, engaging in discussions, playing games, and so on.

- *Supervised practice in lessons* Include partner or small-group practice as a bridge between teacher demonstrations and individual practice.

- *Extended practice* Plan ongoing partner practice, using flash cards for building accuracy and fluency on math facts, for enhancing vocabulary, and so on.

- *Structured discovery* Pairs of students or groups may work together to discuss the examples and nonexamples and to discover the concept or rule.

- *Informal presentation* As extended practice, students may form debate teams and prepare arguments based on the information presented.

- *Behavior management* Teams may earn points for quick transitions with students helping and reminding each other of the rules.

Notice that, in all of these examples, partner or group work builds on teacher instruction. It does not replace it.

Many formal cooperative learning and peer tutoring programs can also be very effective in a diverse classroom. Individual teachers may implement some of these programs, and some are schoolwide programs. See the suggested readings at the end of the chapter for information on cooperative learning and peer tutoring programs.

Potential Problems

Although there are many benefits to using peers in instruction, there are potential hazards as well. Simply telling students to work together is rarely enough. Most people have had experience working with others at school or at work when much time was wasted, when one person did all of the work, or when nothing was accomplished. Using peers, like all other teaching techniques, requires careful planning to avoid time spent chatting, fighting, exchanging misinformation, or chaos as students are forming groups or moving furniture. Students will not necessarily know how to work together—how to cooperate, to share, to listen, to encourage, or to challenge each other. It is important to establish and communicate procedures and to assess and teach necessary cooperative social skills.

 Planning for Using Peers in Instruction

Many variables must be considered as you plan for using peers in instruction.

When to Plan

The time and effort that teachers spend planning for using peers depends on how they are going to be used. If teachers intend to use peer partners or groups often (as an active participation strategy, as part of supervised practice, or as a regular part of the reading or math or spelling program), then it is most efficient to plan and teach direct instruction lessons on the procedures in advance. That time will be well spent because it will help avoid more planning and teaching time later. For example, in plans for reading lessons, you may simply write, "Find your reading partner and follow the oral reading routine." That will be sufficient if students have previously been taught the routine and have established partners. If you teach and provide practice on using the "Numbered Heads Together" procedure, then, in activity and lesson plans, you only need to write "Form your Heads Together groups, count off, and discuss . . ." (Kagan, 1992).

In some cases, teachers will plan for the use of peers as a one-time event. For example, suppose you are planning an inquiry activity in science. For that particular activity, you must plan the membership, the meeting places, and the procedures for the groups to follow. In that case, you would write detailed directions into the "activity middle" component of the activity plan.

Planning Decisions

Regardless of when you plan for using peers in instruction, it is always necessary to make decisions about why, how, who, and where. Consider the reason for using peers, the size of the groups, how tasks will be shared, the prerequisites, who will work together, and the management and logistics. The following suggestions are adapted from Arends, 1997; Johnson, Johnson, and Holubec, 1991; and Slavin, 1995.

Why Use Peers in a Lesson or Activity?

Do not assume that using peers is always superior to individual work. It is necessary to consider the reason for using partners or small groups. For example, in an activity, the benefits of having students work on group projects rather than on individual projects might be to generate more ideas, provide the opportunity for individuals to study one narrow topic in depth, and provide practice on cooperative social skills. To bring about a higher success rate, you may use peers as part of supervised practice to provide additional support as students are attempting new skills. Be sure that all students involved in peer practice will benefit from it.

Determining the Size of Groups

Decide which it is preferable to use—pairs of students or small groups. Small-group size typically ranges from three to six members. Consider the following factors when trying to determine the most appropriate group size:

1. *More cooperative social skills are needed in larger groups.* It is easier to share materials, take turns, or reach consensus with one other person than it is with five other people. Also, in larger groups, equal participation is more difficult to achieve. The decision about group size, therefore, should be partly based on the level of cooperative skills the students have.

2. *All groups do not necessarily have to be the same size.* Diversity can be accommodated by having some smaller and some larger groups. This may need to be done anyway, depending on the total number of students in the class. For example, if you have 23 students, you can form five groups with three members and two groups with four members.

3. *The type of task may influence the group size.* If students are to take turns reading aloud, students will get more practice in groups of two than in groups of three or more. Larger groups may be appropriate if the task is a project where each student has something different to do, such as researching a different topic, and all tasks can be done at once.

4. *The task may logically divide itself.* Peers may be divided by needed roles, such as a reader and a writer, or according to the content, such as reporting on the three branches of government.

5. *Time is a factor.* Typically, more time will be needed, the larger the group. For example, if the students are to discuss or solve problems together, more time will be needed for larger groups so that each member gets a chance to contribute.

6. *Sometimes more mundane elements must be considered.* Group size may be affected by the number of materials or equipment available, the size of tables, and so on.

Determining How Students Will Share Tasks

It is important to consider what each student will do during the partner or group work and to communicate this to the students. It is usually not enough to simply tell students to work together, cooperate, help each other, teach each other, or discuss. It is essential to be much more specific. For example, for partner practice on vocabulary, you might say, "Partner 1 will define the first word, and Partner 2 will use it in a sentence. Then switch for the second word."

Teachers may think about the typical roles needed in partner or group work, such as reader, recorder, checker, encourager, and timer. Then they may decide which roles are needed in a particular task. It is most efficient to directly teach those roles that will commonly be used, so all students know how to carry them out. It is also necessary to decide whether roles will be assigned by the teacher or by the group.

If it is difficult to figure out what each student will do, ask yourself whether this is a task that can be shared or whether the size of the group is appropriate. Remember that not all learning is best done in group situations.

Determining Prerequisite Skills and Knowledge

In addition to analyzing whether students have the necessary content knowledge and skills, it is essential to analyze whether they have the interaction skills required to be successful at the task. The following examples illustrate how you may consider required academic and social skills as you plan:

1. Summarizing paragraphs with a partner would follow teacher instruction on summarizing. This way, you would know that all students have the necessary preliminary content knowledge on how to summarize. However, you would also need to decide whether students have the skills to listen to each other, to accept criticism, to take turns, and so on.

2. Before planning to have students discuss a particular topic in small groups, you would decide whether they had the necessary information or knowledge about the topic to make a discussion productive. You would also need to analyze the students' discussion skills, such as making relevant comments, criticizing ideas rather than the person, and asking for clarification.

3. To form groups and pick a subject to investigate, students would have to possess not only the necessary research skills, but also skills in offering ideas, reaching consensus, and so on.

Several options are available for teaching students who do not have the prerequisite cooperative social skills to be successful at the task. First, avoid the problem by changing the lesson or activity to eliminate the use of peers or structure the task carefully to help students be successful, that is, provide clear and specific directions, change the group size, assign specific roles, and so on. Finally, you may wish to preteach the necessary social skills, using the direct instruction model. Have students practice by role-playing. (See Chapter 11 for more detail.)

Deciding Who Will Work Together

Teachers may sometimes choose to form groups at random or to allow students to decide. More typically, they will want to plan the membership of pairs and groups carefully. When students will be working together for more than brief periods of time (for a one-hour science experiment or a month-long reading partnership), consider the following factors when planning who will work together:

1. *Skills* Consider the task and purpose when choosing whether to pair or group homogeneously or heterogeneously. For example, if you intend to individualize the content of the tasks, with some students needing to practice addition facts, some working on multiple-digit addition, and some working on multiplication, then choose homogeneous pairs so both students are getting practice on the skills they need. On the other hand, if all students are practicing the same skills, it makes sense to pair a high achiever with a low achiever. In that way, stu-

dents who are skilled at the task can help the low achievers, while reinforcing their own learning by giving those explanations. When forming pairs and groups, it is important to consider the study and interaction skills of the students, in addition to academic skills.

2. *Compatibility* It is also necessary to consider how students get along together when forming pairs and groups. Students should not be put together who actively dislike each other or who distract each other, unless the purpose is to provide practice on conflict resolution or on ignoring distractions.

3. *Integration* Another consideration in forming pairs and groups is that of promoting social integration. Mixing boys and girls, individuals with and without disabilities, and students from varied cultural backgrounds can increase tolerance and promote friendships in the classroom. However, the teacher must carefully plan for this outcome.

When students will be working together briefly, as in active participation strategies, it makes sense for students who sit near each other to be grouped together. Teach students who their "neighbor" is (for example, the person to their left), and who is included in their small group. If desks are in rows, plan for odd numbers and for the person at the end of the row when thinking about partnerships. Think about and teach students how to turn or move their chairs to form small groups. (Note that you will not want much furniture moving for brief group work.) If desks are in clusters or students sit at tables, teachers may designate partners. Consider whether peer practice will be used often when making desk arrangements and seating plans.

Planning for Management and Logistics

Consider the many management, logistical, and organizational issues when having students work with their peers. Of course, issues will vary, depending on what students will be doing. The following are some management basics for which planning is essential.

1. *Plan where pairs or groups will meet.* If students are to work together, they will need to be phys-

ically close together. If this involves changing seats or moving furniture, carefully plan to avoid too much wasted time. (Note that teaching how to move into groups may be time well spent.) No one should be physically excluded from the group, and everyone should be able to see the materials and each other. The pairs and groups should be situated far enough apart so that groups do not distract each other and so they can be easily monitored.

2. *Plan how to regain attention.* When students are working and talking together, it can be difficult for them to shift their attention back to the teacher. They may not easily see or hear the teacher. Therefore, teachers should provide practice in responding quickly to a stronger signal for attention, such as a bell.

3. *Plan specific rules for partner or group work.* These rules will depend on the needs of the students. Teachers may need to set specific rules regarding staying with the group, how to resolve conflicts, how to correct errors politely, what to do when finished, and so on. Students may be required to ask for help from each other before asking the teacher.

4. *Plan how you will monitor the partners or groups.* Plan how you will help with both the academic and social tasks of the group. Set goals for yourself. Do not just wander. What are you looking for or listening for?

5. *Plan how you will communicate the procedures for working together to the students.* Remember what has been learned about giving directions clearly and efficiently. The following suggestions may provide guidance:

- List groups and their members on a transparency or chart for students to read.
- Display a diagram or map, or put signs up in the room to show where groups meet.
- Demonstrate how to move desks and chairs, if that is necessary.
- Show and tell how students should work together, that is, demonstrate taking turns, reaching consensus, and so on.

- Provide a list of the steps to follow to complete the assignment.
- Tell students the individual and group objectives, the time lines, and the evaluation procedures.

Summary

Having students work with partners or in small groups during lessons and activities is a strategy with many potential benefits. However, careful planning is needed to ensure that students work together effectively and efficiently. Planning is necessary to determine the size and membership of groups, to decide how students will share tasks, to evaluate the knowledge and skills needed by students, and to figure out how to manage the classroom.

References

Arends, R. I. (1997). *Classroom Instruction and Management.* New York: McGraw-Hill.

Arreaga-Mayer, C. (1998). Increasing active student responding and improving academic performance through class-wide peer tutoring. *Intervention in School and Clinic, 34*(2), 89–94.

Goodwin, M. (1999). Cooperative learning and social skills: What skills to teach and how to teach them. *Intervention in School and Clinic, 35*(1), 29–33.

Hock, M. F., Schumaker, J. B., & Deshler, D. D. (2001). The case for strategic tutoring. *Educational Leadership, 58*(7), 50–52.

Johnson, D. W., Johnson, R. T., and Holubec, E. J. (1991). *Cooperation in the Classroom.* Edina, MN: Interaction Book.

Kagan, S. (1992). *Cooperative Learning.* San Juan Capistrano, CA: Resources for Teachers.

Lovitt, T. C. (2000). *Preventing School Failure: Tactics for Teaching Adolescents* (2nd ed.). Austin, TX: Pro-Ed. (See Chapter 11 in particular.)

Mastropieri, M. A., Scruggs, T. E., Mohler, L. J., Beranek, M. L., Spencer, V., Boon, R. T., & Talbott,

E. (2001). Can middle school students with serious reading difficulties help each other and learn anything? *Learning Disabilities Research and Practice, 16*(1), 18–27.

Mathes, P. G., & Babyak, A. E. (2001). The effects of peer-assisted learning strategies for first-grade readers with and without additional mini-skills lessons. *Learning Disabilities Research and Practice, 16*(1), 28–44.

Olson, J. L., and Platt, J. M. (2000). *Teaching Children and Adolescents with Special Needs* (3rd ed.). Columbus, Ohio: Merrill, an imprint of Prentice Hall. (See Chapter 10 in particular.)

Slavin, R. E. (1995). *Cooperative Learning: Theory, Research, and Practice.* (2nd ed.). Needham Heights, MA: Allyn & Bacon.

Slavin, R. E. (1994). *A Practical Guide to Cooperative Learning.* Needham Heights, MA: Allyn & Bacon.

Utley, C. A., Mortweet, S. L., & Greenwood, C. R. (1997). Peer-mediated instruction and interventions. *Focus on Exceptional Children, 29,* 1–23.

Vaughn, S., Hughes, M. T., Moody, S. W., & Elbaum, B. (2001). Instructional grouping for reading for students with ld: Implications for practice, *Intervention in School and Clinic, 36*(3), 131–137.